T0247671

FINTECH FEMINISTS

FINTECH FEMINISTS

INCREASING INCLUSION, REDEFINING INNOVATION, AND CHANGING THE FUTURE FOR WOMEN AROUND THE WORLD

NICOLE CASPERSON

WILEY

Published by John Wiley & Sons, Inc., Hoboken, New Jersey.
Published simultaneously in Canada.

For general information on our other products and services or for technical support, please contact our Customer Care Department within the United States at (800) 762-2974, outside the United States at (317) 572-3993 or fax (317) 572-4002.

Wiley also publishes its books in a variety of electronic formats. Some content that appears in print may not be available in electronic formats. For more information about Wiley products, visit our website at www.wiley.com.

Library of Congress Cataloging-in-Publication Data is Available:

ISBN 9781394273584 (Cloth)
ISBN 9781394273607 (ePub)
ISBN 9781394273591 (ePDF)

COVER DESIGN: PAUL McCARTHY
COVER IMAGE: © ANTON BRIONES

SKY10083333_083024

To the Fintech Is Femme community, thank you for inspiring and supporting my work over the years. Keep pushing the boundaries.

And to my dashing partner, Anton Briones, whose endless patience and support made this book possible.

CONTENTS

CONTENTS

Each time a woman stands up for herself, without knowing it, possibly, without claiming it, she stands up for all women.

—Maya Angelou

INTRODUCTION

"Y ou need to choose between fintech or women, but you can't do both."

Those words from my editor struck me like a blow to the stomach. Why should I have to choose? Shouldn't there be ample space for women's narratives in our publication? Why are women's perspectives deemed separate from the fintech beat, while men's are not?

In my journalism career, I have devoted a decade to reporting on auto finance, mortgages, wealth management, and fintech. I have contributed to prominent business-to-business industry publications, reaching financial services professionals and influencing decision-makers in the economic system from behind the newsroom. My work has consistently aimed to inform and shape the perspectives of those leading the financial industry.

As I rose in my career from reporter to editor, I noticed a troubling trend in every newsroom: they are predominantly male led. Globally, only 22% of 180 top editors across 240 news outlets are women, despite women making up 40% of journalists in the 12 markets studied across five continents, according to research by the 2023 Reuters Institute for the Study of Journalism.[1] Women are significantly underrepresented in editorial leadership roles and news coverage, leaving their voices muted in a global news industry still dominated by men.

This imbalance leads to skewed news coverage favoring male perspectives, neglecting the viewpoints of half the global population. Women make up only 25% of the individuals heard, read about, or seen in newspapers, television, and radio news, according to the Global Media Monitoring Project, which has tracked gender representation in the world's news media every five years since 1995. From 2000 to 2020, women's representation in business-related occupations in the news – like businesspeople, executives, managers, and stockbrokers – barely increased from 12% to 20%. In contrast, women's stories are most represented in occupations like sex workers at 95% and homemakers at 68%.[2]

Due to this bias, stories centering on women's perspectives are often labeled as activism or ideology and relegated to the "diversity" or "women's" sections of online and print publications. Consequently, our daily news media predominantly reflects the male perspective, implying that women's viewpoints are less relevant or suitable for the public's regular consumption. This pervasive bias silences women's experiences and insights, perpetuating a narrow and incomplete narrative in the media landscape that ignores the indispensable role women play in shaping our society.

In business media, these biases look like the false narratives fed to women about money that disregard their experiences and viewpoints. You've heard them before: articles that claim the pay gap is a woman's decision, or that women don't like to invest, or women are frivolous spenders. I can tell you that none of those ridiculous storylines are true. But media shapes the narrative, business controls the money, and when business media does not adequately cover women as the brilliant founders, innovators, investors, and leaders that they are, it perpetuates inaccuracies about women, money, and their roles as business leaders.

To change the story, we have to change the storytellers. We must learn how to be innovative entrepreneurs, investors, and CEOs by listening to and learning from the women building in fintech. Throughout this book, the stories of female leaders will rewrite the narrative with the truth: women have always played an integral role in shaping our finance and technology innovations, maybe you just haven't read about them yet. The media has the power to shape beliefs and drive change. By accurately highlighting women's contributions in business and finance, we can shift the narrative and ensure that women's voices are heard, and their businesses are valued.

As a journalist, my job is to observe and critique the industries I cover. It is also my job to amplify voices that need to be heard, spread awareness, and describe perspectives that are otherwise overlooked. The lack of women's stories in sectors so crucial to our society, economy, and culture can't continue. To combat this, I have decided to concentrate my reporting on women-led companies while examining fintech's future through a feminist perspective.

Women do not simply operate feminist fintech companies, and "fintech feminism" goes beyond just a "feminine" approach to fintech. Instead, "fintech feminism" critically analyzes the industry as a whole, scrutinizing how systemic flaws stem from an inequitable representation of women and the global majority. This perspective challenges the status quo and advocates for action to lead to a more inclusive fintech landscape that genuinely reflects diverse voices and experiences. Feminism isn't exclusive to any gender or ethnicity; it advocates for social, political, and economic equality between everyone – women and men. Historically, men's perspectives have been the default, shaping our financial system in one direction. Amplifying women's stories, promoting women into leadership roles, and funding their businesses is crucial to creating a financial system that serves our economy in many directions. This, in turn, will help to prevent the crises and wealth disparities at the root of many current societal issues including healthcare and climate change.

Given the biased media landscape, it's no surprise that women are underrepresented in fintech. We've been bombarded with stories that perpetuate outdated narratives creating cycles of systemic oppression: men lead in business, and women lead in homemaking. The reality is much more of a "yes, and" situation – it's not mutually exclusive to be a businessperson and homemaker; in fact, most women are handling both. But when we tell stories from one perspective that present women as only one role and do not showcase their leading roles in different spaces, these stories create vicious cycles of homogeneity. The founders who receive funding secure media attention, hire their friends, and ultimately shape the structure of our economy and society. In turn, media plays a critical role in the lack of funding, equitable pay, and promotion of women in fintech as operational leaders.

As a result, the dominance of a single voice in the leadership of financial services and technology institutions has created significant gaps in innovation, increased fraud, revenue losses, and recurring economic crises. Products designed predominantly by men tend to be skewed toward male users, highlighting a critical issue: the need for a more inclusive approach to financial services. The hopeful question arises: How will financial services become more functional, equitable, and impactful for everyone when women and people of color drive the innovation?

By the end of this book, we will answer that question by showcasing that when women lead, they create financial products that cater to the unique needs of women, people of color, students, caregivers, mothers, entrepreneurs, small business owners, and underserved communities. These products address gaps in traditional financial services, promote financial inclusion, and arm a broader spectrum of society with economic independence, ultimately fostering a more resilient economy for everyone.

When people ask why I chose to dedicate my journalism career to covering fintech, my answer is simple: it's because of the incredible women building it. Over the past decade, I've been inspired by female leaders who are scrappier, more flexible, innovative, and resilient than their male counterparts. Despite receiving less funding and media attention, these trailblazers are creating fintech companies that are innovative, valuable, and unlock the economy for the most underserved. They target long-overlooked demographics – small business owners, the care economy, and low-income female entrepreneurs in international markets – unlocking revenue streams and delivering social good. As I researched women in fintech for this book, a recurring pattern emerges among them: they often view their achievements or advantages as a duty to contribute to their communities. Their ethos mirrors the adage of "build longer tables, not higher walls." No matter in the face of success or failure, they remain steadfast to sustainability and progress. Female leaders in fintech are not only reaching more communities; their actions create a ripple effect in a world where everything is connected. Women in fintech are driving significant economic activity for our global GDP, addressing climate change, solving high healthcare costs, opening access to wealth building, establishing sustainable businesses, and reshaping the financial services industry with innovative approaches. What could be more powerful than that?

This is why, after all these years, I believe fintech could be more inclusive of the global majority – and yield different results – than traditional finance or technology ever could. What truly inspires me about the fintech industry is the rise of female leaders who aren't deterred by past financial crises. Instead, they are driven by a solid resolve to learn from the past and fix what's broken in order to build a better future for the world.

Throughout my years of reporting, interviewing, and traveling, I've discovered that the most impactful leaders are driven by their first-hand experience with the challenges they address. They represent immigrants, mothers, and entrepreneurs who deeply understand the problems of their communities and are motivated to leverage fintech as the tool to create innovative solutions. It's true what they say – necessity is the mother of invention. This drive for innovation leads to greater financial inclusion, which is a key part of broader social inclusion. After all, having access to and effectively using financial services is crucial to fully participate in our economy.

Statistics are one form of data, but so is human experience. Throughout this book, you'll be provided with both. You'll read about the start-up concepts that originate from the lived experiences of leading women in fintech, and be presented with the data that backs up a consistent theme of this book: diversity, in all its forms, is valuable in building successful businesses.

BECOMING A FINTECH FEMINIST

In late May 2020, as a 26-year-old reporter for a popular trade magazine specializing in investment news and analysis for financial advisors, I found myself navigating the quickly evolving fintech landscape. Among my older, predominantly male colleagues, I was the young blood in the newsroom. When investing apps surged in popularity and financial literacy went viral on TikTok during the pandemic lockdowns, my interest piqued while my colleagues dismissed these changes. They clung to the belief that the financial services industry, with its centuries-old institutions, was immutable, impervious to the whims of a pandemic or viral videos.

Our morning pitch meetings, held over video calls, often included scoffing at my suggestions that financial advisors should pay attention to social media or the growing number of retail investors using smartphone financial apps. While my colleagues overlooked the transformative impact of modern technology and social media on the financial sector, I was witnessing firsthand a phenomenon reshaping the intersection of finance, technology, and culture.

Reporting on the burgeoning influence of technology on traditional financial institutions and changing consumer expectations, I frequently found myself explaining the significance of fintech to my editor. Unlike my colleagues, I sensed early on that the blend of finance, technology, and media would spark a dramatic rise in financial education and awareness. Perhaps my time spent on TikTok allowed me to see the trends unfolding online that others missed.

To me, the fintech field was explosive, brimming with opportunities to modernize our outdated financial system and prioritize financial inclusion through advanced technology. I embraced the challenge of covering this revolution.

As the youngest, and the only female and person of color reporter on staff, I also became the unofficial go-to for stories on female leadership, social justice, and financial inclusion. Though occasionally assisted by a colleague, I felt a personal responsibility to cover these topics because I uniquely understood them from experience.

Day after day, amid pandemic-fueled lockdowns, I worked remotely in my tiny Manhattan apartment down the block from Wall Street. Being a fintech reporter during the height of COVID-19 meant writing about the collapse of our economy in real-time. Most importantly, I chose to use my fintech coverage to highlight the glaring wealth disparities the pandemic exposed between gender, race, and socioeconomic status as the first year of the pandemic knocked 54 million women (about twice the population of Texas) out of work worldwide, widening the gender gap in employment. It could take years for that gap to narrow again. Almost 90% of women who lost jobs in 2020 exited the labor force altogether, compared with around 70% of men.[3]

It was an economic disaster that set the progress women had made in the workforce back by generations, and the downstream impact on our economy would also be felt for years. As a reporter, I was eager to explore how fintech start-ups could harness technology to drive progress for the female workforce and the economy, especially after the setbacks they faced. I interviewed sources, gathered research material, and pitched story after story, only to have my editors approve *after* I covered Goldman Sachs earnings calls. While I endured doing double the work to ensure the publication covered the female perspective, it felt like the financial system was carved in stone, with front-page reporting reserved only for established incumbents, not for the agents of change.

Once again, I noticed a shift that my older male colleagues overlooked – a silver lining to the pandemic-fueled layoffs and increased household responsibilities women were subjected to due to societal norms. As more women exited the labor force, they returned to work as entrepreneurs. It was one of the most dramatic economic shifts since the pandemic. Women made up nearly half – 47% – of new business owners, up from 29% in 2019, according to data reported in 2023 by Gusto.[4] This increased rate of entrepreneurship among women has continued, with women comprising 49% of new business owners in 2021 and 47% in 2022.

The steady influx of women into entrepreneurship correlates with economic shifts sparked by the pandemic. In 2020, 32% of women started new businesses because they were laid off. In 2021, 28% created businesses in response to increased childcare responsibilities. By 2022, 64% became entrepreneurs due to the need for work flexibility. The rise in women business owners is encouraging since women build businesses that better serve their employees and communities.

However, a stubborn statistic remains: only 2% of venture capital funding goes to female founders, despite women starting nearly half of all new businesses.[5] This disparity has significant implications beyond the frustrations of underfunded founders, especially given the critical role financial services and fintech play as the lifeblood of our economy. To get more money into the hands of women, fintech must not only provide female entrepreneurs with the tools to grow their wealth and businesses but also ensure that women are involved in creating fintech products tailored to serve the female demographic. The future of fintech, and indeed our economy, will thrive when women are fully represented and supported in their entrepreneurial and operational ventures.

Fintech, short for financial technology, is a catch-all term for digitizing traditional financial services. Fintech is used by banks, small businesses, legacy financial institutions, and consumers, and it encompasses tasks like depositing checks, transferring money, paying bills, and applying for loans. Do you remember the last time you transferred money from your Venmo account to your bank or used tap-to-pay to buy groceries? If so, you're using fintech – likely every day.

Fintech also represents a paradigm shift, expanding access to financial services for overlooked populations to accumulate wealth and challenging the established norms of the Wall Street-driven financial world, which has systems in place – from the FICO score to redlining – that have historically excluded women, people of color, and the 99% from achieving greater wealth.

By June 2020, covering the fintech beat without addressing societal inequities became nearly impossible. I may have been a B2B fintech reporter, but I was not going to ignore what was happening in the world and its direct impact on my beat. The murders of George Floyd and Breonna Taylor ignited a social reckoning, and the pandemic further highlighted deep-seated inequalities. This compelled me to communicate the significance of fintech in including communities typically excluded from the wealth-building narrative. Traditional finance has historically favored the wealthy and disadvantaged the poor, particularly women, people of color, and individuals with disabilities. For instance, how can wealth accumulation be based mainly on hard work and merit when more of the wealth acquired by new billionaires comes from inheritance rather than entrepreneurship?[6] It is essential to address systemic oppression, such as racism, sexism, ableism, classism, and ageism when discussing money, finance, and technology. Business is built on relationships, finance is personal, and technology influences our culture. If you believe human issues are irrelevant in business conversations, you are missing the fundamental piece to every successful and sustainable business strategy.

By bridging finance and technology together, creating fintech, I witnessed a surge of female entrepreneurs and business leaders who recognized that placing humanity at the center of our financial systems was the key to unlocking growth.

Over time, I discovered that women leaders were centering their work on a greater purpose. These women, whether founders of fintech companies or executives at the world's largest banks or financial institutions, were deeply passionate about reshaping a world where all people are equitably served by financial services.

Without equal female leadership, fintech faces its most devastating inadequacy – its failure to serve 50% of the global population. However, technological advancements make this disparity not just a problem; it's an opportunity to address and narrow the pay, wealth, funding, and investing gap that women have faced for generations.

This leads me to my following observation and one of my goals for this book: we need to stop trying to "fix" women and start listening to and learning from them to fix the system. For far too long, we've been teaching women to "girlboss" their way to success by mimicking men. Instead of demanding that women change, we must demand that companies pay women equally. We need to ensure that female founders receive fair funding instead of being repeatedly told that their companies are too "hyper-niche" or "high-risk" or that there's no "ROI" in investing in women. Every story and data point you'll read throughout this book proves that just isn't true. Research shows, over and over, that women build more profitable businesses, drive greater returns, and show stronger leadership qualities while receiving only a fraction of the money to do so. Meanwhile, male founders underperform their female counterparts despite receiving 98% of the funding year after year.

We must invest more capital in female fintech founders and develop systems where women can build start-ups, hire more women, and accumulate enough wealth to fund the next generation of female leaders. I uncovered that this goal can be achieved, in part, by rewriting the narrative.

Feeling isolated in my male-dominated newsroom, I decided it was up to me to initiate the cycle of women receiving the media coverage they deserve, enabling them to attract the funding and networking opportunities they need to succeed. Consequently, I left my secure position in traditional media and ventured into entrepreneurship, hoping not to drown.

In November 2021, I founded Fintech Is Femme, my media company, to create the change I wanted to see in both the media and fintech landscapes. I needed to prove that a feminist lens on fintech would attract a massive audience and kickstart a cycle of money flowing into the hands of more female founders in fintech.

I started writing a twice-weekly newsletter, filled with doubts. Not only was I seemingly the only independent journalist covering fintech for industry professionals (most other industry newsletters are written by former operators), but I was also the only woman, person under 30, and person of color doing it.

Insecurities flooded in at the start. I'm not a fintech operator – and people love to remind me. However, I've learned that what seemed disadvantageous at the start was my greatest superpower – that's what strengthens my observations of the industry. My entire education in this field comes from conducting hundreds of interviews (I've lost count) with leading CEOs, founders, investors, and executives – both women and men. My insights are a cumulative reflection of their stories and perspectives.

Still, as a female-led independent publication in fintech, I often feel isolated. But I put those insecurities aside and, like clockwork, sent out a newsletter covering women-centric stories in fintech every week. Ten months later, Fintech Is Femme attracted 50 000 subscribers who loved reading my feminist perspective, insights, and news coverage on fintech. (That's more readers than a sold-out concert at Madison Square Garden.) It turns out my former editor, and my insecurities, were wrong; I could cover fintech and women, and plenty of industry leaders found it valuable.

The newsletter evolved into my podcast, *Humans of Fintech*, where I've interviewed various fintech leaders since 2021. Many of the insights in this book come from those interviews. The podcast aims to show that your story drives your leadership, which drives your success, whether you're a fintech founder, operator, investor, or executive leader. I release monthly episodes showcasing how the most impactful leaders in fintech use their narratives to fuel their business growth. Those stories are now distilled in this book for your reading pleasure.

As I continued to build Fintech Is Femme, plenty of people put many limitations on me. "Your content makes people uncomfortable" is the limitation that a former colleague said to me on repeat. "Can you focus more on fintech and less on women?" is another one. That criticism was the rocket fuel I needed to propel past limiting beliefs and keep going, thriving, and pushing toward my greater goal: to rewrite the narrative in fintech by covering the innovations of women-led businesses that ultimately are solving problems in our economy that have been overlooked for decades.

Given that women represent a $31 trillion economy, thrive as entrepreneurs, own more homes, earn more degrees, and consistently deliver higher revenue and ROI, investing in women is a statistical no-brainer.

I had come to learn throughout my own journey as an entrepreneur that real power is knowing you never need permission from anyone but yourself. And when you have a community of other women in your corner – there are no limitations to what you can achieve.

Almost three years into building my media company, the movement and community has grown. Fintech Is Femme's success hinges on our core pillars:

1. **Amplify Her Story:** You can't be what you can't see, and we need more people to see and hear female stories in fintech, an industry that sits at the intersection of two of the most powerful business sectors on the planet.

2. **Share Her Blueprint:** After sharing her story, we break it down into actionable, bite-sized pieces, creating a roadmap for others to follow.
3. **Build Her Community:** We need a supportive network of women in fintech to sustain us through successes and failures.

Following this winning strategy, Fintech Is Femme has graced billboards in Times Square, secured brand deals with the largest financial institutions in the world, hosted events across the US and globally, and I am a public speaker who uses her time on stages to spread this message far and wide: Women are the key to unlocking a better financial future for the world.

However, the most significant measure of success comes from the countless messages from women who have used insights from the Fintech Is Femme newsletter or podcast interviews to secure funding, get promoted, or land jobs in fintech. I'm incredibly proud of how many women have decided to build fintech companies because of Fintech Is Femme. This is critical – not only do women need to be finance experts, but they need to be entrepreneurs building the tools that make our economy function equitably. With the *Fintech Feminists* book, my ultimate goal is to mint more female founders and operators in fintech to close the wealth, pay, and investing gaps once and for all.

WHAT TO EXPECT

Fintech Feminists is more than just a book – it's a blueprint for women in the fintech industry. The narrative delves deep into the insights necessary for building better businesses and increasing female leadership and innovation. Through a series of meticulously conducted interviews and extensive research, this book illuminates the indispensable role women play in the future of our global financial system. The women's stories ahead will show you how female innovators in fintech are reshaping finance and redefining success, transforming the digital revolution into a goldmine for entrepreneurial success.

This book is perfect for you if you're interested in contributing to solving financial and societal inequities by fueling our economy with innovative solutions. In preparation for *Fintech Feminists*, I interviewed more than 300 leaders in finance and technology and wrote hundreds of articles chronicling fintech. These women and their companies are adding value to the industry and contributing significantly to society. However, their stories have often been overlooked or simply not associated with great leadership in finance and technology. This book aims to change that narrative by highlighting these women's exceptional qualities that correlate with outstanding leadership and innovative business models.

Throughout my reporting for this book, I found that the intersection of their personal narratives fuels their business models, leadership techniques, and funding strategies. The women in the coming chapters showcase that building profitable businesses does not come at the expense of social good – they prove that the two fuel each other.

I also discovered that women building in fintech are more likely to include varied perspectives in decision-making, which enhances their ability to empathize with colleagues and customers. These leaders often lead with vulnerability, a willingness to explore business opportunities outside the status quo, and a focus on achieving a greater purpose beyond profits. Despite their innovative approaches, these women's contributions have frequently been underestimated and undervalued simply because of their gender. You'll have to read the book to truly grasp the depth of their impact. The book doesn't fully capture the diversity and the number of women leading in fintech, as there are too many for me to write about all of their incredible stories in one book – but with 36 profiles and a handful of features detailing the stories of trailblazing women in fintech, it's a start. Whether you're interested in learning about the pivotal role of women in digital finance, exploring the $31 trillion female economy, or seeking actionable strategies for operational and entrepreneurial success, this book is your comprehensive guide to leading in the fintech revolution.

In writing this book, I wasn't just testing my hypothesis that women are the key to unlocking a better financial future for the world – I was also learning how to navigate the financial system better myself. The chapters ahead are organized thematically, with profiles of women interwoven with relevant research. Plus, you'll read the story of how they have influenced fintech and my work as a journalist dedicated to covering this space.

Get ready to meet a series of fintech trailblazers, each a powerhouse in their own right, from Sallie Krawcheck, who boldly transitioned from banking to spearhead the first fintech venture by and for women, to Sheila Lirio Marcelo, the pioneering Filipina immigrant and the seventh woman to lead a company to its public debut, and Mary Ellen Iskenderian, a visionary who has steered Women's World Banking for nearly two decades. My hope is that the strategies and stories highlighted in *Fintech Feminists* serve as a valuable resource for anyone, regardless of their background, looking for ways to succeed in finance and technology. The practical takeaways in this book are drawn from the real experiences of female leaders who have navigated the challenges of the fintech industry. These lessons are not just theoretical – they are proven strategies that have led to tangible success.

Remember, patriarchy allows these inequitable systems to flourish, but let me be clear: The opposite of patriarchy is not a matriarchy. Today, we live in a patriarchal society where men hold positions of dominance and privilege, but a matriarchy is an entirely different system designed to work well for everyone involved. That's what I see for the future of fintech. With our economy and society facing widening inequities, the insights from these women are table stakes.

Fintech Feminists provides a comprehensive guide to understanding how female innovators are reshaping the future of finance. By offering a blend of practical advice, inspiring stories, and insightful research, this book is poised to be an invaluable resource for anyone looking to understand women's integral role in the digital revolution and the future of our global financial system. Join me as we delve into these powerful narratives and discover how women in fintech are not just changing the game – they're rewriting the rules for everyone, and we need their perspectives now more than ever.

NOTES

1. Reuters Institute. *Women and Leadership in the News Media 2023: Evidence from 12 Markets.* Accessed May 20, 2024. https://reutersinstitute.politics.ox.ac.uk/women-and-leadership-news-media-2023-evidence-12-markets#header--1.
2. Global Media Monitoring Project. *Who Makes the News? GMMP 2020 Report.* July 13, 2021. Accessed May 20, 2024. https://whomakesthenews.org/wp-content/uploads/2021/07/GMMP2020.ENG_.FINAL20210713.pdf.
3. *Washington Post.* "The Pandemic Is Threatening Women's Progress. Will It Push Them out of the Workforce for Good?" Accessed May 20, 2024.
4. Gusto. "The Rise of Women Entrepreneurs." Accessed May 20, 2024. https://gusto.com/company-news/the-rise-of-women-entrepreneurs.
5. PitchBook. "The VC Female Founders Dashboard." Accessed May 20, 2024. https://pitchbook.com/news/articles/the-vc-female-founders-dashboard.
6. UBS Global. *Billionaire Ambitions Report 2023.* Accessed May 20, 2024. https://www.ubs.com/global/en/family-office-uhnw/reports/billionaire-ambitions-report-2023/download.html.

CHAPTER ONE

WHAT THE FINTECH?

On 15 February 1999, *Time* magazine featured Former Federal Reserve Chair Alan Greenspan alongside former Treasury Secretaries Larry Summers and Robert Rubin on the cover. Big, bold yellow letters proclaimed that the trio were on the committee to save the world from a global economic meltdown.[1] However, the cover also suggested that the group only prevented a global crisis *for now*.

That cover foreshadowed the inevitable – the 2008 global financial crisis hit less than a decade later. The collapse of investment bank Lehman Brothers on 15 September 2008 marked the ominous dawn of this era of uncertainty, sending shockwaves rippling through the global financial bedrock.[2] Greenspan eventually conceded that the global financial crisis exposed a mistake in the free market ideology – trusting that free markets could regulate themselves – which guided his 18-year stewardship of US monetary policy.[3]

Fast forward to 24 May 2010, and this *Time* magazine featured a cover with three female regulators: United States Senator Elizabeth Warren, 19th Chair of the US Federal Deposit Insurance Corporation Sheila Bair, and 29th Chair of the US Securities and Exchange Commission Mary Schapiro. They were dubbed "the women charged with cleaning up the mess," portrayed with serious expressions – tasked with addressing the aftermath of unchecked corporate greed and the systemic failure of the banking system.[4]

I first noticed the juxtaposition between these two covers while researching for this book. I came across a 2011 research paper by Julie Nelson, a professor of economics at the University of Massachusetts Boston known for applying feminist theory to questions about the definition of economics, its models, and methodology.[5] Feminist economics advocates for a fuller exploration of economic data. It argues that traditional economic thought is shaped by social norms and its models and methods are biased, focusing mainly on male-associated topics and assumptions with women's contribution to the economy routinely ignored.[6] As a result, important issues like unpaid care work, unequal power relations between men and women, and labor market outcomes for women of color have been overlooked by the mostly male-dominated field. For example, mainstream economics seems to have overlooked the value of unpaid domestic and care work predominantly carried out by women in the home, which is essential to a well-functioning economy.[7] GDP measurements consider the value produced through wage labor, but not through unpaid care work, which represents a contribution to the global economy of at least $10.8 trillion per year, more than three times the size of the global tech industry.[8] When feminist economics is applied to the 2008 financial crisis, it makes me think of the gaps in our system and ask: Could having women in leadership roles have prevented the global financial crisis?

The heart of the problem was risk, a responsibility largely taken for granted by male Wall Street professionals and left for female regulators to manage. Author Jay Newton-Small shares in her book *Broad Influence: How*

Women Are Changing the Way America Works, that many world leaders, including Bair, International Monetary Fund chief Christine Lagarde, British Labour deputy leader Harriet Harman, and Japanese Prime Minister Shinzo Abe, believed the global financial crisis would not have occurred if more women had held senior positions on Wall Street.[9] The crisis was seen by many as a signal for Wall Street to diversify its leadership.

Then there's the crisis that shaped the "tech" side of fintech – the 2001 dot-com bubble. This bubble saw a rapid and ultimately unsustainable surge in the value of stock market shares in internet service and technology companies, often referred to as "dot-com." It included new businesses or start-ups with little to no profitability record or unrealistic business models, leading to the overvaluation (and subsequent crash) of Wall Street's young internet technology industry.[10]

Could the popular and well-known "bro style" culture, which preferred male leadership during the 1990s tech boom and was characterized by entitlement, hubris, and risk-taking, have led to its eventual failure?[11] Similar to its role in the financial crisis, this culture caused the downfall, making me wonder: If more women had held leadership roles in the tech industry back then, could they have prevented or lessened the impact of the disaster?

The dot-com bubble and the global financial crisis originated from industries that men predominantly led, and it's not a coincidence that these industries face a crisis or crash every 10 years or so. Have you heard of the phrase: "Insanity is doing the same thing repeatedly and expecting different results?" When 98% of venture capital dollars go to male founders, who then predominantly hire male leaders, perpetuating a cycle that sees money continuously funneled into the next male-led start-up, ultimately leading to economic crises, it's a classic case of insanity.

Today, these industries are still largely male-dominated, creating an environment often described as "pale, male, and stale" – a phrase used to highlight the overwhelming presence of men in these spaces for generations.

While the words may elicit a quick eye-roll and an uncomfortable laugh, the missed opportunity for diversity to drive innovation has a significantly negative impact on our economy.

Before we continue, I want to be clear: this is not a book about hating men. I hope thousands of brilliant men are reading this book so they can join the *Fintech Feminists* movement, too. The reality is that when a single perspective dominates decision-making in industries that shape our society, it can create dangerous blind spots, stifle innovation, and close off vast areas of economic potential – it's that simple. We've already seen groupthink as a commonality at the root of financial and tech failures that, unfortunately, impact the people who did not make those decisions the most. Also, none of this is a zero-sum game. As we follow women's lead in fintech, we will all benefit from the outcomes. Closing gender gaps benefits countries and companies as a whole, not just women.

In this book, you will encounter numerous fintech pioneers launching start-ups to fill the gaps in the financial system. Many of them concentrate on meeting women's unique financial needs, tapping into a revenue source from half of humanity that their male counterparts have historically ignored. These women identified opportunities to solve root problems in our economic system by learning from past failures, recognizing that profit and purpose are not mutually exclusive but rather mutually reinforcing. They built diverse teams because they understand innovation lives in diverse perspectives and experiences. These women are paving the way for billions of dollars in revenue to enter fintech.

What makes these women even more remarkable is how they have persevered in spite of systems that have not been so welcoming. As evidenced in the fintech industry's own crises, fintech has inherited some "bro" cultures that have trickled down from our predecessors in the finance and technology sector, particularly in terms of funding and leadership.

Globally only 1% of total venture capital goes to fintech start-ups founded solely by women.[12] As a result, female-led fintechs raise 54 cents for every dollar raised by their male counterparts. On top of that, less than 6% of CEOs and less than 4% of chief innovation or technology officers are women.[13] This is a huge, missed opportunity. Fintech is uniquely positioned to drive economic change, promote equitable financial services, and boost financial inclusion for overlooked groups, many of whom are women. The commercial case is clear: by failing to identify, understand, and connect with the female market due to the lack of women in leadership, firms are leaving substantial amounts of money on the table to the tune of $700 billion, according to a 2020 analysis by Oliver Wyman.[14] This glaring disparity costs our economy a lot of money, especially considering the potential for female entrepreneurship to contribute $5 trillion to the global GDP.[15]

These harrowing statistics are not limited to fintech but also affect our related industries that feed the fintech ecosystem. There are 4071 FDIC-insured banks, and fewer than 5% of publicly traded banks have a female CEO.[16] Meanwhile, more than half of bank employees are women. Jane Fraser, who became the CEO of Citi in March 2021, is the only woman currently leading one of the 50 largest banks in the country. The percentage of women serving as CEOs in technology is roughly 17%, according to data reported in 2024.[17] Women hold 8.2% of CEO positions at S&P 500 companies, or 41 out of 459 CEOs, as of 2023. Not only is that number a new record, but it also marks the first-time female CEOs outnumber CEOs with the first name John, per an analysis from Bloomberg.[18]

Clearly, fintech is following the lead of finance and technology a bit too closely. The problem with mimicking the spaces of our predecessors is constructing on a faulty foundation will tend to be, well faulty – it's a flawed system to change, and we need to confront it directly and comprehend the context. Otherwise, what we build will persist in being flawed.

For example, fintech faced an industry-specific crisis that included cultural awareness with the rise and fall of the cryptocurrency sector. This was exemplified by the well-documented demise of cryptocurrency exchange FTX and its founder, Sam Bankman-Fried, in 2022.[19] This sent shockwaves across the industry, eroding trust in a once-hailed sector for its potential to enhance financial inclusivity and prosperity. The subsequent collapse of crypto-friendly banks, Silvergate Capital Corp. and Signature Bank, in 2023 further complicated the narrative, diverting attention from broader conversations about what blockchain technology was invented for – financial inclusion. Additionally, fintech suffered a significant blow during the banking crisis of March 2023 when herd mentality triggered a bank run, cascading into multiple bank failures within five days. Once again, these crises expose the pattern of being led by a male-dominated industry.

While these hardships bruised the fintech industry and its traction, we bounced back quickly – proving there's still a ton of resiliency and room for growth. In fact, after years of hypergrowth – as of July 2023, publicly traded fintechs represented a market capitalization of $550 billion – the fintech industry has entered a new era of value creation, where the focus is on sustainable, profitable growth.[20] To achieve our industry's primary goal of making profits in a way that lasts and includes everyone and to prevent another economic crisis, we need to deliberately increase the number of women who lead companies and start new businesses in fintech.

Research shows the correlation between gender-diverse leadership and profitability, revealing that companies with at least 30% female leadership were 6% more profitable.[21] There's no reason to believe fintech would be an exception. If more women had led during previous financial crises and the dot-com era, we might have seen fewer "unicorns" and "too-big-to-fail" banks. Instead, we could have had a more resilient landscape with crisis-resilient banks and technology start-ups built on sustainable profitability. Our actions will determine the fate of the fintech industry and its impact on the global economy. Let us not look back 15 years from now with a new crisis under our belts as we ask ourselves: What preventions and economic advancements could be if women were leading in fintech?

For now, 2024 data from the World Economic Forum gives us a sense of the key role female representation plays in the success of the fintech industry both in executive roles and as one of the most significant growth markets we've ever seen. Fintech companies with more than 30% women leaders were more likely to outperform less gender-diverse companies, suggesting that fintechs can harvest competitive financial results in terms of market performance by keeping a higher-than-global-average rate of female leadership. Plus, fintech companies with female executives will experience a 12% increase in their female customer base. This positive trend extends to product offerings, with a substantial 30% increase in products designed to target female customers.[22] The significance of these findings reverberates on a global scale. Fintech companies that embrace gender equality in leadership contribute to financial success and the broader goals of reducing inequalities and promoting gender equality worldwide. Ultimately, the infusion of female leadership in fintech is a game-changer, unlocking new possibilities for market performance and customer base expansion. As the industry evolves, fostering diversity at the top levels is not just a matter of representation – it's a strategic imperative for sustained commercial success and global impact.

A BRIEF FINTECH HISTORY

One positive outcome of the past crises is the spark of innovative ideas. Many successful start-ups today, some of whom you'll meet in the pages to come, emerged during the dot-com bubble and the 2008 financial crisis. Addressing economic exclusion will take time, but the innovators in this book will show how you, as a reader, can play a pivotal role in closing wealth gaps while building profitable businesses. This book provides a blueprint for achieving that type of success in fintech.

Before we delve into those insights, it's important to revisit the history of the fintech industry so that we understand how to shape its future. Several historical events have led to the fintech industry evolving from operating behind the scenes to becoming a significant part of cultural consciousness.

Fintech, short for "financial technology," refers to any digital services consumers use to manage their money. These services include online banking, payments, investing, savings, budgeting, borrowing, education, and goal-setting. The industry is massive, and while I will not be able to cover every moment of history or innovation that has led us to where we are today, consider this a concise version. I've compiled this history based on the standout headlines I've written while reporting on fintech as part of my journalism beat.

The origins of fintech can be traced back to several historical moments. In the nineteenth century the New York Stock Exchange (NYSE) installed a specialized form of teleprinter known as a stock ticker to transmit financial orders.[23] Then, in September 1958, Bank of America mailed 60 000 credit cards to consumers in Fresno, California, revolutionizing the way people conducted financial transactions.[24] By October 1959, more than two million credit cards had been issued in California alone. The introduction of the Automated Teller Machine (ATM) by Barclays in 1967 further transformed banking by providing customers with access to cash and basic banking services outside of regular banking hours.[25]

However, the true intersection of banking and technology, or the fintech we are familiar with today, began in the internet era. Digital banking emerged in the 1990s, with Wells Fargo launching wellsfargo.com in 1994 and becoming the first bank in the US to offer free internet access to checking account balances in 1995.[26] This allowed consumers to manage their finances from anywhere with internet connectivity and a computer.

Subsequently, PayPal, founded in 1998, pioneers peer-to-peer payment processes for goods and services.[27] In 2000, Roy Fielding and a group of experts invented the Representational State Transfer Framework (REST), which became a standard for allowing two servers to communicate and exchange data. Thus, it changed the way computer applications communicated and altered the application program interfaces (APIs) landscape, laying the groundwork for fintech.[28]

These technology advancements coupled with learning lessons from the financial crisis made one of the goals of fintech to lower the costs of providing more personalized and extensive banking and wealth management services to a broader audience – the everyday consumer – not just the wealthy 1%. This would drive market growth for businesses, and bring more women, people of color, and other overlooked demographics into the mainstream of the global financial system, stimulating more economic activity. As fintech has contributed to achieving this goal, the industry's value has increased. This growth is driven by rapid consumer adoption, with businesses and small and medium-sized enterprises increasingly turning to fintech for banking and payments, financial management, financing, and insurance.

Fintech came into its own after the 2008 financial crisis, when traditional banks and financial institutions faced new regulations with the formation of the Consumer Financial Protection Bureau following repeated crises, prompting an overhaul of the banking industry. At the same time, society was rapidly progressing, thanks to the widespread use of the internet and smartphones. These devices have become the primary means of accessing the internet and using various financial services, allowing millions worldwide to access financial services via mobile applications. This set the stage for the emergence of a new wave of fintech companies that challenged the banks. As the banks and incumbent financial institutions dealt with the aftermath of the crisis, it left an opening for fintech founders – many of whom were former Wall Street employees turned entrepreneurs as a result of the financial crisis – to unbundle the banks' services and build tech start-ups that offered singular pieces of the banking experience, becoming best-of-breeds while breaking down financial services into different tech sectors.

Early fintech brands emerged, like SoFi in 2011, for example, which started as a student loan refinancing platform to provide more affordable options for those taking on debt to fund their education. In payments, start-ups like Square, Stripe, Toast, Plaid, and Wise have made transferring money internationally easier and less expensive. Companies such as Lending Club, Revolut, and Kabbage gained attention and market share in credit. Insuretechs (insurance technology) like Goji and Root made inroads in the insurance market, while robo-advisers from Betterment, Wealthfront, and Ellevest attracted customers with low-cost, algorithm-driven investing advice.

Even big tech companies like Apple and Google have stepped into fintech – wanting their piece of the pie with Google Wallet launching in 2011 and Apple Pay following suit in 2014. Today, large fintech players, primarily the neobanks, are now rebundling financial services by offering banking, savings, personal loans, auto insurance, mortgages, and investing – thus becoming like a bank itself. In fact, in 2024, fintech SoFi became the official bank of the National Basketball Association (NBA).[29] Even Apple teamed up with Goldman Sachs as its banking partner to venture into consumer credit card issuing and start bundling banking services with the launch of the Apple Card but terminated the agreement in 2023.[30]

Fintech companies have been disruptive because they can innovate and differentiate. Their agility in using new technologies to anticipate and solve customer needs sets them apart, as legacy systems and processes do not burden them. Throughout my reporting, I observed that these fintech start-ups do not disrupt their industry in the way that, say, Uber disrupted the transportation sector or Netflix disrupted movie-going. Instead, fintech carves out value propositions in unique niches among and between much larger players in financial services. For fintech entrepreneurs, it's not just about surviving in the shadow of financial giants like Citigroup, Vanguard, and JPMorgan Chase & Co. It's about comprehending their strategies, spotting gaps in the market, and devising ways to enhance value for these incumbents. This strategic comprehension is a key to survival and a pathway to success in the competitive fintech landscape. Collaboration is crucial in the rise of fintech as the banks rebounded from the financial crisis, and we stepped into the next era.

A key advancement that enabled more companies to offer financial services to more people is the rise of banking-as-a-service, or BaaS – a model in which financial institutions provide access to their core banking functions through APIs. This enables third-party businesses to build their own financial products without needing to become banks. Fintech companies no longer need to be specialists to offer traditional financial services as long as they have a bank partner to provide that expertise. On the other hand, tech-savvy legacy banks can fend off the encroaching threat of fintechs by moving into the BaaS space to share their data and infrastructure. Research conducted in the past year found that 77% of fintechs and banks reported an increase in correspondent banking relationships, where infrastructure is provided for fintechs to support their own products.[31] Today, BaaS continues to grow, allowing traditional banks, insurers, and wealth managers to reach a wider range of customers at a lower cost by partnering with non-financial businesses. Consumers increasingly use these platforms to access e-commerce, travel, retail, health, and telecom services. For example, a financial service could be someone taking out a small loan when paying for a holiday on a travel site or instantly calculating and selling micro-insurance for newly purchased luxury clothes.

This advancement enabled non-financial businesses to distribute financial products under their own brand, providing customers with the experience of buying a product from that brand, while a financial institution actually provides the financial product. To offer BaaS via a distributor, a financial institution can set up a platform for this purpose based on the latest low-cost, cloud-native, scalable technology, which will reduce its cost to serve customers.

For financial institutions, BaaS offers a compelling opportunity to expand their customer base at a significantly reduced cost, thereby promoting financial inclusion. As per Oliver Wyman's analysis, the average cost of acquiring a customer typically ranges from $100 to $200. However, with the adoption of a new BaaS technology stack, this cost can plummet to as low as $5–35.[32] This substantial cost reduction paves the way for new revenue streams and fosters deeper customer relationships and cross-selling opportunities, bolstering the institution's profitability and growth potential. However, the BaaS model has not been without controversy. Take Synapse, for instance – they filed for Chapter 11 bankruptcy on 22 April 2024.[33] As one of the pioneering BaaS providers since 2014, their collapse left hundreds of thousands of users locked out of their accounts. In response, Synapse had to shut down its services to some of its fintech or bank partners, including Evolve Bank & Trust. This situation highlights a key issue: companies that look like banks do not have the same regulatory protections. As fintech keeps growing and evolving, it's clear that strong regulatory frameworks and consumer protections are essential to prevent such crises.

As financial institutions began catering to a larger and more diverse customer base, they started amassing more consumer data, particularly with the surge in our digital footprints. This data empowered fintechs to assist financial institutions in delivering financial products not just through conventional finance apps, but also in tailoring and personalizing the products to resonate with individual customers' unique needs. This adaptability was particularly evident during the global pandemic, when our industry confronted the coronavirus – the greatest test to the global economy since World War II.

FINTECH'S MASS ADOPTION MOMENT

The World Health Organization declared the coronavirus outbreak a pandemic on March 11, 2020.[34] This led to state-imposed shutdowns to control the spread of COVID-19. The resulting economic downturn caused significant job losses in early 2020. Government restrictions and fear of the virus kept people at home and closed businesses, leading to a sharp economic decline. Federal policymakers put relief and recovery measures in place – like stimulus checks and the payroll protection program (PPP) – in 2020 and 2021.

These measures played a key role in supporting the economy. Their impact was significant, leading to an economic recovery that started in May 2020. According to the National Bureau of Economic Research, the pandemic recession was the shortest since World War II, lasting only two months.[35] The recovery was faster than expected, and by the end of 2023, job creation and economic activity had exceeded pre-pandemic levels. As governments implemented measures to control the virus and stabilize the economy, the use of fintech rapidly increased – subsequently, so did a heightened awareness of financial disparities. The impact was not the same for everyone, with workers in low-wage industries, women, workers of color, those without a bachelor's degree, and foreign-born workers being affected the most.[36] They experienced large reductions in employment and earnings, showing that the pandemic had a greater economic impact on them and their recovery.

The shutdown of our in-person economy led to the mass adoption of fintech during the pandemic out of pure necessity. Lockdown measures limited in-person interactions as consumers and businesses could not purchase goods and services, or even make deposits at a bank branch or ATM, leading to increased use of mobile devices for economic activities. In 2021, mobile finance apps reached 573.1 million downloads in the US, up nearly 19% from the year prior.[37] Between 2020 and 2021 the proportion of US consumers using fintech grew from 58% to 88% – a 52% year-over-year increase, according to 2021 research by Plaid.[38] This surge in adoption exceeds the timeframes of previous technological innovations: refrigerators took 20 years, computers took 10, and smartphones took 5 to reach comparable consumer usage levels. This widespread adoption marked a new era where fintech is no longer behind the scenes of the financial system but center stage as a key player in the economic landscape. Investors noticed and began pouring record amounts of investments into the fintech sector. Benefiting from the acceleration in digitization triggered by the pandemic and a financial system flooded with liquidity, fintech funding in 2021 increased by 177% year over year to $92.3 billion.

ENTRANCE INTO CULTURAL CONSCIOUSNESS

During the pandemic, two fintech segments experienced increased mainstream adoption and fueled each other's growth. First, there was a surge in investing, with more than 10 million Americans opening new brokerage accounts in 2020.[39] Due to increased leisure time and surplus cash, many consumers turned to stock investing. As there are no formal ways to educate customers on investing in the stock market, these new users turned to social media to learn. Plenty of personal finance experts (and non-experts) on social media platforms were willing to share knowledge about finance, breaking down barriers and making it more accessible. This content became viral, with 48% of Gen Z investors learning about investing and finances through social media.[40]

When you type the hashtag #personalfinance into the TikTok app's search bar, you'll find thousands of 60-second videos offering financial advice on topics like savings, budgeting, investing, and explanations of economic terminology. One of the videos that started the popular trend of finance content on TikTok was from Humphrey Yang, a content creator who gained millions of views in February 2020. He posted a video showing a billion dollars worth of rice, with each grain representing $100 000. The visual comparison of a huge pile of rice to illustrate the net worth of Amazon founder Jeff Bezos compared to an average person's single grain highlighted the wealth disparities in America. These disparities only worsened as the fallout from the pandemic continued.

Wealth inequality is higher in the United States than in other developed countries and has risen for 60 years. Notably, global billionaire wealth surged by $4.4 trillion between 2020 and 2021, while more than 100 million individuals fell below the poverty line.[41] This stark dichotomy highlights the pandemic's profound impact on widening wealth gaps and emphasizes the urgency of addressing systemic inequities. As more consumers learn about these flaws in our financial system, they expose these systemic barriers by sharing that new found knowledge on social media. The influx of millions of new investors was now using their purchasing power to express their values and support causes they believe in, such as climate change, healthcare, and women's rights. One financial expert grew her financial education platform into a multimillion-dollar business by showing millions of women how to use their wealth to fight for causes they believe in.

REWRITING MONEY NARRATIVES

Tori Dunlap grew up thinking that learning about finance was a regular part of every child's education. Her parents taught her finance basics, like saving and not overspending on credit cards. However, when she entered college and adulthood, she realized how privileged she was to have received such an education. In an interview in January 2024, Dunlap told me that her financial expertise had become a point of interest among her friends, particularly her female friends, who often sought her advice and guidance. The sheer volume of advice she was providing made her realize the dire state of financial literacy in America. The estimated average amount of money that lacking knowledge about personal finances cost people was $1,506 per year in 2023.[42] According to a 2022 National Financial Educators Council (NFEC) survey, in total Americans lost more than $436 billion due to financial illiteracy.[43] "It's crippling," Dunlap said. "It creates all of the disparities that we see."

After graduating college in 2016, Dunlap decided to climb the corporate ladder. It would not take long before the rose-colored lenses came off and the reality of corporate America, especially for women, sunk in. "I was working for men who were abusive and saying weird sexual comments to me," she recalled. "I became very disillusioned very quickly." Then, in the 2016 election, Dunlap was optimistic that the US was getting its first female president, and, instead, Donald Trump was elected. "I was entering adulthood and womanhood in a very different country than I expected," she said. "It honestly radicalized me."

The convergence of the two experiences – being the go-to finance expert among friends and realizing that girl-bossing your way up the corporate ladder is toxic – led her to believe in the power of financial knowledge. As Dunlap shared in our interview and throughout her book *Financial Feminist*, when women have our financial health together, we can get out of that job we do not want to be in, or we have the option to start a business or donate to the causes we want to support. "That was the kind of moment where I was like – so what am I going to do about it?" she said. At 22, Dunlap started a financial education blog and began saving money to amass $100 000 by age 25. In 2019, Dunlap made it happen and soon appeared on

Good Morning America to discuss how she did it. Three weeks later, she quit her job to build a full-time company, Her First $100 K. Audiences, especially women, were hungry for financial education.

Dunlap began sharing the same financial advice she shared with her friends via her podcast that she launched in 2021, *Financial Feminist,* with a $99 mic off Amazon. Within two days, it was the number one business podcast in the world – and is now the most popular show about money for women. By 2022, her book *Financial Feminist* emerged and immediately landed a *New York Times* Best Seller accolade. On social media, Dunlap shares all of her insights and her accomplishments on social media platforms like TikTok and Instagram.

The timing could not be more perfect. Financial education gained newfound cultural relevance in 2020, primarily due to pandemic-fueled lockdowns spurring increased engagement in personal finance content on TikTok. This carried into the world of fintech, with 79% of users looking for education around starting an emergency fund, improving credit scores, and creating a savings habit from their fintech applications, according to Plaid's 2022 fintech effect report. Until personal finance content exploded with billions of views on TikTok, the average person had limited access to financial advice due to account minimums or a lack of knowledge. However, technology has enabled anyone with a smartphone to access the same level of financial guidance that was once limited to the wealthy and well-informed. The most notable spike in interest has come from those traditionally underserved by financial services.

A 2023 survey commissioned by Forbes Advisor and conducted by market research company Prolific found that 78% of millennials and Gen Z believe they have more access to financial advice now, thanks to social media like TikTok, than they would have as part of previous generations because of their identities, such as race, gender, or income. Creators like Dunlap have leveraged the TikTok platform to build businesses and spark movements toward financial inclusion and knowledge sharing, catering to these untapped demographics. On TikTok, Dunlap has garnered an audience of 2.4 million as she continues to build the "financial feminist" movement, inspiring women to own their financial independence as the greatest tool for fighting patriarchal barriers. This is based on the principle that "having a financial education is a woman's best form of protest," said Dunlap.

During the pandemic in 2021, I followed Dunlap's recommendations and opened a high-yield savings account through SoFi to build up my emergency fund. Thanks to this, by December 2023, I could use my saved money to take my media company, Fintech Is Femme, independent and pursue my entrepreneurial journey full time. This is the power of fintech fueling female entrepreneurship. I've experienced it myself.

As fintech leaders, builders, investors, and operators, we are critical in enabling women to access financial services. Money, indeed, does mean options. And especially if you are a member of the global majority, when you have money, you do not have to be in a situation that does not respect you, does not honor you, and does not make you feel safe. You have the freedom to choose. "That's the feeling I want every single woman on this planet to feel," Dunlap said. "We will not have equality for any marginalized group until financial equality."

As women, we are often taught that pursuing wealth is terrible. It stems from a long line of gender inequities when it comes to women and their finances. It wasn't until 1974, when the Equal Credit Opportunity Act passed, that women in the US were granted the right to open a bank account independently. Technically, women won the right to open a bank account in the 1960s, but many banks still refused to let women do so without a signature from their husbands. It's 2024, and we are still playing catch-up.

Ultimately, Dunlap's mission and content give women the confidence to understand that it's not greedy or morally corrupt to be a high earner or to want money to establish one's independence. "At the end of the day, money is a stack of government-issued paper," Dunlap said. "It has no inherent moral value. It's morally neutral, and what you do with it is where morality starts."

As a journalist covering the intersection of finance, technology, and gender parity, I have the opportunity to interview women who have reached a point where they feel compelled to pay it forward. They're determined to establish a fintech company that will transform the financial system, making it more accessible to their communities. Yet, this endeavor has its challenges related to the money narrative. Not only do women have to grapple with the mental hurdle of entering a VC room without being pigeonholed, but they also face skepticism, mainly due to gender.

It's disheartening when even female founders of innovative companies with impressive revenue growth and strategic planning encounter questions in VC rooms about their plans for parenthood rather than focusing on the business's potential for social good and profitability. It's a stark reminder that despite their accomplishments, they are often viewed through a narrow lens instead of being recognized for the innovative and lucrative ventures they are building.

So, how do we move forward? Per Dunlap's advice, we need to be proud of the businesses we are building, and "we need more women unabashedly pursuing money," she said. "When a woman has money, she becomes uncontrollable." When you are an uncontrollable person, the patriarchal, racist system that exists panics.

"I want to highlight that I am almost obnoxious about our business," Dunlap said. If you follow Dunlap on social media, you'll notice that she posts about her business daily and its positive impact. I find it inspiring and hope that it motivates you, too. Women must showcase their achievements, inspiring others to do the same. After all, you cannot aspire to be something you have never seen.

Women are not individually at fault for lacking the self-confidence to put themselves out there. Society often conditions us to avoid taking risks, minimize our accomplishments, and wait for opportunities to come to us.

A common challenge women entrepreneurs face is the gap between their efforts and the need for systemic change. While it's often suggested that women should ask for the funding they deserve, the reality is that without an environment that actively supports women, these efforts may not yield lasting results. For instance, even if a woman has a brilliant business proposal, it may not matter if she presents to a group that does not value or support female entrepreneurs.

So, while there's undoubtedly a lot we can do as individual women and every step toward progress matters, larger leaps require systemic change. Institutions must recognize that investing in women is morally right and financially lucrative.

Moreover, the support we need extends beyond just the workplace. Our government's lack of support adds another layer of complexity to our challenges. "It's a frustrating situation, to say the least, but it's one I'm determined to change," Dunlap said. "The only thing that wins by you playing small is patriarchy."

Throughout history, women have been subjected to various false narratives that aim to limit their potential and encourage them to strive for unrealistic standards of perfection instead of being courageous. Society has conditioned women to pursue perfection, which is ultimately unattainable. As a result, instead of embracing their imperfections and taking action, many women hesitate or avoid taking on new challenges, such as investing or starting a company. Pursuing perfection often leads to experiencing misogynistic schemes like impostor syndrome, which can be a barrier to success.

An example of these misogynistic schemes was made viral in 2023 when the founder of Girls Who Code, Reshma Saujani, told the story of how imposter syndrome is modern-day bicycle face during a commencement speech at Smith College. During the cycling boom of the 1890s, the sport gained traction in Europe and North America, particularly among women.

However, just as its popularity peaked, a novel medical condition emerged, posing a threat to women's health: bicycle face.

This peculiar affliction targeted women who dared to venture on bike rides, purportedly manifesting in symptoms such as flushed cheeks, bulging eyes, and a countenance ranging from anxious to stony. Curiously, while men also participated in cycling, bicycle faces exclusively haunted women, suggesting a deliberate attempt to dissuade them from embracing the activity. Far from being a genuine medical syndrome, bicycle faces appeared more as a tactic to deter women from the liberating act of cycling. In an era where the bicycle symbolized burgeoning feminism, enabling women to traverse greater distances independently, it's evident that bicycle faces served as a tool to hinder this progress. So, the next time you think you need to be perfect to be great at building in fintech – think of bicycle face.

"As an entrepreneur, my top rule is 'done is better than perfect,'" Dunlap said. "I firmly believe in getting things done rather than endlessly striving for perfection, which I see as a common barrier for women." Dunlap works with women who fear making mistakes or feel overwhelmed by the idea of needing everything in place before starting. "I've learned firsthand that you do not need to have all the answers or resources upfront," she said.

The key is to start and adapt as you go. Waiting until you have all the knowledge or resources is a recipe for never getting started. "Learn by doing," Dunlap said. "Embrace a philosophy of getting things done and refining them as we progress, acknowledging that perfection is an illusion. Sure, mistakes happen, but they are growth opportunities."

As women, it's essential not to shy away from asserting our needs – that's the essence of networking. Many of us were taught that networking involves donning business suits, shaking hands, and visiting vendor booths. But networking is about reciprocity. It's about helping others while also being open to receiving support in return.

Remember what American cultural anthropologist Margaret Mead taught us, Dunlap reminds me: Never underestimate a small group or individual's impact on the world. It's often these dedicated, modest groups that drive significant change.

FINANCIAL ILLITERACY EXPOSED

Social media can be an excellent tool for financial education, but things can get tricky for consumers when fintech apps start using social media-like tactics. Take Robinhood, for example. They make investing feel like a game, which is fun but risky if people do not know what they are doing.

Robinhood's user base increased from 12.5 million in 2020 to 22.7 million in 2021, largely because of its gamified investing and unlimited day trading features.[44] However, this rapid growth did not come without controversy. In June 2020, a 20-year-old named Alex Kearns tragically took his own life after mistakenly believing he had lost $730 000 on Robinhood.[45] This heartbreaking incident underscored the risks that free-trading platforms can pose for inexperienced investors.

By December 2020, Robinhood was hit with a lawsuit from Massachusetts Secretary of the Commonwealth, William Galvin, accusing the fintech start-up of using gamification to attract and manipulate users. This led to a $7.5 million settlement in January 2024.[46] The GameStop stock surge in January 2021 further showcased the significant impact fintech can have on the market while highlighting Robinhood's controversial payment for order flow (PFOF) model, which made up about 75% of its revenue in 2020.[47] Critics argue that while Robinhood claims to democratize investing, it actually profits by selling user data, essentially turning its main street users into products that Wall Street benefits from.

BE A TROJAN HORSE

Not all gamification is terrible. Some fintech founders are positively using these techniques to boost financial education, especially for communities that traditional banks have left out.

For instance, African Americans frequently face financial challenges that the broader US population, particularly whites, does not experience. This disparity arises from entrenched systemic discrimination within our financial institutions. A prime example is the decades-long practice of redlining – a discriminatory banking policy that began in the 1930s and prevented people of color from obtaining mortgages and accessing the same wealth-building opportunities through homeownership. The federal Home Owners' Loan Corporation created color-coded maps that marked areas where households of color resided, designating these "redlined" zones as risky for lending.[48] One crucial step to addressing this issue is increasing financial literacy. A 2019 study by TIAA Institute found that while 66% of African Americans say they are doing okay financially, the number is 78% for whites. The median household income for African Americans was $35 400 in 2016, compared to $61 200 for whites.[49]

Angel Rich has made it her mission to use gamified experiences to promote financial literacy and equity. As a Black woman in fintech, she has broken barriers and reinvested in her community. In her powerful 2018 TED Talk, Rich illuminated the critical importance of strategic success, underscoring how methodical planning and execution can amplify one's influence and drive meaningful change. She highlighted the inspiring journeys of Beyoncé and Oprah, two iconic figures who meticulously crafted and expanded their platforms. Once established, they harnessed their immense reach and resources to become formidable advocates for the Black community, demonstrating that strategic success is not just about personal achievement, but about using one's power to uplift and inspire others.

Rich calls this the "Trojan Horse" strategy: letting people underestimate you, using their egos against them, and then changing systems from within.[50] Her version of trailblazing came as a fourth generation Washingtonian who reverse-engineered the FICO credit scoring system to invent a globally recognized financial education mobile game app.

Rich knew from the age of six that she wanted a career in finance. She attended Hampton University, graduated with honors, and earned a bachelor's degree in marketing. She studied Chinese business culture and language at the University of International Business and Economics in Beijing to broaden her knowledge.

After college, she started as a global market research analyst at Prudential Financial in 2009. She conducted more than 70 financial behavior studies there, including the Obama Administration's Veterans Initiative. After leaving Prudential, she and her college friend, Courtney Keen, founded their first company, The Wealth Factory, in 2013. Their mission was to provide equal access to financial literacy worldwide.

The Wealth Factory encompasses several brands focused on fintech and financial literacy, including Wealthy Life, which offers financial education through games and curricula. In 2016, Rich deepened her community involvement by launching Black Tech Matters, a social impact organization dedicated to increasing diversity in STEM. This organization brings together students, entrepreneurs, and professionals committed to investing more than $30 million in Black-led companies.

Rich's career as a fintech entrepreneur hit a significant milestone in 2017 when The Wealth Factory launched the full version of their app, CreditStacker. Imagine Candy Crush, but instead of swapping candy, you swap credit types to pay off debt, improve your credit score, and answer multiple-choice questions about personal finance. Each level introduces a new aspect of personal finance that players need to understand to advance in the game. It's simple yet effective. Within two weeks, the app exceeded 200 000 downloads in 60 countries and 21 languages.

Since then, CreditStacker has received widespread acclaim. It was recognized by Michelle Obama's White House team as the best financial literacy product in the country and garnered accolades from the Department of Education and JP Morgan Chase, which awarded Rich a $10 000 grant for her innovative solution to reducing poverty.[51] The United Nations named her one of five global icons in 2018 for her influence within the African diaspora. Forbes even dubbed her the "Next Steve Jobs."[52]

However, Rich has been very open about the significant hurdles she still faces in the tech industry, which often discriminates against women and people of color. Despite her success and numerous accolades, she still receives a fraction of the funding her male counterparts do. In a 2017 interview with Forbes, she shared her frustration: "My competitor raised $75 million. I won best financial product and best learning game. My company raised only $200 000."

Black founders receive less than 0.5% of the $140.4 billion of venture capital funding of US start-ups in 2023, according to data firm Crunchbase.[53] Before 2021, only 93 Black women had raised $1 million or more in venture capital.[54] To shed light on these disparities, Rich wrote a book titled *The History of the Black Dollar*, which explores the economic challenges faced by the Black community.

Despite the challenges, Rich has stayed true to her mantra of "being the Trojan Horse." These obstacles have pushed her to build a lean company on limited resources, making her fintech start-up more sustainable and a better investment. "I have to have guts, I have to have grit, I have to be patient," she said. "And when the time is right, I will take down their walls."

Continuing her mission with unwavering dedication, Rich broke new ground in 2021 by founding CreditRich and forging a partnership with Experian, becoming the first Black woman to secure an institutional alliance with a major credit bureau.[55] CreditRich empowers users by turning spare change into a powerful tool for financial improvement, helping them pay bills and boost their credit scores. This simple yet innovative platform truly embodies the ethos of tech for the people. Rich's pioneering work not only challenges industry norms but also sets a vibrant example of how technology can be harnessed to create equitable opportunities for all.

In 2022, Rich and Keen took their efforts another step forward by launching the CreditRich Visa debit card in collaboration with Visa. Digitally issued by FDIC bank member Sutton Bank, this card gives account holders an instant bank account and digital card via the CreditRich app, making it the first Black woman–owned neobank.[56] This service is aimed at women, millennials with high student debt, and people of color who need more financial services and literacy.

The CreditRich app offers more than just payments. Users can check their credit reports, connect their accounts, make online payments, and directly link their paychecks. It also provides options to download investment and spending tips designed to help improve credit scores and encourages building savings by adding spare change from everyday purchases to their bank accounts. The app's launch comes at a time when US wealth inequality is growing worse, with the pandemic and the subsequent recovery exacerbating that gap.[57]

Rich's story demonstrates the power that comes from being underestimated. Inspired by her favorite book, *The Iliad*, she teaches others to embrace underestimation as a strategic advantage to fix broken systems from within. "Whether you are too Black, too white, too big, too tall, too short, too bald, or whatever it is," she said, "there is power in being underestimated." She emphasizes that patience, guts, and grit are essential when building within systems not designed for you. Rich believes that even when underestimated, those working for change are already making significant progress, from Silicon Valley to Hollywood and now, even in our credit reports.

Rich's success – fueled by grit and determination – highlights how fintech has reached a crucial point where innovators like her use their expertise to address systemic issues and close the wealth gap. Her presence paves the way for more Black founders to enter fintech, driving innovation across the industry and bringing equity to diverse communities. Rich's impact has not gone unnoticed; in June 2023, she became the youngest African American HBCU graduate to receive the Presidential Lifetime Achievement Award, signed by President Joe Biden.[58]

"I encourage you to go forth and be Trojan horses," she said. "Oh, do not worry if they are still underestimating us. We want them to underestimate us because they do not realize they are already surrounded."

Rich sees success in fintech as a long-term legacy rather than a one-off solution. "Books will be written, murals will be painted, museums will be erected, and when they come to Broadway 1000 years from now," she said, "they will see the ruins of how we globally built a new empire from being Trojan horses." For Rich, continuing in fintech is a given because, as she says, "A winner does not quit on themselves."

BITCOIN'S BRIEF GLORY

In addition to the rise of investing and financial education, Bitcoin, the world's largest cryptocurrency, also experienced a meteoric rise during the pandemic era of 2020–2021. This marked it as undoubtedly the most hyped asset on the block, with prices reaching a record high of $64 000 in 2021. However, the value came crashing down after the bankruptcy of FTX, a Bahamas-based cryptocurrency exchange, began in November 2022. Other crypto exchange bankruptcies, including Genesis, BlockFi, and Celsius Network, followed suit. Thus, fintech has made headlines and gained cultural relevance in a way it never had before, for better or worse.

Still, cryptocurrency allured people with the idea that it could be a means to attain financial prosperity. It was seen as an escape from the traditional financial systems that have deep-rooted racial biases and do not cater to the needs of underserved communities and people without a conventional source of income. Unfortunately, in pursuing this new financial frontier, the same voices have shaped its course, veering from its original intent.

The core mission of cryptocurrency – to craft a new financial ecosystem unmarred by the inequities of the existing one – demands that individuals from diverse backgrounds, notably women and people of color, lead in its construction. Leaders such as Cleve Mesidor, the executive director of the nonprofit Blockchain Foundation and a former official in President Barack Obama's administration. She has dedicated her career to promoting justice in politics and crypto and continues to advocate for policies that will ensure the flourishing of people of color in the crypto economy.

The COVID-19 pandemic spurred an unprecedented surge in cryptocurrency adoption, with historically low interest rates encouraging borrowing and speculation in high-risk assets. This was evident in 2021 with the proliferation of crypto apps, trading platforms, and even crypto-dispensing ATMs, making digital assets seem easy. However, the euphoria of these developments was short-lived, with a dramatic crash in 2022 leading to massive losses and insolvencies. As a largely unregulated asset, cryptocurrencies are inherently volatile and lack protective mechanisms like deposit insurance – leaving them vulnerable to fraud, hacking, and other schemes.

Despite these challenges, approximately 20% of Black, Hispanic, and Asian American adults in the United States have engaged with cryptocurrency through purchase, trade, or usage, according to surveys conducted by the Pew Research Center in 2021 and 2022.[59] Plus, cryptocurrencies still offer a tantalizing prospect of peer-to-peer transactions devoid of intermediaries such as banks or governmental bodies, providing individuals with avenues of wealth accumulation that may otherwise be inaccessible. I, for one, believe that blockchain technology and cryptocurrency can still be used as a force for good and financial inclusion – as long as we diversify the voices we listen to and the founders we fund building toward the sector's future.

RECLAIMING MY TIME

Congresswoman Maxine Waters, a prominent Democrat on the House Financial Services Committee, has voiced her concerns over dollar-pegged stablecoins, expressing deep concern in August 2023 over PayPal's stablecoin launch without a solid federal framework for oversight and enforcement.[60]

Stablecoins have been like the anchored best friend in the wild world of cryptocurrencies. Think of Tether (USDT) and the promise of blockchain tech without the heart-stopping roller coaster ride of crypto prices. And stablecoins are really popular. In 2022, stablecoins reached a transaction volume of $6.87 trillion, overtaking traditional payment giants like Mastercard and PayPal.[61]

Unlike their crypto cousins, stablecoins don't come with a set supply or issuance schedule. Instead, their quantity relies on market demand and economic conditions. These digital gems are backed by collateral, adding a pinch of stability that soothes investors' nerves. They've become the go-to bridge between the crypto and traditional financial realms. Transactions can zip along with blockchain efficiency, all while sidestepping the volatility that haunts most cryptocurrencies.

As stablecoins soar in popularity, they catch the watchful eye of regulators like Waters, a seasoned Democrat who has represented California's 43rd congressional district since 1991. She's not just any politician; she's a heavyweight in financial services regulation. With a hefty tenure on the House Financial Services Committee, Waters has shaped financial policy since before most of us had heard of Bitcoin.

Her career is marked by tireless advocacy for consumer protection, affordable housing, and diversity in the financial sector. These principles are etched into her DNA and have shaped her views on regulating fintech and financial innovation.

Waters' journey into financial policy started long before she hit the national stage. Before her illustrious career in Congress, she served in both the California State Assembly and the California State Senate.[62] Here, she sharpened her understanding of the intricate world of financial services regulation, setting the stage for her pivotal role in national financial policy.

But it was her spot on the House Financial Services Committee that catapulted her to the forefront of financial regulation matters. This committee wields immense power and influence, overseeing a vast array of financial and economic issues, including fintech. In June 2022, the committee even hosted a hearing about combating bro culture in fintech.

Waters' time on this committee made her a central figure in shaping national financial regulations, especially those involving emerging fintech innovations.

Throughout her career, Waters has been a relentless champion of affordable housing. Her efforts to make housing more accessible and to combat discriminatory lending practices directly impact fintech, especially in the realm of housing finance. This demonstrates her nuanced grasp of how fintech intersects with critical issues affecting ordinary Americans.

Waters has also been an active voice in discussions about regulating fintech companies, covering everything from digital payments and peer-to-peer lending to blockchain-based solutions.

When it comes to fintech, Waters has expressed concerns about consumer protection, data security, and fair lending practices. Her commitment to safeguarding consumers and ensuring fairness in financial services is unyielding and, dare I say, commendable.

Remember the 2008 financial crisis? Waters played a pivotal role in shaping the nation's response. She threw her weight behind the Dodd-Frank

Wall Street Reform and Consumer Protection Act, a monumental piece of financial regulatory legislation. Dodd-Frank brought in a slew of regulations affecting both traditional financial institutions and fintech companies, marking a major milestone in financial sector regulation.

Her advocacy for consumer protection stands out. Waters has been a vocal proponent of beefing up oversight of financial institutions to prevent predatory practices. This stance is hugely relevant to fintech companies, which often deal directly with consumers. Her commitment to protecting everyday Americans is a cornerstone of her career.

But that's not all. Waters has consistently championed diversity and inclusion within the financial industry. She's been a forceful advocate for financial institutions and fintech companies to promote diversity at all levels. Her belief in ensuring underserved communities have access to financial services underscores her commitment to a fair and equitable financial landscape.

As the cryptocurrency and fintech landscape hurtles forward, regulators and policymakers face the formidable challenge of balancing innovation with protection (a tale as old as time).

Waters's clear call for federal oversight and bipartisan cooperation underscores the urgent need for a comprehensive regulatory framework equipped to tackle the unique challenges posed by stablecoins in today's ever-evolving digital financial landscape. Only through such cooperation can we steer stablecoins toward fulfilling their potential as valuable financial tools while curbing associated risks.

While innovation is essential, it must walk hand in hand with thoughtful regulation to shield consumers and ensure the stability of our financial system.

Vice President Kamala Harris has made it clear she rejects the false choice suggesting we can protect the public or advance innovation. Regulation doesn't stifle innovation; the lack of funding for women and diverse entrepreneurs does. What we need is regulation that protects consumers and brings economic opportunity for all founders. To strike that balance we have to take a comprehensive and adaptive approach.

There are so many ways to do this, including establishing regulatory sandboxes to allow fintech start-ups and innovators to test their products and services, crafting comprehensive and technology-agnostic regulatory frameworks, forming partnerships between regulators, industry players, and innovators, and prioritizing consumer protection.

Additionally, regulators should require digital asset businesses to obtain licenses or register with regulatory authorities, explore the use of regulation technology to streamline compliance processes, invest in public education and awareness campaigns, cooperate with international regulatory bodies, review and update regulations regularly, provide incentives for businesses to comply with regulations, establish innovation hubs within regulatory bodies, mandate periodic third-party audits, encourage ethical considerations, and define different types of tokens.

Balancing financial regulation and innovation in the digital asset space is an ongoing process that requires collaboration, adaptability, and a commitment to both consumer protection and technological progress. Striking this balance will be crucial as digital assets continue to reshape the financial landscape.

As Waters stated in a May 2024 press release: "My message to the crypto industry and everyone else: Democrats will always press for compliance, investor protection, and market integrity."[63]

AI: FINTECH'S NEW PARADIGM OF GROWTH

Today, fintech is facing a relatively challenging environment after the boom – and eventual bust – of the pandemic-fueled hype cycle. The funding surge of 2021 quickly decreased, returning to normal levels, as worsening economic conditions and horrific geopolitical events destabilized the business environment. This led to a drop in fintech valuations, with many private firms facing financial challenges and publicly traded fintechs losing significant market capitalization.

However, there are a number of opportunities to keep us aspirational about the future of our industry and its growth potential as we generate more value creation in financial services. In fact, McKinsey research shows that revenues in the fintech industry are expected to grow almost three times faster than those in the traditional banking sector between 2022 and 2028. Emerging markets will fuel much of this revenue growth, which I'll address later in this book.

As we transition into the new growth paradigm, one technology poised to drive our industry's next wave of expansion is artificial intelligence (AI). Since OpenAI's ChatGPT launched and reached 1 million users in just 5 days – compared to Instagram's 2.5 months and Spotify's 5 months – the potential for AI in the financial sector has become undeniable.[64] This rapid adoption signifies a huge opportunity, but we must be intentional about who is discussing AI and who is listening to avoid repeating past mistakes. Historically, every technological revolution has marginalized women's voices, leading to crises. AI, while promising, already mirrors the gender bias in society.

For example, on 7 December 2023, the *New York Times* reported an article titled: "Who's Who Behind the Dawn of the Modern Artificial Intelligence Movement" and out of 12 figures listed, not one was a woman.[65] Seeing this headline was annoying, considering I was able to rewrite the list featuring 12 leading female figures in AI including women like Dr. Fei-Fei Li, Dr. Latanya Sweeney, and Dr. Daphne Koller. It did not take me long to do this. This shows the level of due diligence we must do as entrepreneurs, investors, and innovators to ensure that we amplify and follow the women leaders in these spaces. Mainstream media has shown a disinterest in spotlighting them. As we have discussed, diverse perspectives on building these technology innovations directly impact whether these tools succeed or fail the users they aim to serve.

There are a number of applications where AI can improve financial services. One of the most promising is improving lending practices. By collecting a broader range of data points, AI can enable lenders to offer credit to more people, addressing the inadequacies of traditional credit scores, which often fail to reflect a consumer's true ability to repay.

The readiness to embrace AI in financial services is evident from a consumer perspective. According to a 2023 report by Plaid, 60% of Americans believe AI will revolutionize financial services within the next five years.[66] They see AI's potential in lowering bills, solving customer service issues, providing budgeting advice, managing subscriptions, and offering financial education. However, consumers also express caution, with 70% preferring to review AI's financial decisions before fully trusting it. This indicates a desire for transparency and control in the decision-making process. Therefore, fintech must champion the cause of making AI-infused financial services trustworthy, avoiding the pitfalls seen in the crypto sector.

Millennials and Gen Z are particularly open to new fintech apps incorporating AI, with 60% and 51% respectively willing to embrace these technologies. As economic uncertainty affects 89% of Americans, fintech offers a lifeline, with more than half turning to digital financial tools. These tools help users understand their spending, achieve financial goals, and reduce inflation-related stress.

A significant concern is the inadequacy of traditional credit scoring, with 63% of consumers questioning its fairness. This underscores the need for AI to drive transformative action, especially to avoid perpetuating societal inequities that disproportionately affect Black and Brown Americans. The shift toward consumer-permission data, supported by 60% of consumers, promises a more accurate financial portrait.

OPEN BANKING AND GENERATIVE AI

Open banking has revolutionized how consumers interact with their financial data, and how much alternative data financial institutions are able to collect on their users. Open banking is the term used to describe the structured sharing of data by consumers with (and between) their financial service providers. It gives consumers the ability to connect data from their various banking, investment, and other financial accounts, creating a real-time snapshot of their financial health like they have never seen before. While the US has embraced this primarily through private sector initiatives, the Consumer Financial Protection Bureau's 1033 rule is set to shake up the banking industry by paving the way for open banking to make it mandatory.[67] The rule would accelerate the transition toward open banking, giving consumers control over their financial data and introducing new protections against misuse by companies. It would stimulate competition by preventing financial institutions from hoarding personal data and requiring them to share it with other companies offering better products at the consumer's request. The proposed rule has a goal to empower people to leave banks that provide poor service and prohibit companies that receive data from misusing or improperly monetizing sensitive personal financial information. This allows generative AI to play a crucial role by providing a comprehensive view of customers' financial lives by analyzing both structured and unstructured data, from check images to customer service transcripts. Yet, biases and discrimination embedded in AI algorithms remain a concern. Researchers like Timnit Gebru, Rumman Chowdhury, Safiya Noble, Seeta Peña Gangadharan, and Joy Buolamwini highlight how lack of diversity in training data contributes to biased outcomes in hiring and credit algorithms.[68]

While the rise of AI and open banking is exciting, fintech professionals must address the real-world consequences by adopting ethical AI training practices, ensuring clean data, and promoting transparency. Otherwise, AI will be another innovation that fails to serve most consumers' financial needs. One fintech company working on making data more accessible is NTropy, founded by CEO Naré Vardanyan, who launched the platform in 2020. Despite recent advancements in open banking and AI that have made data more accessible, the problem of understanding this data to create real value remains largely unsolved. This data powers decisions from credit scores to loan agreements and enables various financial products that impact lives. Vardanyan saw an opportunity to provide a developer-first and scalable platform that helps businesses make sense of their transaction data, from which customers can benefit in the future.[69]

As a result, more businesses can use AI to create economic opportunities instead of fearing the technology. For instance, Reshma Saujani, the founder of Girls Who Code, advocates for using AI to drive economic progress by expanding financial services. Her organization, Moms First, introduced an AI-powered platform, PaidLeave.ai, in 2024 to assist New York parents in accessing paid leave benefits, with plans for nationwide expansion.[70]

THE WOMEN WHO KICKED DOWN FINTECH'S DOORS

In the history of finance and technology, the pioneers in these fields were women who often balanced activism and entrepreneurship, shaping the future of finance and working toward a more equitable world. Before I open the door to the stories of all the women building in fintech today, it's important to honor the trailblazers who came before us. Today, we continue their legacy.

For example, on 27 December 1967, Muriel Siebert became the first woman to own a seat on the New York Stock Exchange, the lone woman among 1375 members. In 1977, she was appointed Superintendent of Banks for New York State, the first woman to hold the post.[71]

Fast forward to 2021, and Lynn Martin took the reins as the 68th President of the New York Stock Exchange, suggesting Siebert's journey wasn't a solitary leap but the first domino in a chain reaction of female leadership on Wall Street.[72] From Juanita Kreps, who in 1972 became the first woman to sit on the board of directors of the NYSE,[73] to Stacey Cunningham in 2018, who became the first woman to lead the NYSE as president.[74] Their stories echo a common belief: Fortune favors the bold, and one woman's milestones pave the way for others to follow her.

Yet, despite the remarkable contributions of women pioneers in finance and technology, the fintech landscape often seems marred by a scarcity mindset. The myth persists that there's not enough funding, talent, or women to lead. Well, let us call it what it is – *bullshit*. Historically, women have built the foundation of the fintech industry, but cultural norms have iced them out of these spaces over time.

For example, software programming was once an almost entirely female profession. As recently as 1980, women held 70% of the programming jobs in Silicon Valley. That ratio has completely flipped today. Female technicians once outnumbered male workers on the Valley's hardware assembly lines by more than two to one. Those jobs are now nearly all overseas. In 1986, 36% of those receiving bachelor's degrees in computer science were women. The proportion of women never reached that level again.[75]

The decrease in women in these spaces is largely due to the shift to bro culture in recent decades, including the industry's long-standing and enthusiastic reliance on hiring by employee referral and the tiresomely persistent fiction of a gender-blind "meritocracy." Still, the women who laid the foundational bricks in finance and technology were anything but your typical finance or tech bros.

Grace Hopper, Margaret Hamilton, Ada Lovelace, and Maggie Walker, to name a few, were the architects of the digital age. But their stories are buried beneath a narrative that insists on maintaining the status quo. We see it in articles today from mainstream media highlighting men as the leaders of the digital finance revolution, ignoring the contributions of women who have been quietly pulling the strings from Wall Street to Silicon Valley.

Women have been writing codes, breaking barriers, and building empires in finance and technology for ages. In the 1800s, when women were supposedly confined to corsets and embroidery, Ada Lovelace was busy concocting the first-ever algorithm for Charles Babbage's Analytical Engine.[76] Her visionary work laid the cornerstone for modern computer programming. That's right; history's first computer programmer was a woman.

Grace Hopper, a mathematics Ph.D. and rear admiral in the US Navy, invented the first compiler called "A-0" which translated mathematical code into machine-readable code – laying the foundation for modern programming languages.[77] Her determination to translate complex ideas into machine-readable code led to the creation of COBOL (short for "common business-oriented language") and set the stage for the language of fintech. Hopper's work in programming the Mark I during World War II and her promotion of COBOL in both military and private sectors highlighted women's crucial role in developing financial technologies. When you think about fintech, remember that a woman built the rails to begin with.

In 1903, Maggie Lena Walker made history by becoming the first Black woman to charter a bank, the St. Luke Penny Savings Bank, and also the first African American woman to serve as its president.[78] When the stock market crashed in 1929, Walker kept things going by merging with another bank, creating the Consolidated Bank and Trust, which was the nation's oldest continually run Black-owned bank. Walker's financial expertise and leadership opened doors for diverse voices to lead and be heard in the financial sector.

While men were making "small steps" on the moon, Margaret Hamilton took a giant leap for womankind. Hamilton was the lead software designer for NASA's Apollo program, and her visionary work was crucial in saving the 1969 Apollo 11 mission. The innovative asynchronous processing flight software she designed successfully circumvented critical error messages, ultimately enabling the historic landing of the Eagle and bringing the first humans to the moon.[79] Her foresight laid the groundwork for the reliability we demand in our financial software today.

Three women who played a vital role in advancing NASA's missions were Katherine Johnson, Dorothy Vaughan, and Mary Jackson. As seen in the movie *Hidden Figures*, these African American women were human computers who played a vital role in 1962 when they helped send the first American astronaut, John Glenn, into orbit.[80]

In 1974, Betsy Cohen made history by founding Jefferson Bank in Pennsylvania, where she served as Chairman and CEO, becoming one of the nation's first female bank CEOs. In 1999, she launched The Bancorp, a virtual bank that provided services to thousands of fintech companies, including PayPal. She led The Bancorp as CEO for 15 years, offering internet banking and financial services to approximately 1600 fintech firms.[81]

After 15 years of building strong relationships with these companies and knowing the benefits of being in the public market, Cohen ventured into the world of special purpose acquisition companies (SPACs). SPACs allowed her to provide capital to fintech companies that had the necessary infrastructure to succeed as public companies. A SPAC is a vehicle that transforms private companies into public ones, granting them access to public markets and crucial capital for growth and scaling.

Cohen was an early player in the reverse merger trend that lasted roughly between late 2020 and early 2021 when SPAC deals exploded in popularity, rising from 59 SPACs in 2019 to 247 in 2020. Cohen's investment firm Cohen Circle – which she runs with her son, financier

Daniel Cohen – helped take seven companies public through SPACs between 2015 and 2021, as *Forbes* reported in 2023.[82]

Like these trailblazers, the women featured in this book have made remarkable contributions to the rise of fintech, illustrating the powerful intersection between social good and capitalism. They have not only paved the way for today's fintech start-ups but have also redefined the industry's narrative, moving beyond the mantra of "move fast and break things." These visionary women show us that it's possible to create meaningful change and profoundly impact our economy while still generating substantial profits. Their stories inspire us to believe that innovation can be both ethical and lucrative, setting a new standard for future generations in fintech.

NOTES

1. Time. "Time Magazine Archive Article." Accessed May 20, 2024. https://content.time.com/time/magazine/0,9263,7601990215,00.html.
2. Encyclopædia Britannica. "Bankruptcy of Lehman Brothers." Accessed May 20, 2024. https://www.britannica.com/event/bankruptcy-of-Lehman-Brothers.
3. The Guardian. "Greenspan Admits to 'Flaw' in His Market Ideology." October 24, 2008. Accessed May 20, 2024. https://www.theguardian.com/business/2008/oct/24/economics-creditcrunch-federal-reserve-greenspan.
4. Time. "Time Magazine Cover." May 24, 2010. Accessed May 20, 2024. https://content.time.com/time/covers/0,16641,20100524,00.html.
5. Nelson, Julie. "Women Leaders and Economic Crisis: Evidence from a Panel of Economic Experts." Working Paper, Boston University, June 2011. Accessed May 20, 2024. https://www.bu.edu/eci/files/2019/06/11-03NelsonWomenLeaders.pdf.
6. European Parliament. *Feminist Economy: Background Note for Workshop*. Accessed May 20, 2024. https://www.europarl.europa.eu/cmsdata/254870/Briefing_Background%20note_Workshop_Feminist%20economy_.pdf.
7. Women's Budget Group. "What Is Feminist Economics?" Accessed May 20, 2024. https://www.wbg.org.uk/article/what-is-feminist-economics/.

8. Oxfam. "Not All Gaps Are Created Equal: The True Value of Care Work." Accessed May 20, 2024. https://www.oxfam.org/en/not-all-gaps-are-created-equal-true-value-care-work.
9. Newton-Small, Jay. Broad Influence: How Women Are Changing the Way America Works. New York: Time Books, 2016.
10. Encyclopaedia Britannica. "Dot-Com Bubble." Accessed May 20, 2024. https://www.britannica.com/event/dot-com-bubble.
11. Chang, Emily. *Brotopia: Breaking Up the Boys' Club of Silicon Valley*. New York: Portfolio, 2018.
12. Findexable. "First Global Benchmark of Gender Diversity in Fintech by Findexable Reveals Systemic Underrepresentation of Women and Investment." Accessed May 20, 2024. https://findexable.com/news-and-insights/first-global-benchmark-of-gender-diversity-in-fintech-by-findexable-reveals-systemic-underrepresentation-of-women-and-investment.
13. Findexable. *Fintech Diversity Radar Report 2021*. November 2021. Accessed May 20, 2024. https://findexable.com/wp-content/uploads/2021/11/FDR-Report-2021-v1.0-3-November-2021.pdf.
14. Oliver Wyman. "A $700 Billion Missed Opportunity." Accessed May 20, 2024. https://www.oliverwyman.com/our-expertise/insights/2020/apr/risk-journal-vol-9/redefining-business-models/a-700-billion-dollars-missed-opportunity.html.
15. Boston Consulting Group. "Creating Necessary Opportunities for Women." Accessed May 20, 2024. https://www.bcg.com/united-states/work-and-culture/equity-empowers/creating-necessary-opportunities-for-women#:~:text=A%202019%20BCG%20study%20found,having%20equal%20access%20to%20capital.
16. American Banker. "The Women Who Are Bank CEOs." Accessed May 20, 2024. https://www.americanbanker.com/list/the-women-who-are-bank-ceos.
17. What's the Big Data. "Women in Tech Statistics." Accessed May 20, 2024. https://whatsthebigdata.com/women-in-tech-statistics.
18. Bloomberg. "Women CEOs at Big Companies Finally Outnumber Those Named John." April 25, 2023. Accessed May 20, 2024. https://www.bloomberg.com/news/newsletters/2023-04-25/women-ceos-at-big-companies-finally-outnumber-those-named-john.
19. Associated Press. "Timeline of Sam Bankman-Fried's FTX Fraud Case." Accessed May 20, 2024. https://apnews.com/article/sam-bankman-fried-ftx-fraud-timeline-be13e3fc0e074e2edd50ba59d1f8960e.

20. McKinsey & Company. "Fintechs: A New Paradigm of Growth." Accessed May 20, 2024. https://www.mckinsey.com/industries/financial-services/our-insights/fintechs-a-new-paradigm-of-growth.

21. Peterson Institute for International Economics. "Gender Diversity and Profitable: Evidence from a Global Survey." Working Paper, April 2016. Accessed May 20, 2024. https://www.piie.com/publications/working-papers/gender-diversity-profitable-evidence-global-survey.

22. World Economic Forum. *The Future of Global Fintech 2024.* Accessed May 20, 2024. https://www3.weforum.org/docs/WEF_The_Future_of_Global_Fintech_2024.pdf.

23. Science Museum. "Boom and Bust: Telegraphy and Wall Street Crash." Accessed May 20, 2024. www.sciencemuseum.org.uk/objects-and-stories/boom-and-bust-telegraphy-and-wall-street-crash.

24. Washington Post. "The Day the Credit Card Was Born." November 4, 1994. Accessed May 20, 2024. https://www.washingtonpost.com/archive/lifestyle/magazine/1994/11/04/the-day-the-credit-card-was-born/d42da27b-0437-4a67-b753-bf9b440ad6dc.

25. Barclays. "From the Archives: The ATM is 50." June 2017. Accessed May 20, 2024. https://home.barclays/news/2017/06/from-the-archives-the-atm-is-50.

26. Wells Fargo. "First in Online Banking." Accessed May 20, 2024. https://history.wf.com/first-in-online-banking.

27. PayPal. "History and Facts." Accessed May 20, 2024. https://about.pypl.com/who-we-are/history-and-facts/default.aspx.

28. Microsoft. "API Design Best Practices." Accessed May 20, 2024. https://learn.microsoft.com/en-us/azure/architecture/best-practices/api-design.

29. National Basketball Association. "SoFi and NBA Partnership." Accessed May 20, 2024. https://pr.nba.com/sofi-nba-partnership.

30. Reuters. "Goldman Sachs Faces Rocky Exit from Apple Credit Card Partnership." December 18, 2023. Accessed May 20, 2024. https://www.reuters.com/business/finance/goldman-sachs-faces-rocky-exit-apple-credit-card-partnership-2023-12-18.

31. Forbes Technology Council. "Lessons from the History of Fintech." Forbes. July 24, 2023. Accessed May 20, 2024. https://www.forbes.com/sites/forbestechcouncil/2023/07/24/lessons-from-the-history-of-fintech/.

32. Oliver Wyman. "The Rise of Banking as a Service." March 2021. Accessed May 20, 2024. https://www.oliverwyman.com/our-expertise/insights/2021/mar/the-rise-of-banking-as-a-service.html.

33. Associated Press. "Synapse, Evolve Bank Face Fintech Account Freeze." Accessed May 20, 2024. https://apnews.com/article/synapse-evolve-bank-fintech-accounts-frozen-07ecb45f807a8114cac7438e7a66b512.

34. World Health Organization. "WHO Director-General's Opening Remarks at the Media Briefing on COVID-19 – 11 March 2020." Accessed May 20, 2024. https://www.who.int/director-general/speeches/detail/who-director-general-s-opening-remarks-at-the-media-briefing-on-covid-19-11-march-2020.

35. National Bureau of Economic Research. "Business Cycle Dating Committee Announcement." July 19, 2021. Accessed May 20, 2024. https://www.nber.org/news/business-cycle-dating-committee-announcement-july-19-202.

36. Center on Budget and Policy Priorities. "Tracking the Recovery from the Pandemic Recession." Accessed May 20, 2024. https://www.cbpp.org/research/economy/tracking-the-recovery-from-the-pandemic-recession.

37. eMarketer. "Finance Apps Downloads." Accessed May 20, 2024. https://www.emarketer.com/content/finance-apps-downloads.

38. Plaid. *The Fintech Effect 2021: Mass Adoption.* Accessed May 20, 2024. https://plaid.com/the-fintech-effect-2021-mass-adoption/.

39. Deloitte. "The Future of Retail Brokerage." Accessed May 20, 2024. https://www2.deloitte.com/us/en/pages/financial-services/articles/the-future-of-retail-brokerage.html.

40. CFA Institute. *Gen Z and Investing.* Accessed May 20, 2024. https://rpc.cfainstitute.org/-/media/documents/article/industry-research/Gen_Z_and_Investing.pdf.

41. Scientific American. "COVID Has Made Global Inequality Much Worse." March 31, 2022. Accessed May 20, 2024. https://www.scientificamerican.com/article/covid-has-made-global-inequality-much-worse/.

42. PR Newswire. "Lack of Financial Knowledge Costs Americans Money – Over $1,500 on Average in 2023, New Survey Shows." April 27, 2023. Accessed May 20, 2024. https://www.prnewswire.com/news-releases/lack-of-financial-knowledge-costs-americans-money-over-1-500-on-average-in-2023-new-survey-shows-302028634.html.

43. International Federation of Accountants. "The Cost of Financial Illiteracy." Accessed May 20, 2024. https://www.ifac.org/knowledge-gateway/discussion/cost-financial-illiteracy.

44. Robinhood. "Robinhood Reports Fourth Quarter and Full Year 2021 Results." Accessed May 20, 2024. https://investors.robinhood.com/news/news-details/

2022/Robinhood-Reports-Fourth-Quarter-and-Full-Year-2021-Results/default.aspx.

45. CNN. "Robinhood Faces Scrutiny After Customer's Suicide." June 19, 2020. Accessed May 20, 2024. https://www.cnn.com/2020/06/19/business/robinhood-suicide-alex-kearns/index.html.

46. Reuters. "Robinhood Settles Massachusetts Regulators' Trading Case for $75 Million." January 18, 2024. Accessed May 20, 2024. https://www.reuters.com/legal/transactional/robinhood-settles-massachusetts-regulators-trading-case-75-million-2024-01-18/.

47. Bloomberg Law. "Capital Markets Professional Perspective: Payment for Order Flow." Accessed May 20, 2024. https://www.bloomberglaw.com/external/document/X1RP679S000000/capital-markets-professional-perspective-payment-for-order-flow-.

48. Habitat for Humanity. "Historic Housing Discrimination in the U.S." Accessed May 20, 2024. https://www.habitat.org/stories/historic-housing-discrimination-us.

49. TIAA Institute. "Financial Literacy, Wellness, and Resilience among African Americans: Introduction." Accessed May 20, 2024. https://www.tiaa.org/public/institute/about/news/financial-literacy-wellness-and-resilience-among-african-americans-introduction.

50. Rich, Angel. "Be a Trojan Horse: The Power of Being Underestimated." TEDxBroadway. Accessed May 27, 2024. https://www.ted.com/talks/angel_rich_be_a_trojan_horse_the_power_of_being_underestimated.

51. Roberts, Alayna. "A New Way to Teach Kids About Money and Debt: How the Award-Winning CreditStacker App Has Turned Financial Literacy into a Popular Game." The 74 Million. Last modified February 20, 2018. https://www.the74million.org/article/a-new-way-to-teach-kids-about-money-and-debt-how-the-award-winning-creditstacker-app-has-turned-financial-literacy-into-a-popular-game.

52. Stengel, Geri. "The Next Steve Jobs? A Black Woman Only Gets Funding Crumbs." Forbes. May 3, 2017. Accessed May 20, 2024. https://www.forbes.com/sites/geristengel/2017/05/03/the-next-steve-jobs-a-black-woman-only-gets-funding-crumbs/?sh=2d92751e3c33.

53. Crunchbase News. "Venture Funding for Black-Founded Startups in 2023: Data and Insights." Accessed May 20, 2024. https://news.crunchbase.com/diversity/venture-funding-black-founded-startups-2023-data/.

54. Holmes, Tamara. "Black Female Founders Have Raised Millions in VC This Year." Business Insider. September 15, 2021. Accessed May 20, 2024.

https://www.businessinsider.com/black-female-founders-raised-millions-in-vc-this-year-2021-9.

55. Forbes Fellows. "Fintech Disrupter Angel Rich Becomes First Black American to Partner with a Major Credit Bureau." Forbes. April 21, 2021. Accessed May 20, 2024. https://www.forbes.com/sites/forbesfellows/2021/04/21/fintech-disrupter-angel-rich-becomes-first-black-american-to-partner-with-a-major-credit-bureau/.

56. Black Enterprise. "HBCU Grads Partner with Visa to Launch First-Ever Black Woman-Owned Neo-Bank." Accessed May 20, 2024. https://www.blackenterprise.com/hbcu-grads-partner-with-visa-to-launch-first-ever-black-woman-owned-neo-bank/.

57. Reuters. "U.S. Wealth Inequality Grew Worse Through Current Recovery, NY Fed Study Shows." February 7, 2024. Accessed May 20, 2024. https://www.reuters.com/world/us/us-wealth-inequality-grew-worse-through-current-recovery-ny-fed-study-shows-2024-02-07/.

58. Black News. "Angel Rich Becomes Youngest Black Person to Receive Presidential Lifetime Achievement Award." Accessed May 20, 2024. https://blacknews.com/news/angel-rich-youngest-black-person-receive-presidential-lifetime-achievement-award/.

59. Associated Press. "Cryptocurrency Investing Lures More Minority Investors." January 21, 2023. Accessed May 20, 2024. https://apnews.com/article/crypto-bitcoin-minorities-investors-banks-distrust-46c8e064d6a38d4d47581653959dc209.

60. U.S. House Committee on Financial Services. "Press Release: Committee Democrats Address Economic Inequality." Accessed May 20, 2024. https://democrats-financialservices.house.gov/news/documentsingle.aspx?DocumentID=410725.

61. Crypto Briefing. "Stablecoins Surpass Mastercard and PayPal in Transaction Volume." Accessed May 20, 2024. https://cryptobriefing.com/stablecoins-surpass-mastercard-paypal-in-transaction-volume.

62. U.S. House of Representatives. "About Maxine Waters." Accessed May 20, 2024. https://waters.house.gov/about-maxine.

63. U.S. House Committee on Financial Services. "Press Release: Committee Democrats Introduce Legislation to Address Economic Inequality." Accessed May 20, 2024. https://democrats-financialservices.house.gov/news/documentsingle.aspx?DocumentID=411444.

64. Exploding Topics. "ChatGPT Users." Accessed May 20, 2024. https://explodingtopics.com/blog/chatgpt-users.

65. Moreno, J. Edward. "The Key Figures in AI." *The New York Times*, December 3, 2023. Accessed May 20, 2024. https://www.nytimes.com/2023/12/03/technology/ai-key-figures.html.

66. Plaid. "Consumer Insights Reshaping Finance." Accessed May 20, 2024. https://plaid.com/blog/consumer-insights-reshaping-finance/.

67. Consumer Financial Protection Bureau. "CFPB Proposes Rule to Jumpstart Competition and Accelerate Shift to Open Banking." Accessed May 20, 2024. https://www.consumerfinance.gov/about-us/newsroom/cfpb-proposes-rule-to-jumpstart-competition-and-accelerate-shift-to-open-banking/.

68. Business & Human Rights Resource Centre. "These 5 Women Activists Have Been Raising the Alarm about the Human Rights Risks of AI for Years." Accessed May 20, 2024. https://www.business-humanrights.org/en/latest-news/these-5-women-activists-have-been-raising-the-alarm-about-the-human-rights-risks-of-ai-for-years/.

69. Fintechna. "Ntropy Announces $32M Round to Help Financial Companies Make Sense of Data." Accessed May 20, 2024. https://www.fintechna.com/press-releases/ntropy-announces-32m-round-to-help-financial-companies-make-sense-of-data/.

70. PR Newswire. "Moms First Launches PaidLeaveAI to Help Parents in New York Access Paid Family Leave." Accessed May 20, 2024. https://www.prnewswire.com/news-releases/moms-first-launches-paidleaveai-to-help-parents-in-new-york-access-paid-family-leave-302005318.html.

71. National Women's History Museum. "Muriel Siebert." Accessed May 20, 2024. https://www.womenshistory.org/education-resources/biographies/muriel-siebert.

72. Yahoo Finance. "NYSE President Lynn Martin on Her Journey from Tech to High Finance." Accessed May 20, 2024. https://finance.yahoo.com/news/nyse-president-lynn-martin-on-her-journey-from-tech-to-high-finance-214551804.html.

73. Encyclopaedia Britannica. "Juanita Morris Kreps." Accessed May 20, 2024. https://www.britannica.com/money/Juanita-Morris-Kreps.

74. National Public Radio. "It Was Never About My Gender: NYSE's First Female President Thanks Her Trailblazers." June 10, 2018. Accessed May 20, 2024. https://www.npr.org/2018/06/10/618271798/it-was-never-about-my-gender-nyse-s-first-female-president-thanks-her-trailblaze.

75. MIT Technology Review. "Tech Fix: The Gender Problem." August 11, 2022. Accessed May 20, 2024. https://www.technologyreview.com/2022/08/11/1056917/tech-fix-gender-problem/.

76. Encyclopaedia Britannica. "Ada Lovelace: The First Computer Programmer." Accessed May 20, 2024. https://www.britannica.com/story/ada-lovelace-the-first-computer-programmer.
77. Yale University Office of the President. "Biography: Grace Murray Hopper." Accessed May 20, 2024. https://president.yale.edu/biography-grace-murray-hopper.
78. National Women's History Museum. "Maggie Lena Walker." Accessed May 20, 2024. https://www.womenshistory.org/education-resources/biographies/maggie-lena-walker.
79. Wired. "Margaret Hamilton, NASA, and the Apollo Program." October 13, 2015. Accessed May 20, 2024. https://www.wired.com/2015/10/margaret-hamilton-nasa-apollo/.
80. National Geographic. "Women at NASA." Accessed May 20, 2024. https://education.nationalgeographic.org/resource/women-nasa/.
81. YouTube. "Arta: Q&A with Betsy Cohen." YouTube video, 5:28. Accessed May 20, 2024. https://youtu.be/ba-iVWMmw3M.
82. Hyatt, John. "Why Dealmaker Betsy Cohen Believes SPACs Will Make a Comeback." Forbes. June 1, 2023. Accessed May 20, 2024. https://www.forbes.com/sites/johnhyatt/2023/06/01/why-dealmaker-betsy-cohen-believes-spacs-will-make-a-comeback/.

CHAPTER TWO

GET IN, WE'RE RESCUING THE ECONOMY

When Liza Landsman got the call to take over as CEO of one of today's largest fintech companies, she immediately thought of her "shoulder angels," as she calls it. "Rather than an angel and a devil," she told me, "I have my 'social good' angel on one shoulder and my 'capitalist' angel on the other." Landing a job in fintech provided her the opportunity to satisfy both. However, it would take a lengthy career journey – and a ton of introspection – to find her way into fintech.

Landsman started her career in traditional finance. She has experience in operations and venture capital, having worked at Citigroup, BlackRock, E*Trade, and New Enterprise Associates. She was also one of the founding executives at Jet.com, where her strategic leadership contributed to the company's $3.3 billion acquisition by Walmart. Over the years, she gained insights from those experiences, but one pattern kept standing out.

"I observed that those businesses are structurally designed to cater to and serve the country's mass affluent population extremely well," she said. However, significantly less is available for the 99% of US households that don't meet the top 1% criteria. "It never made sense to me that the overwhelming majority of Americans should be so drastically underserved by the largest financial institutions out there," she said.

In the past, investors had to hire a stockbroker to place trades. These brokers earned a commission on the trades, so working with sizable investments was only worth their while. In other words, you had to be rich for a stockbroker to work with you. However, technology has changed this, and now, several investing applications are available for consumers to invest small amounts.

Landsman understands the power of good financial habits because she doesn't come from a family with money. She was the first woman in her family to attend college, and her daughter will be the second. Landsman earned her bachelor's degree from Cornell University, which was great, except it came with student loan debts that she soon realized her fresh-out-of-college literary agent job couldn't pay. So, she entered the finance industry to make enough money to afford her student loans.

BETTING ON BLACK

As Landsman advanced in her career, moving through various traditional finance roles, it was during her time at Citi that she started to contemplate what she wanted for herself. She was fortunate to have an executive coach who challenged her constant talk about the "next job" she desired. "That keeps your mindset narrow when you need to look at a much broader universe of opportunities," she said. "When you talk about the job you want, you're essentially betting on 17 on the roulette wheel instead of betting on black." Translation: Consider what you want from your life instead of thinking about your job to attract the best outcome.

To figure out what she wanted, she made a list of non-negotiables. "It's a key superpower for clarity, and this list must be the shortest," she said. "The turning point in my career came when I started using this."

During our interview, Landsman recounted a story where she established a non-negotiable. In a previous job when one of her colleagues left, she was asked to take over his position. This led her to question the structure of her division. Before taking the role, Landsman believed there was a better way to organize their business and told the company that she was the right person to lead it. This enabled her to expand her responsibilities significantly. More importantly, this experience prompted her to contemplate how she wanted to allocate her time and what she aspired to achieve in her career. This shift is critical as it will unlock your next phase of personal and professional growth as you navigate through your fintech career.

To understand what she wants, Landsman starts by religiously conducting a self-inventory every year. She recommends asking yourself:

- What skills do I want to build?
- What experiences do I want to have?
- What are my goals?

"Doing self-inventory every year is crucial because starting with a North Star is important," she said. "But we are not static. We are nonlinear. And this evolution is something we have to bring into our process actively." She considers this self-inventory a "portfolio rebalancing" and credits the practice of self-reflection to a gift her mom gave her and her brother when they turned 21. Every year, her mother wrote Landsman a letter, giving her insights into what was happening with her, what was happening with the world, and how she thought about the things around her. Landsman encourages everyone to do it for their children if they can and credits this "incredible gift" as an inside look into her parents' lives before they got divorced, what her mom was like in her 30s, and her perspectives on raising children of different genders – something that fueled her own introspection and career development.

Because she desired to have her two "shoulder angels" combine forces in a place where she spends so much of her time – her work – Landsman decided she could have a job that filled her cup and gave her room to make an impact. It turns out that job was in fintech.

In February 2023, she became CEO of Stash, an investing platform founded in 2015 by Brandon Krieg and Ed Robinson, who realized that wealth creation systems – mainly investing – were underutilized by everyday Americans. Today, Stash is an investing platform helping about 2 million active subscribers invest, with $3 billion in assets managed.[1] Stash raised $40 million in October 2023, positioning itself for a future Initial Public Offering (IPO) shortly after Landsman joined as the CEO.[2] This is just one of several rounds raised by Stash since it was founded, but the mission has never been more relevant in today's macroenvironment.

The number of Americans without an emergency fund is growing yearly – more than 1 in 5 Americans have no emergency savings[3] – and there's a dire need for easy and reliable wealth-building solutions like Stash. "More than half of Americans don't know how money works or how to acquire it, keep, preserve, or grow it," she said. Landsman wanted to spend time with Stash because its model also psychologically understood investor behavior. Stash's founders modeled the fintech after Weight Watchers, understanding that humans easily get overwhelmed by significant changes in their behavior – especially anything that feels restrictive.

Like Weight Watchers breaks down the idea of losing 30 pounds at once to just losing 1 pound a day for its users, Stash proposes that you don't need $3000 to invest but rather as little as $5. The platform constantly rebalances its Smart Portfolio based on market conditions for its customers. So, all investors need to do is invest a small amount of money consistently over time, which can help build wealth through compounding – when money grows exponentially.

CONSUMER FINTECH IS ALIVE AND WELL

When I interviewed Landsman on 28 March 2023, just a month after she took the helm of Stash, the industry sentiment around consumer fintech was melancholy. There was a reason – the industry was coming off the heels of the Silicon Valley Bank failure, which spurred a crisis that took down two other banks and triggered a sharp decline in global bank stock prices.[4] I'll always remember the moment when the news broke, and I received numerous text messages from founders asking if fintech was dead. This discussion spread throughout the fintech community, with LinkedIn posts, tweets, and blogs questioning the future of consumer fintech and whether the sector would recover.

During our interview, I asked Landsman a routine question about her take on what was happening in the industry, given the timing. Without pause, she reassured me that consumer fintech is still alive and well despite market uncertainty. "As long as people still have unmet financial needs," she said, "technology will play an increasingly important role in enabling these transactions."

To remain motivated by the potential of consumer fintech, which has arguably grown oversaturated and has lost the interest of investors over the years, Landsman advises separating pessimism for capital markets from the ability of fintech companies to bridge wealth gaps and provide financial tools and services to those who need them most.

"As long as we believe consumers will want to buy and sell stuff to have money later in their lives – no matter what the capital markets are doing – this criticism will remain a fallacy," she said. "There are billions of underserved people who don't have access to financial services – the power of fintech is its ability to bridge this gap."

When building consumer fintech companies, founders should prioritize financial fundamentals. Consumers are primarily seeking fintech applications to help with understanding how to create an emergency fund, check and improve their credit scores, and develop better savings habits. It's crucial to redirect the focus toward creating solutions that cater to the genuine financial needs of the average person rather than developing tools based on assumptions about consumer preferences.

One key to consumer fintech companies' success is creating better customer financial habits. Rather than just adding more products, fintech companies should focus on helping people break through mental barriers and develop healthier financial behaviors. Of course, building these habits takes time, and it can be challenging to judge success in the short term. But for companies committed to the long game, there's a huge opportunity to make a difference in people's lives while capturing market share – Stash exemplifies this strategy.

For example, through better financial literacy education and budgeting tools, consumers can take control of their finances and create generational wealth. This kind of long-term impact is invaluable and something that companies should strive for when developing their user engagement strategies. The future of consumer fintech lies in its ability to create experiences, not just services. "To do this, companies must learn to maximize micro-moments and raise anticipation in building financial stability," Landsman said.

Consumer fintech is not dead since it has yet to solve the fundamental financial demands of most Americans. Even more alarming, fintech still needs to address the financial sector's most detrimental failure – its inadequate service to women.

HOW WOMEN BECAME A GROWTH MARKET

The world often treats men as the standard and women as different, which leads to bias and discrimination in our systems, especially in finance. The financial world assumes the default human experience is male, while the female experience, representing half of the global population, is considered niche. However, this overlooks that women represent one of the most significant growth markets for financial services to tap into. Not only are they half the population, but women represent nearly half of the US workforce, and they are the majority when factoring in self-employment.

The surge in female employment is closely tied to education. By 2019, nearly half of employed women aged 25–64 held a bachelor's degree or higher, a remarkable increase from 1970 when this figure was four times lower.[5] As of spring 2021, women constitute 59.5% of college students.[6] Despite the ongoing wage gap, educational and employment trends have led to a significant boost in women's financial power. American women now control more than $10 trillion in assets, a figure that is expected to triple in the next decade.[7]

Women are not just becoming the primary breadwinners and financial heads of households; they are also responsible for 85% of daily spending decisions and 80% of healthcare expenditures for their families. This underscores their economic influence and the need for financial services to cater to their needs. If the gender gap were closed, global GDP could be raised by 20% across countries, a World Bank study released in March 2024 shows.[8]

We witnessed the growing influence of the female dollar, recently, throughout the summer of 2023. Women from diverse backgrounds exuded a newfound confidence, propelling the economy forward through ventures close to their hearts – think concerts and movies authentically representing the female experience, fueled by powerhouse artists like Beyoncé and Taylor Swift, whose record-breaking concert tours left audiences – and economies – enriched. For example, Beyoncé's Renaissance tour generated an estimated $4.5 billion for the American economy, about as much as the 2008 Olympics did for Beijing.[9] On top of that, the Barbie movie, directed by Greta Gerwig and produced by Margot Robbie, shattered box office records. Women across industries were making an indelible mark on the global economy.

Women's consumer spending translates into more than $31 trillion annually.[10] This astronomical figure represents a goldmine for fintech, a sector that ironically remains significantly underrepresented by women. However, fintech companies led by women have a strategic advantage in serving the untapped market of financial products for women from different demographics. This is because these companies can relate to the problems that their target customers face and can create unique solutions to address those issues. By embracing female consumers' unique needs and experiences, fintech can pave the way toward financial independence and inclusivity for women. This will have a monumental impact on our economic landscape. But we need more women building in fintech to make it a reality.

HARNESSING THE POWER OF THE FEMALE DOLLAR

I first met Sallie Krawcheck in 2020, interviewing her over the phone for a story about how the global pandemic disproportionately impacted women and people of color. Over a 30-minute call, Krawcheck was able to explain the gender gaps in finance that permeate all around us and connect the dots to what became particularly prominent at the height of the 2020 financial crisis spurred by the pandemic – a "she-cession," as she called it, happening all around us. Women, who constitute a larger share of essential workers, were at a higher risk, reflected in the higher job loss rate among women, particularly in service sectors. Even women who could work from home experienced a decline in productivity, while men benefited from the remote work setup. The increased burden of household duties, childcare, and parental care pushed more mothers to consider leaving the workforce in droves. "This is such a significant issue that it's hard to believe we're discussing anything else," Krawcheck told me. "We need to address this with the urgency it deserves."

The topic for Krawcheck is much more than an inequitable workforce that leads to the gender pay gap, which reveals that women earn 82 cents for every dollar men earn for the same job.[11] An even bigger problem is the gender wealth gap, which tracks how much women own and keep in assets including cash, investments, and real estate. Women only keep 32 cents for every dollar earned by a white man. For Black and Latina women, it's just one penny.[12] To make matters worse, Krawcheck explained that the retirement savings crisis in the US affects women disproportionately because they tend to live longer than men. A 2020 Wells Fargo study shows that working men report a median retirement savings of $120 000, compared to $60 000 for working women.[13] Krawcheck notes that the industry tends to forget that money is the top source of stress for women.

A decade ago, Krawcheck embarked on a mission to dismantle financial myths and misconceptions so women could step into their power grounded in financial knowledge and independence. For example, one pervasive myth is the stereotype that women are spendthrifts with an addiction to shopping for shoes and clothes. Yet, an analysis by LendingTree based on the Bureau of Labor Statistics 2021 data reveals a different story: single men actually spend more than single women, averaging $41 203 annually compared to $38 838.[14]

Building on her background in research and her credibility on Wall Street, Krawcheck chose to start building in fintech with the intention to equip women with tools to reclaim control over their financial lives. Although women possess the inherent power to manage their finances, they have been fed a lifetime of falsehoods, starting with the erroneous belief that girls aren't good at math. This myth persists because girls are often conditioned to feel anxious about math, mistakenly believing it aligns with societal expectations. In adulthood, these damaging messages continue with advice like "stop buying lattes," Krawcheck said.

Such pervasive misinformation can lead women to avoid budgeting or defer financial decisions to men, perpetuating a vicious cycle. Reflecting on her experiences with these stereotypes, Krawcheck underscores the importance of normalizing conversations about money among women, even if internalized gender norms remain a work in progress. The goal is progress, not perfection. With advanced technology, Krawcheck could amplify this message, reaching wider audiences more rapidly than ever before.

Fintech integrates the driving forces of the economy, influencing capital flows and catalyzing investment. "There's nothing more important – or powerful – than that," Krawcheck stated. "Helping women and their allies grow their wealth is immensely powerful. As they build their financial resources, they direct funds toward worthy causes. And technology exponentially enhances the capabilities of financial services."

Over the years of interviewing her, I have learned that Krawcheck's knowledge and frankness around this topic come from a storied career on Wall Street. In 1995, she broke onto the scene through an avenue she knew was her best: Research. She learned that being the numbers person meant the senior executives couldn't ignore her, so she started as a research analyst before landing her first high-profile role as CEO of Sanford C. Bernstein & Co. in 2001, an independent research boutique. By 2002, she was gracing the cover of *Fortune* magazine titled "The Last Honest Analyst." The cover put her in the spotlight of the financial services industry as one of the most visible women on Wall Street. That year, Krawcheck rose through the ranks and was eventually approached by Citigroup CEO Sandy Weill to become CEO of Citigroup's Smith Barney. Shortly after, she was elevated to Citi's CFO. It was a significant responsibility, and Krawcheck, now dubbed the most powerful woman on Wall Street, was looking forward to reforming the broken structures as an insider of one of the world's largest financial institutions.

However, the financial crisis hit within a few months, and the American economy was in freefall. Krawcheck soon discovered that before she stepped into the role, Citi had mis-sold products to their clients, she recalled. It was a mistake, but it was products that were supposed to be relatively low risk and ended up being high risk in a challenging market. Krawcheck advocated for partially reimbursing the clients for it to do right by their customers, even though the company had told their clients there was a risk of losing everything. She approached the idea with Citi's new CEO at the time, Vikram Pandit. Krawcheck said he refused to reimburse their clients. So Krawcheck went straight to the board, and they agreed with her. Now, Krawcheck was faced with battling thoughts around deciding to keep the job she loved (the CEO was going to fire her for going over his head) or go through with the reimbursement and do right by their clients.

"That's when I had an epiphany," she remembered. After talking to her "personal board of directors," they were split. Some people told her to fight for it. Others reasonably said, "Keep your job and live to fight another day." Ultimately, when it came down to making a final decision – she thought of her kids, she told me. "If my kids were with me in the board meeting, what would I want them to see?" In the end, Krawcheck did right by the clients. It cost her a ton of money and a job that she loved.

"By the way, years later, over just a few months, a number of the board members from the time apologized to me and said, 'We shouldn't have let the CEO fire you after that. You were trying to do the right thing. You did the right thing. It was good for the company. We're sorry.'"

That apology didn't put the money she lost back into her pocket – including bonuses and stock that didn't get vested. So, while Krawcheck did right by the company, she says the company never did right by her.

Krawcheck encountered a glaring example of the systemic barriers that hinder women from ascending to the upper echelons of corporate America. In this case, she became a victim of the glass cliff. This is when women executives are elevated, or more accurately, pushed to the edge when business is in turmoil or during crises, and no one else is willing to take the reins (see the *Time* magazine cover references in Chapter 1). These female leaders are expected to rectify the situation but often end up shouldering the blame – and the consequences. The term was coined by two researchers in the UK who found women were 63% more likely to be recruited into leadership roles that were already unstable.[15] After facing off with Wall Street executives, Krawcheck was about to embrace the following challenge: entrepreneurship.

First Fintech for Women, by Women

After a couple of years and some initial apprehension, Krawcheck decided in 2014 to build the first fintech company built by women for women. She called the start-up Ellevest in 2015, surveyed hundreds of women about their investment goals, and pitched her idea to venture capitalists, eventually garnering investments from powerhouses such as Venus Williams, Mellody Hobson, Melinda Gates, and Penny Pritzker. In May 2016, Ellevest launched a digital platform to help women invest and plan for retirement. The platform is a "robo-advisor" that uses an automated investing approach built with a gender-aware algorithm – the first of its kind.

Ellevest's investing algorithm incorporates gender lens portfolios, including the Intentional Impact portfolio, which divests from companies harming the environment, a cause disproportionately affecting women.

The algorithm factors the differences between men and women, including salary gaps, career breaks, and longer life expectancy. "Are our portfolios anti-racist as well?" Krawcheck asked. "You can't advance women without being anti-racist, addressing significant issues faced by Black women and women of color."

Consequently, she updated Ellevest Intentional Impact portfolios with an anti-racist lens. Ellevest's impact portfolios are built to tackle issues that disproportionately affect women, like gender inequality, racial injustice, and climate change. Krawcheck wanted to ensure that Ellevest was available to all women, not just affluent women; therefore, she launched Ellevest with low fees and no investing minimum. Today, the company offers a digital plan that costs $12 monthly, including automated investing and retirement goals, workshops, worksheets, email courses, and discounted financial planning sessions. Ellevest's Private Wealth Management is also available for high and ultra-high-net-worth individuals and institutions. As it turns out, an even better investment philosophy than the 60/40 is investing in other women.

What sets Ellevest and Krawcheck's leadership apart is her innovative approach to the business model. Unlike traditional financial services firms, Krawcheck prioritizes the resources her customers need to improve their finances. "The sky's the limit for us because we have defined ourselves by our mission: to get more money in the hands of women. So everything under that umbrella is fair game for us," Krawcheck explained.

Through her research, Krawcheck identified distinct behaviors in women investors compared to their male counterparts. She used these insights to build a platform specifically designed to address women's unique financial realities that traditional financial companies often ignore. For example, while men might take an educated guess at their risk tolerance, women often leave the platform to figure it out on their own. This behavior indicates a broader hesitation among women to ask questions about investing, negotiating raises, or starting businesses, opting instead to solve these issues independently.

Recognizing this, Krawcheck integrated an educational component into the platform. She focused on writing and sharing data that countered negative stereotypes about women and their financial habits, which evolved into her popular newsletter, "What the Elle?"

"It's been a journey of challenging conventional narratives and building a business that rejects outdated stories, creating something tailored for women," Krawcheck said. "In an industry lacking diversity, I would argue our industry was built for him."

Krawcheck consistently highlights how women can be better investors than men, supported by data from Fidelity Investments showing that women tend to achieve positive returns and outperform men by 40 basis points.[16] Based on 5.2 million accounts, this analysis also found that women often hold too much cash and need to know more before investing. "At Ellevest, we challenged the notion that women don't invest as much because they're more risk-averse," she said. "It's not about having a uterus; it's about how the industry has been built."

In an industry where men manage 98% of mutual fund dollars, 86% of financial advisors are men, and companies owned by white men manage 99% of investment assets, the products and marketing are often tailored to men. Women often feel unseen and unrepresented in the industry due to these statistics. "Maybe women aren't risk-averse; perhaps we haven't built a product or campaign that engages them," Krawcheck said. It's more accurate to say that women are not risk-averse but risk-aware, willing to take risks when they fully understand them.

Krawcheck believes this behavior is partly because the patriarchy demands perfection from women. Women often seek more complete information before taking action, which is a gender difference, not a flaw. This makes the content and financial education element of the Ellevest platform crucial. Ellevest has also fostered a community where women can openly discuss money, breaking the isolation and patronization they've historically faced. Over time, Ellevest evolved from a digital-first investing platform to a holistic financial wellness platform, offering services, products, knowledge, insights, and coaching.

"By the way, we've succeeded despite industry skepticism," Krawcheck noted. "People dismiss us as small because we started from nothing, but there's a nervousness about us being tech-driven and outspoken."

Despite criticism, Krawcheck remains unfazed. Even during the challenging market of March and April 2020, Ellevest experienced net positive inflows weekly, with an annual attrition rate rounded to zero. This counters the notion that tech-first approaches only work in strong markets. Ellevest extends beyond investment management to provide strategic advice on career paths, salary negotiations, budgeting, and more, contributing to its growth.

Krawcheck combines drive with humility, not yet considering Ellevest a complete success. "I think of us as having cleared several high hurdles," she said. Her sense of success comes from the gratitude of Ellevest's users. "One moment that stood out was when I was standing in line to vote during the 2020 election in New York City," she recalled. "The woman behind me saw my Ellevest bag and told me we changed her life."

Krawcheck's impact is not just for Ellevest's users but for the fintech industry, too. The industry average for women on leadership teams is 23%. Ellevest's leadership team is made up of 84% women. About 11% of the industry's teams are people of color, while Ellevest's team is 50% people of color. Only 20% of women are board members by industry average. Ellevest's board members are 83% women.[17] Talk about putting your money where your mouth is. Ellevest's most significant advantage is that the product looks and feels like her because the company culture represents its diverse client base. As a result, Ellevest has earned something every fintech company strives for from its users: a lifetime of trust.

Catering fintech products to women is a business imperative that will propel your company ahead of the competition. Research from the International Finance Corporation (IFC) dives into this, showing how analyzing gender differences can give fintech firms a leg up in tapping into the $31 trillion female market and boosting financial inclusion for women overall. According to the research, having leaders who understand the value of serving women, both socially and commercially, is key for fintech firms that intentionally target women. If the top brass truly believes in financially including women, it will set the tone for the company. According to the survey, about 58% of firms say their focus on women is driven by leaders who get why it's so crucial to include women in financial services.[18] To understand the trade-off between spending more to get women on board and the value they bring, this study looked at how the economics played out for women versus men. Sure, the customer acquisition costs to attract female clients are higher than their male counterparts. However, about 63% of fintech companies that specifically tailor their products and services for women end up with customers who stick around longer, bringing in more value over their lifetime.

It's been shown before that women tend to be loyal customers, and are less likely to default than men. So, even though it might take a bit more effort and cash to get them on board initially, in the long run, it's worth it because they bring in more value. With this type of engagement, you'd think more companies would target them specifically. But get this: less than a third of these firms are tailoring their products and services for women. They're collecting data on gender but not doing much with it to reach out to more women or make their products more appealing to them. Ellevest capitalizes on this wide-open opportunity.

HOW HARD IS IT TO RAISE A SERIES B?

As a trailblazing figure, Krawcheck's prominence on Wall Street could have led her down many paths. Yet, her roots in Charleston, South Carolina, where she was raised in a humble middle-class household, seemingly informed her decision. Most successful women in fintech I interviewed came from humble origins and were influenced by the work ethic of female family members who transcended gender norms. This characteristic propels them to find purpose in innovation and confidence via representation. "My grandmother worked outside the home at a time when there weren't a ton of career paths for women in South Carolina," Krawcheck told me. "But she was a strong, independent woman."

On the flip side, Krawcheck's parents married in their early 20s, just as her father started law school, and had four children in under four years. "And here, on the one hand, was my strong, independent grandmother. And here were my parents who had no money and were massively in love, and their only fights were around money, and when they fought around money, they fought, make no mistake about it." For Krawcheck, her money story was shaped by that contrast of strength and independence on the one hand and natural friction on the other.

When we talk about "money buying happiness," it's not about material possessions. It's about the freedom of choice – to be your truest, most authentic self. This is the key to breaking free from cycles of toxicity and finding true happiness.

In every conversation, Krawcheck returns to the bottom line – when women have more money, we can leave marriages that don't serve us, jobs that don't fulfill us, and build innovative businesses. Unfortunately, even when the most successful women become entrepreneurs, the odds are stacked against them. Krawcheck recalls the early days of worrying about failure when building Ellevest. We know what the data shows us: 90% of start-ups fail.[19] On top of that, Krawcheck was building a company founded by women, building a product designed for women. So, for Krawcheck, the odds were even worse. Also, as women, research says that we take failure much harder. It can be easier not to try because if you don't try, you don't fail. And then you don't have the embarrassment of failing. "By the way, I've failed publicly so many times I can't even count at this stage," Krawcheck reminds me. I notice that the ownership of her failures and her willingness to share her authentic experiences make her a stronger leader who draws people in because she connects with others.

Starting a women-led, women-focused digital financial services company is a challenging feat. While Krawcheck, 59, had the status on Wall Street to get her in the door for meetings with venture capitalists, it wasn't enough for them to see beyond her gender and age.

When starting Ellevest, she shared that one of the big Wall Street firms came to her about investing in the start-up in one of their earlier rounds, and they said, "We love what you're doing. We love what you've built. The technology is terrific. We love the mission; we love the brand. We want to invest $2 million." Krawcheck pushed back. With her knowledge of Wall Street, she knew the firm could do a double-digit number. She advocated for the company, reminding them the ROI would be worth it. Ellevest could teach their firm a lot about engaging with women, which is essential for a big company. The firm returned, and instead of the $15 million investment, they offered to host a dinner. "Boy, is that patronizing," she said.

Undeterred, she pressed on. She revealed that each investment round Ellevest raised had unique characteristics. For the most part, the seed round was assembled by individuals she had collaborated with on Wall Street. Regarding the later rounds, Krawcheck would meet with individuals from investment firms, and she'd easily convince the individual to invest just by showcasing the market opportunity backed by the financials of Ellevest. However, that investor would typically return to their investment committee, and the investment would fall through. Any doubts any investor had, she could combat with data. But it wouldn't matter if the investor didn't inherently see the big picture value of investing in women.

So, she found two other approaches to make it work. She could go to venture funds that do not need unanimous approval, which led her to the key to Ellevest's large funding rounds: individuals. Instead of focusing on convincing investors to support Ellevest, she flipped the narrative. She met with people already aligned with Ellevest's view of the world – where women are given financial services at the same rate as men, which is a $700 billion opportunity.[20]

"I find it much easier to go to people who have money, who share our view of the world, and then convince them to invest," she said. "So flipping it from approaching people who invest for a living to people who have our view of the world." From the pre-seed to a $34 million Series A and hitting milestones like $1 billion in assets under management in March 2021, this approach to raise capital via like-minded investors, in addition to a top-notch product and content experience, has fueled Ellevest to rise as an innovative fintech firm. So, when Krawcheck and the Ellevest team decided to pursue their Series B round, they were confident it would be a cinch. After all, the markets were hot in 2021, and the fintech sector was riding a wave of investment.[21] It seemed everyone wanted to back fintech, and Ellevest's impressive numbers looked like a surefire ticket to a fat financing round. Little did they know that the journey would be anything but easy.

The ratio of venture dollars raised by women in fintech, specifically for a Series B, is 1 in 10 000, Krawcheck shared. As an industry, we must realize what a burden that is, even for successful women. Krawcheck, the trail-blazer for women in fintech and a well-established powerhouse in financial services, is still walking into meetings with one strike because she's a woman and another because she's over 50. "I'm not anyone's idea of the innovative next-generation founder or Mark Zuckerberg type," she said.

While Kawcheck got her lead and existing investors on board for the second financing round, she still needed help finding new investors interested in funding a female fintech founder's Series B. She did find one – a woman of color investor who ultimately told Krawcheck and Ellevest that the company met 14 of 15 criteria. Because of that, she was not going to invest. "It was heartbreaking," Krawcheck shared. "Not to mention, this investor has 52 portfolio companies – all founded and led by men." Krawcheck and the investor later shared a glass of wine, during which the investor admitted that she would have invested in Ellevest if Krawcheck had been a man. This was because, as the only woman and person of color on her investment firm's leadership team, she would have risked losing her job if the investment in Ellevest had failed. The situation was frustrating. "We have to be successful since we're the only ones doing what we're doing," Krawcheck said. I could feel the combination of passion and disheartenment in her voice. Helping women build wealth should be easier than this.

Then, one day, Krawcheck gets a call from a young woman who works at a seed fund in Portland, Oregon. She had heard about Ellevest raising money and explained that, as an investor, she was obsessed with Ellevest but could not reach the company's minimum at all. However, if she brought together her community of small investors, they could raise Ellevest a couple million bucks. "Ding ding ding," Krawcheck said, "we have a winner." Then, another investor within that group said, "I've got a group of friends who I think would be interested in this too. What if I pull them together?"

That cycle continued, and Ellevest raised a $53 million Series B within three weeks through a series of special-purpose vehicles, each representing a community of women investors. This approach brought in hundreds of new investors, mostly from underrepresented groups.

The moral of the story is that, as Krawcheck eloquently stated, our collective strength as women is our superpower. "We knew it in high school and college when we never traveled alone – always in a pack," she said. "As we grow into our careers, we as women have been convinced to play the game of success as an individual sport, when in reality, the men in our lives have been playing it as a team sport for some time."

Krawcheck calls on all leaders to promise ourselves that we will support all women. We want to help the obnoxious, rambunctious, boring women who seem to be waiting for their turn.

Remember that our restlessness with current affairs is fueled by the belief that progress is always within reach.

As I've interviewed female founders in fintech for years, I see the collective sign that happens when asked about raising money. Women entrepreneurs don't need to try harder; they're already putting in more effort because fewer checks are written for female founders. Achieving their goals just takes much longer, meaning they are already working harder than their male counterparts. If women raise only 2% of venture dollars, that means "it takes 50 times as many meetings, 50 times as many follow-up questions," Krawcheck said. "It's 50 times as many nos." And it doesn't necessarily get easier just because you approach a female check writer.

We know female fintech founders need support raising initial funds. Adding insult to injury, raising early-stage capital from women funders can be a double-edged sword. Research confirms a trend I've heard through multiple interviews and honest conversations with founders and investors: women CEOs have a lower chance of securing next-round funding if they were previously funded by women, regardless of whether they are seeking investments from men or women this time around. These investments can lead to assumptions that the female entrepreneur received special treatment because of gender. The idea that she only received funding because of her gender, in the first place, questions her competency as a founder. This bias also stems from the implicit assumption that receiving funding from women implies they weren't "good enough" to attract investments from more established players, typically men. Understanding the context of this bias can help us learn how to confront it.

Research published in *Organization Science* by Kaisa Snellman and Isabelle Solal examined 2136 start-ups tracked by the Crunchbase database.[22] The researchers found that female-founded firms that received funding from female VCs had more difficulty getting financing in the future. For male-founded firms, there was no difference. The male founders were equally likely to receive future funding regardless of whether their first-round funding came from male or female VCs. The researchers conducted an experiment in which MBA students evaluated identical business pitches with two exceptions: the gender of the founder and the financer. Results showed that female founders were rated less favorably when they had female VC support, suggesting a gender bias. Researchers concluded that observers implicitly believed that the relationship was motivated by considerations other than merit, leading to a discount in perceptions of competence. The women were perceived to have received funding, not because it was well deserved but because female VCs wanted to help out other women who would have needed help to secure financing elsewhere.

This puts female entrepreneurs in a difficult position; if they rely solely on male funding, they are unlikely to receive any, and if they depend on females, they may not get future financing. How do we move forward? First, understand the data that shows that women-run businesses provide as-good or better results than men-run founding teams, on less capital. Next, double- and triple-down your bets on women supporting women, that's what Ellevest did. It's still the most critical part of the solution. As the number of female investors grows and more women invest in each other's businesses, we begin to normalize this practice. Another crucial part of the solution is for female VCs to continue financing women's ventures, including larger sums in later stages. This ensures that female business owners receive the necessary capital to scale their businesses, with late-stage female backers building on the foundation laid by early-stage female financiers. Increasing the representation of women in decision-making positions will also help reduce gender biases in founder evaluations.

However, the success of this shift depends on several factors: the number of female investors, the positions they hold, the industries they invest in, and their networks. Currently, female VCs are primarily involved in early-stage fundraising rounds, which carry the highest risk. This dynamic could change if more women raised significant funds.

This brings up a larger question: Is gender-segregated investment truly the goal? The answer is no. Our industry should promote inclusive investing, where male and female investors collaborate to support promising female entrepreneurs. This collaboration must be genuine, not mere virtue signaling. Only by working together can we create systemic change. To reach this goal, we must first help all investors understand that investing in women is good business for everyone.

"I had a couple of my investors say, 'Do not share the fact that the raise was difficult,'" Krawcheck said. "I was told to position it as people were throwing money at us; we turned the money down." While Krawcheck understands the sentiment, she said it doesn't help. "If I say that, when the next group comes along, and they are raising money, it's hard, then they're more likely to quit because they'll say, well, it's supposed to be super easy."

We have to understand challenges and obstacles to circumvent them. The reality is that for women to venture into entrepreneurship, we must be financially resilient. This resilience requires an extraordinary level of mental strength, a trait women excel in due to the systemic adversity we face. Unlike our male counterparts, we are not afforded the luxury of wasting millions or billions of dollars, given that we already receive a minuscule fraction of the funding available. This heightened aversion to loss cultivates superior risk management skills in women, making us more likely to steer our companies to success. Moreover, women entrepreneurs often prioritize deeper, more meaningful motivations beyond mere profit, focusing on creating positive impacts. This approach not only boosts economic growth but also generates a powerful multiplier effect, as women tend to reinvest a significant portion of their income back into their families and communities. Investing in women is not just about fostering individual success – it's about uplifting entire societies and driving comprehensive, sustainable growth.

YOU CAN'T WAIT TO HAVE FUN

Regarding lessons in entrepreneurship, Krawcheck has a treasure trove of advice. First, it's about remembering that life is a journey and entrepreneurship is not for everyone – so if you're in it, be sure to have fun while you're doing it. "For years, I'd say, 'I'm going to relax after that board meeting or that big project,'" she said. "You can't wait to have fun – and call it quits if you're not having fun along the way because it doesn't get fun. There isn't a moment when you're just like, we did it!"

You have results in that deck that you need to hit. And whenever any of us raise money, you're maybe not 1000% sure how you're going to hit every single metric. And so, you have to start figuring things out. And particularly in fintech, the environment can quickly change on you, as we've seen over the past couple of years.

Krawcheck's efforts have paved the way for countless female entrepreneurs to enter the fintech landscape, many of whom are celebrated in this book. Inspired by her remarkable impact, I posed one final question to her: How do we sustain this momentum of women's economic power?

"I'm a hammer, so everything's a nail – but the solution is you get more money into the hands of women," she responded. "If we can get more women financially secure, it reduces that stress and enables us to take a little more risk in life, such as moving from a corporate job to founding a start-up," she said. Ellevest has found over the years that for men today, the synonyms for money are power, strength, and independence. And for women, it's loneliness, isolation, and uncertainty. "We started to build the community as a place for education and for women to unite and not feel isolated," she shared. Today, Ellevest's network and community surpasses 3 million women, and the company reached a milestone of $2 billion in assets under management in March 2024, celebrating the moment by ringing the opening bell at the New York Stock Exchange.

Reflecting on her career and the advice she can offer other female entrepreneurs following her footsteps, Krawcheck's most significant advice is to stop trying to be great at everything, especially when balancing career and motherhood. "The layer of expectations is toxic," she said. "So, you're CEO, but are you a great mom, too? Are you a great wife as well? I always loved to joke that my goal was a big career. It always was. And in terms of being a mom, I'm average." That doesn't mean Krawcheck wasn't an attentive mother; it just means she didn't always bring the home-baked cookies to school. Sometimes, you'll be the best entrepreneur, founder, and builder; sometimes, you're the best mom, and there's the balance.

"This view that we have to be great at everything simultaneously is a construct that keeps us down because you can't be, and then you're trying to do everything excellently, which means you do nothing well," she shared. "Jessica Calarco, the sociologist, has said what we learned from the pandemic is that other countries have social safety nets, and the US has women."

Positive changes for some women can benefit everyone who interacts with them – whether as business partners, customers, funders, family members, or community members. However, these changes alone are not enough to close the existing racial wealth gap. Systemic change is essential to make real progress in addressing this disparity. On an individual level, one effective way to counteract this inequity is to actively support Black and brown women. This can be done by hiring them, paying them fairly, buying from their businesses, funding their ventures, mentoring them, and more.

The wealth transfer, termed the "Feminization of Wealth" by Ellevest, has the potential to reshape societal beliefs about women and wealth, affecting everyone regardless of whether they directly receive a financial windfall. The impact on women of color, however, remains uncertain. What is clear is that women with more money tend to contribute more to politicians who share their values and to nonprofits aligned with their causes, such as fighting climate change, which disproportionately affects women and people of color. Additionally, financially secure women can invest more in initiatives focused on gender and racial justice.

Krawcheck's mission over the last decade remains as clear today as it was then: get more money in the hands of women because the research is apparent – societies are fairer, families are better off, markets are stronger, and businesses are more effective when women have more money. Ultimately, Krawcheck's persistence to make Ellevest a success stems from her passion to ensure the next generation of female CEOs have footsteps to follow. "That's the responsibility I feel to be successful," she said. "For the next woman who's the founder of the next company."

UNLOCKING THE CARE ECONOMY

On 9 October 2023, history was made when Claudia Goldin became the third woman ever to receive the Nobel Memorial Prize in Economic Sciences.[23] This huge achievement came from her groundbreaking research into women's progress in the workforce. Goldin dug into two centuries of American data, documenting the historical journey of women in the labor market and pinpointing the root cause of the gender pay gap.

Many people think the pay gap between men and women is due to women's choices regarding education or occupation. But Goldin's research tells a different story. She found that when men and women start working in the same job with the same level of college education, they earn the same wages. So, it's pretty unreasonable to assume that women are willingly choosing lower-paying jobs. Goldin's work shows that pay equity takes a nosedive after a woman has her first child, and the gap just keeps widening from there.

This disparity largely comes down to societal norms and expectations that push women to be the primary caregivers for children. It's a clear reminder that to achieve true gender equality in the workplace, we need to tackle the earnings disparity and the heavy caregiving burdens within households, especially those tied to motherhood.

Sheila Lirio Marcelo had a hunch about the enormous importance of the care economy long before it became a massive $6 trillion industry.[24] The care economy covers both paid and unpaid labor, including individuals who provide care services to those who can't support themselves, like children and older adults. With ongoing labor shortages and economic challenges made worse by the COVID-19 pandemic, a significant portion of the US economy is at risk of substantial losses unless business and government leaders come together to address this crisis.

Research by BCG shows that if the care economy remains unchanged, the US could face a GDP loss of $290 billion by 2030 – equivalent to Connecticut's entire GDP. [25] Even more dire forecasts predict a GDP loss of around $500 billion by 2030, underscoring the urgent need for action.[26]

The lack of innovation in the care economy hits women the hardest and comes with high stakes. The COVID-19 pandemic created a major childcare crisis, with mothers often becoming the default solution. This led to four times as many women as men leaving the labor force in September 2020.[27] The media has highlighted the long-term impact of this crisis, likely setting back women across generations. The loss of childcare and school supervision hours has severely affected women's wages, erasing much of the progress made by women in the workforce, and it will take years to recover. Research shows 26% of mothers and 7% of fathers are stay-at-home parents, according to a 2023 Pew Research Center analysis of US Census Bureau data.[28]

Moreover, women make up nearly 60% of unpaid caregivers and more than 80% of paid in-home caregivers for seniors in the United States.[29] Yet, society often overlooks the financial, physical, and emotional toll of caring for loved ones. Lirio Marcelo has been a trailblazer in addressing these issues since she founded Care.com.

Lirio Marcelo grew up in the Philippines, witnessing many business ventures through her parents' entrepreneurial careers. She saw everything from trucking to rice milling, real estate to sugar, and gained valuable insights into the workings of diverse industries. What made a profound impact on Lirio Marcelo was the fact that the gender gap in the Philippines is notably narrow compared to other Asian countries.[30] This meant she was exposed to many strong female role models, including a female president and many female CEOs. The matriarchal nature of the country also meant that Lirio Marcelo's parents did not adhere to traditional and restrictive gender roles. "That left a profound impact on me," she recalled.

"My mother, in particular, was an extraordinary figure – an adventurous risk-taker, a skilled negotiator, and impeccably organized," she shared. "Meanwhile, my father was nurturing, believing in us without question, and fostering our academic growth, even teaching me math alongside my elder brothers." Raised among five siblings, Lirio Marcelo says her parents instilled a sense of resilience from a young age, encouraging her to take risks and explore new horizons.

Years later, her parents boldly decided to immigrate to Houston, Texas, known for its energy technology advancements. In the 1970s, Lirio Marcelo's family of eight immigrated to the United States when she was six. Adapting to life in Houston wasn't without its challenges. It wasn't so much about fear or anxiety as the striking realization that everyone looked different from her and her family.

When Lirio Marcelo turned 10 years old, her parents decided to send her and her younger brother back to the Philippines. She immersed herself in the culture of her homeland, specifically in the province of Candelaria, Quezon. "It was there that we learned the language and developed a deep appreciation for our heritage," she recalled. "Playing with local children on the streets and embracing daily tasks like cleaning classrooms using coconut husks instilled a sense of pride and connection to my roots."

Growing up in her home country gave her an experience that was a grounding force, anchoring Lirio Marcelo to her culture, language, and identity. Moreover, it fostered a heightened awareness of global citizenship and a profound compassion toward diversity, which she credits with shaping her into a more empathetic leader.

As is often the case for children of immigrants, her parents had a predetermined path in mind for their children's future professions to ensure a level of stability immigrant parents never experienced. Being typical Asian immigrants, Lirio Marcelo's parents had specific roles in mind for each of their children, including doctor, dentist, accountant, or lawyer – with Lirio Marcelo being earmarked as the designated lawyer from a young age. *(Similarly, my Filipina mother also expected me to pursue law school.)*

While Lirio Marcelo fully intended to follow her parents' dream, life had other plans. While at Mount Holyoke College, she met her future husband, who was studying at Yale University. Unexpectedly, she found herself pregnant during her sophomore year, which led to a wedding and profound emotional turmoil for her devout Catholic parents. Despite the challenges, Lirio Marcelo remained determined to continue onward, thanks to her incredibly supportive husband and her entrepreneurial spirit.

Despite facing numerous challenges balancing the responsibilities of motherhood and pursuing a career in academia, Lirio Marcelo persevered and applied to Harvard Law School. However, her experience as a young mother prompted her to explore different paths. While attending Harvard Law School, she also enrolled in entrepreneurship courses at Harvard Business School, where she cemented her passion for building, creating, and solving problems – a trait she inherited from her parents.

After graduating, Lirio Marcelo landed a job at a litigation consulting firm. However, she soon realized that the work environment was not conducive to her being her authentic self. As a young mother and full-time worker, she felt constrained and unsupported. By January 2000, Lirio Marcelo had joined a mission-driven company called Upromise, where she embarked on a five-year journey called her "general management tour of duty." This experience exposed her to various roles and industries, including technology and marketing, and provided insights into families' pain points. This understanding was further deepened during her tenure at TheLadders.com, where she learned about people services and the intricacies of job matching.

These early career experiences laid the groundwork for what would eventually become Care.com – a subscription service that addresses families' real pain points, like finding reliable caregivers. However, the inspiration behind Care.com stemmed from personal experiences. Lirio Marcelo relied on her parents for child support until her father's heart attack. She struggled to find dual care solutions via the Yellow Pages and saw the need for a central care matchmaking service.

When she first started building Care.com, Lirio Marcelo admits to being initially insecure about being judged as a female founder who solved a predominately female pain point. With a boost of confidence from mentors, the decision to start Care.com was influenced by three key factors: a solid business model grounded in research and experience, Lirio Marcelo's connection to the problem being addressed, and staying true to her core values and passions.

Launched in 2007, Care.com is an online web portal connecting families, caregivers, and employers for childcare, senior care, housekeeping, pet care, and more. Today, more than 14.1 million members in 16 countries are turning to Care.com to solve their caregiving needs. Having raised more than $110 million in private venture funding Care.com used its cash on marketing and acquired four companies to expand and grow.[31] In January 2014, Lirio Marcelo made history by becoming the first Asian American woman to take a company public and the seventh woman ever to do so. It's worth noting that throughout stock market history, only 40 women have taken a company public, and less than 25 were founded solely by women. The figures become even more striking when we consider the data since 2000, as only one female-led IPO has occurred per year, on average, for the past quarter-century, which amounts to a dismal ratio of 0.49%. This ratio becomes almost negligible when considering the first IPO dating back to 1602. [32]

Lirio Marcelo vividly remembers the day her company went public on the New York Stock Exchange. She recalls embracing her team of all immigrant founders, tears streaming down their faces, and the overwhelming feeling of accomplishment. At the time, Lirio Marcelo tells me, "I just wanted to prove that a company with social impact could grow and be profitable and serve people. That was one of my key drivers." Her unwavering dedication to this mission led her to sell Care.com amidst the unprecedented challenges of the 2020 pandemic. Lirio Marcelo oversaw the acquisition of the platform by IAC for a staggering $500 million.

Looking back on her journey, she emphasizes the importance of humility and flexibility in leadership. She understands that it is crucial to recognize when an approach no longer serves the organization's needs and adapt accordingly. As a start-up CEO, Lirio Marcelo made high-risk decisions that paid off, and as a public company leader, she prioritized data-driven insights to drive success. Her advice to aspiring leaders is to remain committed to evolving and learning from each stage of the journey.

AI FOR CHIEF HOUSEHOLD OFFICERS

After the acquisition of Care.com in 2020, Lirio Marcelo shifted her focus toward policy and advocacy work, with a keen interest in next-generation technologies that create social impact. This led her to delve deeper into the world of artificial intelligence, where she discovered the immense potential of generative AI. Lirio Marcelo recognized the transformative power of AI in creating value for businesses and society at large by completing tasks. "It was like a light bulb went off in my mind once again, prompting me to say, 'Can this technology be applied to assist families?'"

After 20 years of experience in family care, Lirio Marcelo would shift her focus to the daily coordination of care, a persistent challenge that technology is finally equipped to address with the advancements in AI. "The underlying economic imperative of maximizing household productivity remains as crucial to me as it did when founding Care.com," she said. It's about unleashing the economic potential of women, empowering them to reclaim their time and mental bandwidth, and fostering innovation and creativity while revitalizing themselves. Women spend 4.5 hours daily on household tasks, compared to men's 2.8 hours. "If we could just save one hour of women's time at home, accounting for their 44% share of the working population, we estimate potential savings of about a trillion dollars annually, equivalent to the GDP of two countries," she explained. This underscores the economic significance of her latest tech start-up.

Driven by the unmet needs of women and families and the imperative to enhance productivity, Lirio Marcelo is back in the start-up arena with Ohai.ai. Launched in January 2024, this virtual assistant is dedicated to streamlining administrative tasks and everyday care coordination for families, catering not just to women but also acknowledging the vital role of what Lirio Marcelo calls the "chief household officer," the person juggling tasks like managing calendars, planning appointments, and overseeing family well-being, which contributes significantly to the burnout experienced by those managing households and caring for loved ones. Lirio Marcelo designed Ohai.ai as a virtual assistance platform, affectionately dubbed "O," that can alleviate the mental load associated with managing family schedules and delegating tasks.

In a world where the boundary between work and home life is increasingly blurred, Ohai.ai aims to assist users in balancing these spheres by optimizing their time. Combining artificial intelligence with human input, "O" offers basic services for free, including daily schedule summaries and alerts for calendar conflicts among family members. Users can access advanced features for less than $30 per month, such as automatic event scheduling from scanned texts or photos, task delegation, and list management.

The reason behind the founding of this start-up is rooted in a strong belief in the importance of tackling pressing challenges head-on, particularly those related to gender inequality and the financial disparities that women face around the world. Lirio Marcelo is an entrepreneurial mother committed to advocating for women's rights. While managing a household and raising two boys, she realized the immense burden that women carry as chief household officers. For example, even she'll admit that despite her qualifications and professional expertise, she finds it challenging to schedule a routine mammogram amidst the chaos of her daily responsibilities. This experience is a stark reminder of women's unpaid labor and responsibility, often undervalued and overlooked.

Recent studies have highlighted the staggering amount of unpaid labor that women perform globally, with a 2020 report by Oxfam revealing that women would have earned a staggering $10.8 trillion if paid minimum wage for their unpaid work.[33] This figure is three times the total value of the current global technology industry. In the United States, women spend 37% more time on unpaid care than men, leading to significant limitations on their career options, income, and social mobility. The unequal distribution of unpaid labor also has profound effects on mental health and well-being, especially at a time when stress and burnout rates are on the rise. By managing and coordinating tasks, AI has the potential to ease the cognitive load on families, especially those with mothers, and help save them the precious resource of time, which is often more valuable than monetary compensation.

The platform and technology couldn't come at a more perfect time. The pandemic catalyzed demand for flexible work, particularly for women who largely remain the primary caregivers in their households. Entrepreneurship has emerged as the most viable option. Many women are turning to self-employment to navigate the overwhelming responsibilities of managing a career, caring for children, and overseeing household tasks. Since the onset of COVID-19, there has been a notable surge in female entrepreneurship, with the percentage of female entrepreneurs skyrocketing from 29% in 2019 to 47% during the pandemic and further increasing to 49% in 2021.[34] Over the past two decades, women-owned firms in the US have witnessed a staggering 114% increase, with an average of 849 new businesses started by women daily.

"As my friend and colleague, Ai-jen Poo eloquently puts it," Lirio Marcelo said, "Care is what makes all work possible." It's the linchpin that enables more than 50% of the population – primarily women – to participate in the workforce and sustain our economy. "At Ohai.ai, we're tackling this issue," Lirio Marcelo explained. "Our mission is twofold: first, to empower chief household officers – primarily mothers – to reclaim valuable time for themselves and their families." This means freeing up time for meaningful interactions with loved ones, whether helping with homework or preparing nutritious meals. By doing so, we strengthen families and bolster society as a whole. Secondly, Ohai.ai is building a support network for families, especially as the prevalence of single parenting continues to rise. Through the power of AI and a dedicated team of human experts, Lirio Marcelo is creating a user experience that ensures no one has to navigate the complexities of caregiving alone. "Whether coordinating with grandparents, nannies, or co-parents, we aim to foster a sense of community – a care village – that stands ready to assist in any way necessary," she said. In essence, Ohai.ai is not just about leveraging advanced technology; it's about harnessing the collective strength of communities to alleviate the burdens of caregiving and empower individuals to thrive.

Lirio Marcelo is, once again, embarking on a journey to create a tech-driven, female-centric product offering that leverages emerging technologies to provide access to economic growth. As a Filipina immigrant, she is very intentional about her representation as a leader, not only to represent female entrepreneurship but also to show that it's possible to build a mission-driven caregiving company that is profitable, scalable, and positively impacts the world. Today, she sees her role more as a social entrepreneur.

When I asked her for her final advice for the entrepreneurs reading this book, she immediately responded, "Always be raising money."

And here's some tactical advice: "If you're raising an A round and you've already received term sheets, keep pitching," she said. "You could be pitching to potential future B-round investors, and you're already on a roll. You can tell them, 'I've got a full roster of term sheets, and I'd love to talk to you in the future.'" This way, you're starting to develop those relationships early on. That's what Lirio Marcelo did when she raised funds for Care .com – it was back-to-back and fast. People would preempt a round because she had been engaging them since her previous round.

The second advice is to focus on data, data, data. "At Ohai.ai, we had a thesis about the importance of everyday care coordination for families, so we immediately interviewed 200 families," she said. "We even launched an alpha website and ran SEM campaigns to gauge demand and interest. And when we developed the product, we constantly collected data on product features to see what users were engaging with." So, being data-driven is crucial in today's business landscape, especially in technology and digital ventures.

The third piece of advice is a bit more nuanced – it's about balancing intensity with empathy. "In my early days after completing my JD MBA at Harvard, I was very intense, barely sleeping, and setting high expectations for myself and my team," she said. "I demanded a lot, which wasn't conducive to a healthy work environment." Mentors pointed out that while she was intelligent and hardworking, nobody would want to work for her if she continued that way. So, she started to meditate on stress management and self-awareness in her leadership journey. "I reframed my approach to become a service-driven leader, aiming to serve others rather than just driving toward outcomes," she said. "It's an ongoing journey, but it's crucial to balance objectivity and data-driven decision-making with empathetic leadership." Ultimately, Lirio Marcelo's success showcases the importance of embracing all sides of one's identity to successfully build, scale, IPO, and exit a company. The greatest business opportunity could lie in the biggest problem you face today.

While the pipeline of talented women entrepreneurs capable of solving our economy's most pressing issues is abundant, Lirio Marcelo acknowledged that the critical challenge is bridging the gap between seed capital and scaling up. Many female entrepreneurs face obstacles in transitioning from the early stages to achieving substantial growth. But what keeps Lirio Marcelo truly optimistic are the countless women building businesses that drive social impact and challenge and transform corporate culture, just as she did. By following her lead, we can carry on her legacy of building mission-driven and profitable companies while paving the way for the next history-making female entrepreneur.

TAPPING INTO WEALTH TECH

Access to financial advisors plays a pivotal role in achieving financial inclusion, and technology is the key to breaking down the barriers to make this a reality. Historically, financial advisors or certified financial planners (CFPs) were experts hired to manage wealthy individuals' money; the barrier to entry could be between $25 000 and $500 000, $1 million, or even more before a professional money manager would work with an individual. This norm underscores how wealth and resources in the United States have been highly unequal in recent decades, as the share of national wealth owned by the top 1% has increased from less than 25% in the late 1970s to around 45%. In 2022, the top 1% income earners in the US took home 20% of the total income, while the bottom 50% received just 10%. The US has the highest inequality among all developed countries, and more than a quarter of the world's billionaires live there. Though these disparities existed well before the COVID-19 pandemic, the global health crisis has undoubtedly exacerbated the socioeconomic inequality in the US and triggered new concerns over rising inequality.

These realities stressed the necessity for financial advice to be accessible to everyone, emphasizing the need for financial inclusion and broader representation of financial advisors to serve a more diverse clientele. Today,

76.2% of CFPs are male, and 23.8% are female. A staggering 82.1% are white, and only 2% are Black or African American; 3% are Latino; and 4% are Asian, according to May 2024 data by the CFP Board.[35] Given who financial planning and advice is inherently designed for – wealthy white men – and who it isn't, it's about time we reshape innovation to better serve the needs of the diverse demographic stepping into the most significant wealth transfer we're about to see. By 2030, American women are projected to control a substantial portion of the $30 trillion in financial assets held by baby boomers – a wealth transfer of such magnitude that it rivals the annual GDP of the United States, as outlined in a 2020 McKinsey study.[36]

Moreover, the rising wealth generation has an entirely different set of values. As a reporter at *InvestmentNews*, it was pretty standard for me to hear older advisors – and some of my newsroom colleagues – say they don't see value in working with younger investors yet. Undervaluing the upcoming generation just exacerbated the need to leverage technology to understand their holistic worth better and the need for financial advice. Gen Y and Gen Z now collectively represent 47% of the US population, and they already inherit $541 billion each year (which is 30% of the wealth transferred annually – and that percentage is projected only to grow), according to a 2022 report by Fidelity.[37] The generations are just different. They are more progressive, values-driven, and willing to act on those values. This impacts whom they choose to hire as a financial advisor. Gen Y and Gen Z are the most diverse generations to date and value diversity and inclusion in all aspects of their lives – including in a financial advisor. Sixty-two percent of Gen YZ feel it's essential for financial advisors to visibly demonstrate a commitment to social equality and diversity (via their website, social media, or other online content). Despite the growing number of investors and the rise of wealth tech platforms democratizing access to investing and wealth building, the US still faces glaring wealth disparities, particularly affecting women and people of color. For example, 65% of low- and moderate-income working women are interested in investing, but only 4 in 10 are actually doing so, according to 2021 research by Commonwealth.[38]

The median net wealth of white men is 13 times higher than that of Black women. These much lower wealth levels among low- and moderate-income women, especially Black and Latinx women, are mainly due to long-standing racism and sexism that have kept them from traditional ways of building wealth. This inequality not only harms individual households and communities but also deprives the economy of the benefits that come from everyone participating fully and fairly. Wealth creation can take various forms, but participating in capital markets is and will continue to be crucial for generating wealth.[38]

When it comes to the democratization of investing and financial advice – a huge byproduct of the wealth tech revolution we're seeing today – it isn't a true democratization until 50% of the people (i.e. women) use the technology. Financial service firms have a golden opportunity to tap into this global growth by extending financial advice beyond the elite, unlocking economic opportunities for society. However, high acquisition costs, lower asset levels, and outdated banking systems have deterred many financial advisors from engaging with less wealthy individuals.

Technology challenges these norms with the rise of robo-advisory services. These services use algorithms to automate advice with minimal human intervention and present a cost-effective and scalable solution for serving clients with smaller portfolios. Advancements in this technology have revolutionized the landscape, enabling AI-powered robo-advisors to deliver personalized investment solutions in real time at a fraction of the cost of traditional advisors.

Today, financial technology and wealth management, combined with what is called "wealth tech," are at the forefront of humanizing financial advice, expanding access to financial planning, and empowering a diverse demographic to realize their economic aspirations. This evolution has led to the emergence of innovative platforms focused on behavioral finance, attracting increasing support from investors. While these robo-advisors haven't replaced human advisors, they have democratized access to investment services, serving as a tool to enable financial advisors to serve more people. Today, wealth tech is a sub-sector of fintech ripe for growth and innovation with a ton of whitespace left – there are still enormous gaps for start-ups to fill, from retirement planning to investment management. A decade ago, one woman – dedicated to redefining investing – opened the door to this new world and never looked back.

TEN-YEAR OVERNIGHT SUCCESS

Margaret Hartigan started her professional journey as a financial advisor in the Global Wealth Management Group at Merrill Lynch. She was based in San Francisco, and her career took off during the aftermath of the dot-com bubble. Despite this rapid and unsustainable growth period, Hartigan persevered in her role and established herself as a top-quintile financial advisor.

By the end of 2007, she decided to drive across the country and move to New York, which meant she got to have a front-row seat to the 2008 financial crisis. She was still working on Wall Street at Merrill Lynch when Bank of America acquired it. "My deferred compensation went to less than a Levain cookie," she recalled. Corporate greed played a significant role in the global financial crisis of 2008. Greed by the managers of financial institutions led to easy subprime loans with little to no credit checks or down payments. Greed by homeowners led to purchases of houses they couldn't afford, resulting in mass defaults. And one night in 2009, Hartigan was having dinner with a client – "a serial entrepreneur kind of bro," as she described him. He confessed that he was having a midlife crisis, and she shared that she questioned her industry as it currently operates. "That's fascinating – you manage our money. Tell me more," he said. She shared her vision with him and, in the end, asked him to keep their idea quiet. He responded by saying, yes, but it's not our idea; it's your idea, and if you don't do it, you're crazy.

His reaction is not entirely unprecedented. In the past, clients of financial institutions or wealth managers did not expect emotions or human elements to be a part of their relationship with money. They simply wanted someone who could make sure their portfolio grew. In recent years, more and more investors have been interested in leveraging their finances to create social good. Hartigan is a humanities major who works as a financial advisor, so she understands this shift in investor behavior, but most financial advisors aren't factoring human behavior into their practices. This encounter with her client encouraged Hartigan to move forward with her idea for improving financial advice and wealth management using technology.

Hartigan realized clients needed more financial literacy, regardless of their net worth. This was primarily a result of outdated and complex systems on the back end of banks' and advisors' platforms, making it difficult to modernize their work with clients and personalize the experience to be more educational and engaging. A "one size fits all" approach was the norm – what made one person rich would make someone else rich, too (which wouldn't cut it in the future). And finally, a growing number of younger and more diverse clients were inheriting wealth, while the aging advisors needed help managing and serving them. Hartigan was determined to find a new model to serve all three stakeholders: clients, advisors/bankers, and institutions. Eventually, she felt a calling to create this new model. "So, perhaps a bit naively, I departed from a highly successful practice in 2012 and decided I was going to fix this," she recalled.

With more than a decade of experience as a financial advisor, Hartigan felt uniquely equipped to create a hyper-personalized "Apple-like experience on the front end, allowing people to see themselves in their finances," she said. "This would help demystify the process and reduce shame and anxiety about money." In the same way Apple made computer technology easy and accessible to the masses, Hartigan would design an engaging digital investment and wealth planning platform with a mission to enhance financial literacy, deepen financial inclusion, and humanize finance for all.

She called it Marstone and, in 2013, launched an enterprise-ready fintech solution to integrate into financial institutions to efficiently and affordably reach, acquire, and retain clients who seek straightforward information and engagement around their finances. Her decision to build a business-to-business-to-consumer (B2B2C) model instead of a direct-to-consumer was bold – particularly during a time in Silicon Valley when fintech companies like Robinhood were also in development, which gamified and threw digital confetti to entice everyday trading – very sexy – and attracted plenty of venture capital investment. But, Hartigan's strategic move to go B2B2C was an intentional approach to get to the root of the problem within the financial system. "Believe it or not, these banks and major insurance companies operate essentially as fintech companies," she explained. "Many of them rely on highly complex backend services that aren't easily adaptable." So Hartigan developed Marstone to solve this complexity, making it cost-effective for these large financial institutions to serve a wider demographic of investors by integrating directly into the custodian. The custodian handles the backend solutions; whenever you purchase a stock or bond, it's executed somewhere, and there's a record keeper. Major firms like JP Morgan handle this in-house, but most institutions outsource this function. "Custodians are like large energy grids such as ConEd," Hartigan elaborated. "They're a critical and highly commoditized infrastructure that serve thousands of financial institutions by integrating to banking cores and custodial platforms." Hartigan solved a direct pain point that avoided the headache of rebuilding the entire financial infrastructure. It was practical, cheaper, and effective.

It's a common observation I see in female founders, particularly the ones profiled in this book. Instead of applying bandages to solutions, they dive deeper and create solutions that solve the root causes of issues. It's not as sexy, and while research indicates women outperform men with a higher return on investment in their start-up ideas, they receive less funding because, in this case, their products aren't as flashy or attention-grabbing. Hartigan faced this harsh reality 10 fold.

When she pursued venture capital funding, Hartigan would meet with investors, highlighting the convergence of trends and the enormous opportunity at hand. "Most people don't know how to manage their money," she explained. "Large firms require a minimum of $250 000 to engage with clients, and most individuals require financial assistance before reaching that threshold. There's a more cost-effective and simpler approach to address this."

"Investors would lean in," she continued. "And there's this significant wealth transfer underway." Hartigan would outline her strategy to integrate with a custodian – why rebuild the infrastructure when you can lay the groundwork for existing systems to operate more effectively? Unfortunately, due to the lack of subject matter expertise in wealth management among the venture community, Hartigan's B2B approach was not as attractive at the time as the direct-to-consumer robo-advisors.

However, Hartigan pushed forward, continuing her mission. A decade later, she's at the forefront of innovating this space. As the culture around finances and money changed, society began seeing the great wealth transfer unfold. Eventually, investors caught on and began pouring money into these platforms. Wealth tech companies brought in $1.7 billion in venture capital funding across 164 deals in the fourth quarter of 2022, according to CB Insights.[39] That makes wealth tech the third hottest fintech subsector behind payments ($3.4 billion) and banking ($1.8 billion). The confluence of trends Hartigan predicted 10 years ago has come to fruition.

What was deemed super unsexy before is the desire of most VCs today – B2B software as a service (SaaS) – which grabbed 44% of funding in the first quarter of 2023, surpassing B2C fintech, which held a 34% share, according to Dealroom.co.[40] This trend has prompted investors to encourage founders to recalibrate their market strategies, prioritizing B2B models to increase their chances of securing funding.

Today, Marstone is partnered with some of the largest institutions in the world, including Plaid, Blackrock, Interactive Brokers, and Apex Clearing. In January 2024, Marstone raised an $8 million Series B financing round. "The marketplace is finally ready," Hartigan said.

In her journey as a 10-year-old overnight success, as she calls it, Hartigan realizes – looking back – that innovation is enjoyable – it's groovy and sexy, and people love to talk about it. "But it takes a long time for the marketplace to adopt innovation." Reflecting on her journey, Hartigan acknowledges that she initially needed to understand specific venture capital "terminology." "I didn't grasp some of the fintech language, and there are unspoken norms," she admitted. "One is the tendency to define individuals by what they are not. You're not a tech person. You're not a banker. You're not a man, and you're a first-time founder."

Hartigan succeeded not because of these systemic barriers but despite them. She knew that change was coming, and while she thought a B2B approach would be a no-brainer for investors, she's learned that sometimes, the obvious path isn't apparent. "The path is never straight, but always forward – lean into your community," she said. For early-stage founders reading this, look to individuals like Hartigan, who have traversed this path. "But I'm not claiming to have mastered it," she said. "Strangely enough, we're merely at the beginning stages. Sometimes, that's what success entails."

Hartigan is a trailblazer in the fintech industry and a mentor to many. In a recent storytelling event at the 2024 Fintech Is Femme Leadership Summit in New York City, she shared her journey, and imparted some words of wisdom, particularly to women and communities of color. "You won't receive the benefit of the doubt," Hartigan said. "It doesn't matter if I've achieved success previously. My background doesn't matter; I'm a woman, and the established patterns make navigating uncharted territories challenging." You'll find the goalposts constantly shifting. "So, at the very least, set clear boundaries and expectations that align with your values and the needs of your company," she said. Changing the system depends on it.

NOTES

1. Stash. "About Stash." Accessed May 20, 2024. https://www.stash.com/about.
2. TechCrunch. "Armed with $40 M in New Financing, Fintech Stash Is Positioning Itself for the Public Markets." October 13, 2023. Accessed May 20, 2024. https://techcrunch.com/2023/10/13/armed-with-40m-in-new-financing-fintech-stash-is-positioning-itself-for-the-public-markets.
3. Bankrate. "Emergency Savings Report." Accessed May 20, 2024. https://www.bankrate.com/banking/savings/emergency-savings-report/#job-loss.
4. University of Washington School of Law. "SVB Collapse." Accessed May 20, 2024. https://www.law.uw.edu/news-events/news/2023/svb-collapse.
5. U.S. Bureau of Labor Statistics. "Women's Databook 2020." Accessed May 20, 2024. https://www.bls.gov/opub/reports/womens-databook/2020/home.htm.
6. Georgetown University. "Women Increasingly Outnumber Men at U.S. Colleges—But Why?" Accessed May 20, 2024. https://feed.georgetown.edu/access-affordability/women-increasingly-outnumber-men-at-u-s-colleges-but-why/.
7. World Economic Forum. "Unlocking the Trillion-Dollar Female Economy." May 2023. Accessed May 20, 2024. https://www.weforum.org/agenda/2023/05/unlocking-trillion-dollar-female-economy.
8. World Bank. "International Women's Day." Accessed May 20, 2024. https://www.worldbank.org/en/topic/gender/brief/international-womens-day#.
9. The New York Times. "Beyoncé Renaissance Tour." September 27, 2023. Accessed May 20, 2024. https://www.nytimes.com/2023/09/27/magazine/beyonce-renaissance-tour.html.
10. Finding Alpha. "The Trillion Dollar Female Economy Report." Accessed May 20, 2024. https://assets.website-files.com/62eadeaa175d45804906da28/6451cf

78d4b56780ff09e34b_Finding%20Alpha%20-%20The%20Trillion%20
Dollar%20Female%20Economy%20-%20Report.pdf.

11. Pew Research Center. "The Enduring Grip of the Gender Pay Gap." March 1, 2023. Accessed May 20, 2024. https://www.pewresearch.org/social-trends/2023/03/01/the-enduring-grip-of-the-gender-pay-gap.

12. Ellevest. "Closing the Gender Wealth Gap." Accessed May 20, 2024. https://www.ellevest.com/magazine/disrupt-money/closing-the-gender-wealth-gap.

13. Wells Fargo. "COVID-19 Fuels Uncertainty about U.S. Retirement, Wells Fargo Survey Finds." 2020. Accessed May 20, 2024. https://newsroom.wf.com/English/news-releases/news-release-details/2020/COVID-19-Fuels-Uncertainty-about-U.S.-Retirement-Wells-Fargo-Survey-Finds/default.aspx.

14. *The Washington Post.* "Women and Money Myths Debunked." January 16, 2024. Accessed May 20, 2024. https://www.washingtonpost.com/business/2024/01/16/women-and-money-myths-debunked.

15. *Harvard Business Review.* "How Women End Up on the 'Glass Cliff.'" January 2011. Accessed May 20, 2024. https://hbr.org/2011/01/how-women-end-up-on-the-glass-cliff.

16. Fidelity Investments. "Fidelity Investments Women & Investing Study 2021." Accessed May 20, 2024. https://www.fidelity.com/bin-public/-documents/about-fidelity/FidelityInvestmentsWomen&InvestingStudy2021.pdf.

17. Ellevest. "About Us." Accessed May 20, 2024. https://www.ellevest.com/about-us.

18. International Finance Corporation. "Her Fintech Edge Report 2024." Accessed May 20, 2024. https://www.ifc.org/content/dam/ifc/doc/2024/her-fintech-edge.pdf.

19. Startup Genome. "The State of the Global Startup Economy." Accessed May 20, 2024. https://startupgenome.com/article/the-state-of-the-global-startup-economy.

20. Oliver Wyman. "Women as Financial Services Customers." November 2019. Accessed May 20, 2024. https://www.oliverwyman.com/our-expertise/insights/2019/nov/women-as-financial-services-customers.html.

21. CB Insights. "Venture Trends Q1 2024." Accessed May 20, 2024. https://www.cbinsights.com/research/report/venture-trends-q1-2024.

22. INFORMS. "The Gender Diversity Advantage: Evidence from Global Data." Accessed May 20, 2024. https://pubsonline.informs.org/doi/full/10.1287/orsc.2022.1594.

23. The Nobel Prize. "The Sveriges Riksbank Prize in Economic Sciences in Memory of Alfred Nobel 2023: Claudia Goldin." Accessed May 20, 2024. https://www.nobelprize.org/prizes/economic-sciences/2023/press-release.

24. World Economic Forum. "The $6 Trillion U.S. Care Economy: A Major Economic Crisis." January 2023. Accessed May 20, 2024. https://www.weforum.org/agenda/2023/01/care-economy-us-major-economic-crisis-us-davos-2023/#:~:text=The%20%246%20trillion%20US%20care,unable%20to%20independently%20support%20themselves.

25. Boston Consulting Group. "Fighting for a Stronger Care Economy." Accessed May 20, 2024. https://www.bcg.com/united-states/work-and-culture/equity-empowers/fighting-for-a-stronger-care-economy.

26. World Economic Forum. "The $6 Trillion U.S. Care Economy: A Major Economic Crisis." January 2023. Accessed May 20, 2024. https://www.weforum.org/agenda/2023/01/care-economy-us-major-economic-crisis-us-davos-2023/.

27. Center for American Progress. "COVID-19 Sent Women's Workforce Progress Backward." Accessed May 20, 2024. https://www.americanprogress.org/article/covid-19-sent-womens-workforce-progress-backward/.

28. Pew Research Center. "Almost 1 in 5 Stay-at-Home Parents in the U.S. Are Dads." August 3, 2023. Accessed May 20, 2024. https://www.pewresearch.org/short-reads/2023/08/03/almost-1-in-5-stay-at-home-parents-in-the-us-are-dads/.

29. PBS NewsHour. "As America's Population Ages, Women Shoulder the Burden as Primary Caregivers." Accessed May 20, 2024. https://www.pbs.org/newshour/show/as-americas-population-ages-women-shoulder-the-burden-as-primary-caregivers

30. World Economic Forum. *Global Gender Gap Report 2023: Benchmarking Gender Gaps 2023*. Accessed May 20, 2024. https://www.weforum.org/publications/global-gender-gap-report-2023/in-full/benchmarking-gender-gaps-2023/.

31. Harvard Business School. "Founders - Profile." Accessed May 20, 2024. https://entrepreneurship.hbs.edu/founders/Pages/profile.aspx?num=39.

32. Allen, Gemma. "Care.com Founder Launches AI Startup Aimed at $10.9 Trillion Labor Gap." Forbes. February 22, 2024. Accessed May 20, 2024. https://www.forbes.com/sites/gemmaallen/2024/02/22/carecom-founder-launches-ai-startup-aimed-at-109-trillion-labor-gap/.

33. Oxfam America. "All Work and No Pay." Accessed May 20, 2024. https://www
    .oxfamamerica.org/explore/stories/all-work-and-no-pay/.
34. Gusto. "The Rise of Women Entrepreneurs." Accessed May 20, 2024. https://
    gusto.com/company-news/the-rise-of-women-entrepreneurs.
35. Certified Financial Planner Board of Standards, Inc. "Professional
    Demographics." Accessed May 20, 2024. https://www.cfp.net/knowledge/
    reports-and-statistics/professional-demographics.
36. McKinsey & Company. "Women as the Next Wave of Growth in US Wealth
    Management." Accessed May 20, 2024. https://www.mckinsey.com/
    industries/financial-services/our-insights/women-as-the-next-wave-of-growth-in-
    us-wealth-management.
37. Fidelity Investments. *Women and Investing Study 2021*. Accessed May 20,
    2024. https://clearingcustody.fidelity.com/app/proxy/content?literatureURL=/
    9907600.PDF.
38. Commonwealth. "Invest Forward." Accessed May 20, 2024. https://buildcom
    monwealth.org/research/invest-forward/.
39. CB Insights. "Venture Trends 2022." Accessed May 20, 2024. https://www
    .cbinsights.com/research/report/venture-trends-2022/.
40. Dealroom. "Fintech Q1 2023 Report." Accessed May 20, 2024. https://
    dealroom.co/blog/fintech-q1-2023-report.

CHAPTER THREE

DEFYING THE ODDS

Almost all the trailblazing women featured in this book – and within our fintech ecosystem – share a critical commonality: They've successfully secured venture capitalist (VC) funding. Venture capital is the key ingredient to transform audacious technology-based ideas into world-changing institutions that reshape our financial landscape and influence the fabric of our society. Start-ups funded by VC may form the future transformative companies that become drivers of economic growth. For example, many well-known publicly traded technology companies, including Alphabet, Apple, Meta, and Amazon, were once VC funding recipients. Paradoxically, these investments are a part of the origin of the cycle of wealth disparities (notice the companies above are all founded by men). Year over year, I have to report on the same statistic: Of the billions of dollars invested in start-ups across business sectors, only a minuscule 2% of those funds go to women-owned companies.[1]

To be fair, while just 2% of VC capital goes to firms founded solely by women, closer to 20% of VC capital goes to firms with at least one woman as a co-founder. While that is promising progress and those female co-founders deserve to be celebrated, the data suggests VCs need to write checks to far more than just 50% of their portfolio with a female founder as a form of fairness in gender parity. If we benchmark equity in terms of gender parity among mixed-gender founding teams, then 70% of the companies that VCs invest in should have at least one woman founder. Why? A portfolio in which 50% of companies are women-founded doesn't mean 50% of founders are women, according to a 2023 report by Anthemis Group.[2]

In the fintech world, Anthemis reported that global female-led fintech companies raised $1.2 billion across 151 rounds throughout 2023 and the first quarter of 2024. Digging deeper, in 2023 alone, these companies secured $1.19 billion, which accounts for just 3.4% of the approximately $35 billion invested in the fintech sector last year. This highlights both the impressive potential of female-led fintech companies and a significant funding gap. While 3.4% is a step forward, it pales in comparison to the roughly 26% of overall venture dollars going to companies with at least one female founder. Sadly, even this broader figure shows that the industry still has a long way to go in achieving true equity.[3]

Much of the burden for changing the system and behavior of venture capitalists has been placed on women themselves: they've been exhorted to learn to code, major in science, technology, engineering, and mathematics (STEM), and become more self-assertive, which is interesting because women are already taking those steps. Pioneers like Mary Allen Wilkes have been computer programmers since the 1950s. Throughout my years covering the industry, I've heard many of the same excuses for why so few venture capital dollars flow into the hands of women-founded start-ups. Those excuses, coming from defenders of the status quo, range from false narratives like a "pipeline problem," which is an excuse to defend venture capitalists' decision to not invest in more women, claiming there are just fewer women pitching to the VC community. Maybe women just don't want to launch fintech start-ups altogether?

The stories of the women in this book dispel that nonsense; plus, nearly 50% of all businesses are women-owned, showcasing that women interested in creating start-ups exceed the small percentage of women who get access to the benefits of the venture capital system, which not only includes funding but access to mentorship, guidance, and access to a network of potential partners, suppliers, and even customers.

VC firms pool funds from various sources, including pension funds, financial institutions, and wealthy families. They invest in start-ups at the earliest stages of their lifecycles – the first checks are called a seed round. Then, through Series A, B, and C fundraising rounds, VCs provide millions of dollars in the hope of a return years' worth hundreds or even thousands of times their original investment.

WHY WOMEN-OWNED START-UPS ARE A BETTER BET

The gender pay gap is well-known: women earn roughly 80 cents for every dollar a man makes. However, the gender investment gap is less familiar. According to Boston Consulting Group's 2018 research, when women entrepreneurs pitch their ideas to investors for early-stage funding, they receive significantly less funding compared to men – on average, more than $1 million less. Yet, women-owned businesses generate higher revenue, delivering more than twice as much per dollar invested compared to those founded by men. This makes companies founded by women excellent investments for financial backers.[4]

What's particularly notable about the women featured in this book is their ability to achieve more with less. Diving into the BCG's research further, investments in companies founded or co-founded by women averaged $935 000, which is less than half the average $2.1 million invested in companies founded by male entrepreneurs. Despite this disparity, start-ups founded and co-founded by women actually performed better over time, generating 10% more in cumulative revenue over a five-year period: $730 000 compared with $662 000. In terms of how effectively companies turn a dollar of investment into a dollar of revenue, start-ups founded and cofounded by women are significantly better financial investments. For every dollar of funding, these start-ups generated 78 cents, while male-founded start-ups generated less than half that – just 31 cents.

The data is clear: investing in companies founded by women leads to a higher return on investment (ROI). Shall I go on?

- Venture-backed teams with diverse founders, both in terms of gender and ethnicity, tend to innovate more and achieve better financial outcomes, with a 30% increase in multiples on invested capital (MOIC) when companies are acquired or go public, according to McKinsey & Company.[5]
- Additionally, nearly 70% of top-performing US funds have women in decision-making roles.
- Research from the World Economic Forum indicates that companies with above-average diversity scores generate 45% of their revenue from innovation, while those with below-average scores only generate 26%.[6]

In the challenging market of 2022, research from PitchBook found that companies led by female founders exhibited lower median burn rates and greater valuation growth at the early stages compared to their all-male counterparts. At later stages, they also experienced smaller declines in valuation year-over-year. Angel investments and unicorn deal values for female-founded companies have hit their second-highest annual levels. Although exit activity declined significantly across the entire VC ecosystem in 2022, female-founded companies still outperform the broader market in terms of the median time to exit.[7]

Investing in fintech start-ups founded by women is a logical decision backed by statistics. However, most venture capital funding still goes to start-ups founded by men. It's evident that women aren't the issue here – they are excellent at managing money and building successful companies. Who should we seek answers from? The root of the issue lies in the VC system.

MORE DISPARITY THAN DIVERSITY

One solution to the problem is the sheer need for more diversity within the VC firms. In 2022, only 26% of investment professionals were women, according to data by Deloitte.[8] While there are now more female-led investment funds than a few years ago, most venture capital firms still have zero women as general partners or fund managers. Only 19% of the investment partners were female, but 57% of firms had no female investment partners. This highlights the need for more gender diversity in VC firms, especially among decision-makers.

Regarding racial and ethnic diversity, Black professionals made up just 5% of investment professionals, with only a slight increase from 4% in 2020. Hispanic representation remained at 6% of investment positions in 2022. Younger and smaller VC firms tended to have greater diversity among their investment partners. Firms founded within the last decade reported higher percentages of Black (8%), Hispanic (8%), and female (22%) investment partners. While these numbers are still dismal, it does suggest hope that as the industry progresses, it becomes more inclusive and welcoming to diverse talent.

Limited partners (LPs), the financial backers of VC funds, are reportedly interested in diversity, equity, and inclusion (DEI) efforts within VC firms. Data from Venture Forward, the National Venture Capital Association (NVCA), and Deloitte reveals that in 2022, 47% of firms reported that LPs had inquired about their DEI initiatives within the past year. Also, VC firms are no longer merely reacting to LP demands but are proactively seeking DEI information from their portfolio companies. In 2022, 38% of firms reported taking this proactive stance, increasing from 30% in 2020 and 19% in 2018.

Advancing gender equality in VC is not only the right thing to do, but it is also an intelligent money-making move, backed by evidence, to increase the prosperity of the whole industry. A 2021 report by UN Women shows that VC firms with 10% more female investing partner hires make more successful investments at the portfolio company level, have 1.5% higher fund returns, and see 9.7% more profitable exits.[9]

Understanding the data and the realities of the lack of diversity in this business sector is crucial. Venture capitalists play a vital role in determining which ideas, products, and innovations get the opportunity to shape our modern economy and society. They are also pivotal in determining which entrepreneurs will become billionaires and fund the next wave of fintech founders. According to a *Forbes* article in 2021, US fintech billionaires are worth a combined $162 billion.[10] None of these minted billionaires mentioned by *Forbes* are women or people of color.

What are the implications of this? They go well beyond the frustrations of female founders who can't get funded, mainly because financial services and fintech are our economy's lifeblood. The lack of investor and founder diversity has far-reaching consequences. It does not only determine who gets rich. It also shapes the kinds of problems technology companies set out to solve, the products they develop, and the markets they serve. With 98% of venture capital dollars going to white males – our economy is less innovative, less equitable, less safe, and less profitable than it could be.

Think of all those financial services and fintech companies that have not centered their offerings on women's needs. And that, in itself, is a direct result of women not getting funding. The downstream effects mean that women, as individuals, invest less of their wealth than men do, giving up returns that the markets have provided over time. This is one big reason for the data I shared before around the gender wealth gap, which sits at 32 cents to a white man's dollar (and 1 penny for Black women). Think, too, of the businesses not founded, and so the needs that are not met; the investments that have not been made that would have built a more secure future for women and their families; the economic growth we could have seen had that wealth been created. Estimates indicate that VC opportunity costs from withholding investment to diverse founders may be as high as $4 trillion.[11] It simply isn't logical why venture capitalists invest so little funding in these founders, especially when we are in the business of money. And women are good at making money.

This should lead to an increase in interest in such ventures. Instead, venture capital firms continue to gamble on poor investments, such as defunct cryptocurrency exchange FTX. On the other hand, women and founders of color with well-thought-out, substantive business plans remain in the waiting room. Considering that women drive 80% of all buying decisions yet make up only 13% of CEOs, and recognizing that both women and people of color disproportionately face the inequities many fintech businesses aim to address, excluding these groups from product or service creation is a significant missed opportunity for innovation.[12]

Many fintech start-ups that receive funding, like digital banks, investing platforms, and payment processors, specifically target underserved communities disproportionately comprised of women and people of color. Yet, the founders and the leadership teams do not reflect the communities they claim to serve. Fintechs that claim to serve and target these communities without any level of representation in leadership to said communities are a form of financial manipulation, whether unconscious or not. So, when we wonder why women are slower to adopt financial services products or take longer to invest or build wealth, we should reverse the question and wonder what's wrong with the VC system that allows majority of our financial services and fintech products to be designed at the hands of white males. Not only do single-digit percentages of venture capital go to female founders, but Black founders in the US raised 0.48% of all venture dollars allocated in 2023, around $661 million out of $136 billion.[13] And according to McKinsey, Latino founders secured only 1.5% of total VC funding.[14] Even more concerning, just 0.1% of VC funds went to Black and Latino female founders. This glaring gap persisted across all stages of growth – pointing to another reason why the gender and racial wealth gap persists and is growing. Dismissing the lived experiences and perspectives of diverse founders is a detrimental mistake. These lived experiences inform the products we create with the specific needs of our communities in focus. This leads to better outcomes and services for all.

However, the biases that permeate the venture capital industry are so ingrained into the fabric of its system. The scarcity of women in an industry that is so forcibly shaping our society, economy, and culture cannot be allowed to stand. And the idea that men coincidentally build the most innovative companies, are the most talented start-up leaders, and the best networkers, perpetuates a myth of meritocracy that's merely a pipe dream. The reality? A group of wealthy men deliberately created the venture capital system; it didn't happen by chance. The patterns seen today in venture capital firms have been decades in the making.

A BRIEF HISTORY OF THE VC BRO

The first venture capitalists (VCs) in America were wealthy families of the late nineteenth century, such as the Vanderbilts and Rockefellers, who invested in high-return industries like railroads, steel, and oil. However, Silicon Valley became a tech powerhouse in the 1950s due to Cold War spending, which transformed Stanford and filled the Valley with defense contractors. This era gave rise to silicon-semiconductor start-ups, which were all male. By the 1970s, these firms had created hundreds of millionaires, primarily men in their early 30s. Yet, behind the scenes, thousands of women worked in the Valley's microchip fabrication plants and manufacturing facilities from the 1960s to the early 1980s.[15]

The venture business expanded in the early 1970s, led by male semiconductor veterans. Around the same time, in 1974, the Equal Credit Opportunity Act (ECOA) was passed, finally allowing women to obtain their own credit cards. While men were already investing in businesses, prominent figures emerged like Gene Kleiner co-founded Kleiner Perkins, which invested in Genentech, Sun Microsystems, American Online (AOL), Google, and Amazon. Don Valentine founded Sequoia Capital, investing in Atari, Apple, Cisco, Google, Instagram, and Airbnb. These investments laid the groundwork for significant wealth accumulation for men, while women were only just gaining the basic right to access personal capital.

The men leading Silicon Valley VCs didn't just invest; they also mentored and guided the entrepreneurs they funded. They valued individual founders, often over the products themselves, and preferred those they had previously collaborated with successfully. This approach fostered tightly woven networks that repeatedly collaborated on start-ups. Notable groups included "the Traitorous Eight," who left Shockley Semiconductor to found Fairchild Semiconductor, and the "PayPal Mafia," founded by Peter Thiel, Elon Musk, and Max Levchin.

Venture capital firms linked these networks, with Sequoia Capital being an early investor in PayPal. Investors often relied on "pattern recognition," a term used by Kleiner Perkins partner John Doerr, to fund founders resembling past successful entrepreneurs, typically white guys from prestigious universities.

Despite openness to new ideas, VCs like Doerr overlooked Silicon Valley's exclusionary networks, believing in the myth of a meritocracy. This lack of diversity in VC firms impacts who receives funding, with roughly 85% of venture capital check writers being men as of 2021.[16] Male investors are more likely to fund male CEOs, perpetuating a cycle where male-led companies dominate, making it difficult for female entrepreneurs and founders of color to secure funding.

The issue is pervasive, undermining both the economy and the future of technology. Its impact is so significant that policymakers have been compelled to step in and act. On 8 October 2023, California Governor Gavin Newsom signed Senate Bill 54, the Fair Investment Practices by Investment Advisers (New Diversity Reporting Law). This law requires VC companies with ties to California to annually report the demographic information of the "founding team members" at their invested companies. This first-of-its-kind law aims to address the inequitable funding distribution to women- and diverse-owned companies. With more than 5700 VC firms in California, this law is expected to have significant consequences for the venture capital industry in the United States.[17]

On 30 June 2022, the House Committee on Financial Services' task force on financial technology held a hearing to discuss combatting the "tech bro" culture of fintech and address the lack of investment in start-ups founded by women and people of color. The hearing was prompted by the explosive growth of fintech, with venture capital firms investing $35 billion in fintech start-ups in 2021, up from $18 billion in 2020.[18]

During the hearing, Sallie Krawcheck, the founder and CEO of Ellevest, was one of the witnesses. Based on her experience, she addressed the current status of women raising fintech venture funding, sharing during her testimony that the situation includes encouraging and challenging news.[19]

On the positive side, there's been an influx of capital from women investors targeting early-stage venture capital, with some of this funding specifically earmarked for women and underrepresented founders. This marks a significant step forward in diversifying the funding landscape.

However, the challenging news for fintech founders is that the investments women investors make, and the funds women CEOs raise, tend to be concentrated in more traditional, women-focused consumer businesses – not in fintech. This trend indicates a gap in support for women-led fintech ventures.

The even tougher reality is that this initial support has not translated into later-stage funding. Women, particularly in fintech, face significant hurdles when it comes to raising Series B and later rounds. Krawcheck emphasized the importance of these later-stage investments, especially for fintech, which is typically more capital-intensive than other sectors. Unlike other start-ups that can adopt a "build-the-plane-while-you're-flying-it" approach, she said, fintech companies need substantial upfront investment to build infrastructure, develop compliant and secure products, and establish a brand and community before launch.

Moreover, there are still fewer women writing the larger-sized checks needed for these later stages. As of a few years ago, the majority of venture capital firms did not have a single woman partner, highlighting a critical disparity in the industry.

The good news is that female leaders are working to build a VC landscape that intentionally invests in women and diverse leadership, fueling economic innovation.

CREATING NEW SYSTEMS AND PATTERNS

In 2007, Amy Nauiokas observed all the signs that indicated a shifting landscape for financial services – the summer of 2007 saw the release of the first iPhone, soon followed by millions of consumers embracing these devices as indispensable tools. Simultaneously, the 2008 financial crisis compelled traditional banking to navigate new regulatory frameworks in response to recurring crises, opening the doors to new players to enter the market and change how financial services functioned and consumers engaged with their money. "It was all sort of bubbling around," Nauiokas explained to me. She had a strong intuition about financial technology long before "fintech" was even coined. "It became evident to us, my partner Sean Park and me, that how this transformation unfolded and the individuals leading it would significantly shape its trajectory," she said.

After more than a decade working inside Wall Street, in 2008, Nauiokas began warning the "powers that be" in major financial institutions about what was coming – she'd explain that the world was evolving, the financial services infrastructure needed an overhaul, and digitizing the markets was crucial to the future of our economy. She proposed the creation of an investment platform to bring together regulators, financial institutions, investors, entrepreneurs, and academics to work together to invest in women and diverse founders to build the next generation of financial services tools that leveraged technology to solve society's most pressing issues – from improving access to investing for everyday consumers, developing software for more manageable cross-border payments, and using data to help farmers sustainably increase productivity.

"We used to encounter doubts like 'How's that going to work?' or 'There aren't enough women or people of color available,'" she said. "None of these objections felt valid; they seemed more like excuses to resist change."

Those doubters overlooked a vision that eventually crystallized into an industry worth billions – what we now know today as fintech. And amidst a global pandemic and subsequent social reckoning, those banks would, years later, launch funds dedicated to investing in diverse founders. Consider Nauiokas the ultimate fintech trendsetter in the VC world.

When Nauiokas began her career, it was in traditional Wall Street fashion. She started as a junior banker, pursued her MBA, and followed the typical path to establish the credentials necessary for success in that environment. From the start, throughout the 1990s and early 2000s, she noticed the lack of inclusivity on Wall Street, but it wasn't until she reached a more senior position that she felt a responsibility to address it. "Like many in that space," she shared, "I initially focused solely on doing my job, knowing that advancement was uncertain and often discouraged outspokenness."

She rose quickly, eventually working at Barclays, building and leading the company's award-winning and market-leading global e-commerce business. This cemented her reputation as an early pioneer in digital financial services and earned her a promotion to CEO of Barclays' retail brokerage business and the Head of its Wealth Direct business. By age 36, she had become one of the few senior women on Wall Street with a seat at the table.

"It was at this point that I began to recognize the importance of mentorship and representation within the industry," she said. "As a woman in a leadership role, I had a unique opportunity to pave the way for others and provide the support I had lacked earlier in my career." Despite some women's hesitancy in embracing their identity as leaders, Nauiokas understood the significance of being visible and vocal about her experiences. So, she actively decided to advocate for change. As the 2008 financial crisis loomed, and she continued to see the opportunity that her male counterparts on Wall Street so clearly overlooked, she did what many high-achieving but frustrated professionals do when they hit the ceiling with their corporate companies: she became an entrepreneur.

After being "laughed out of rooms" and encountering repeated dismissals while attempting to persuade traditional financial institutions to embrace change, particularly in adopting new technology and injecting more money into the hands of diverse founders, she and Park decided to launch their investment firm. She foresaw it as a long-term endeavor, fully aware that effecting systemic change from within can span decades or even centuries.

In 2010, Nauiokas and Park founded Anthemis Group to become early adopters and leaders in the change they saw coming. Their company believed that making real progress requires a global movement and a flexible infrastructure to attract economic investment for new models, develop human talent for institutional innovation, and nurture intellectual expertise to expand the boundaries of our financial institutions. They built an investment company to foster collaboration within the industry rather than engaging in competition. "We understood that this journey would be more of an evolution than a revolution, which felt like the right approach for us when many were fixated on disruption," she said. This strategy allowed Anthemis to capitalize on Nauiokas's preexisting relationships within the extensive ecosystem of financial services players and bridge the gap to Silicon Valley – a connection that, to be honest, wasn't as prevalent back in 2008.

The ultimate goal is to deploy financial, human, and intellectual capital in service of a better economic system. To pursue that mission, the company supports pre-seed to growth-stage start-ups that embed finance into their products, services, and operations (eventually known as embedded finance). Not only did this concept set Anthemis apart in the early days, but so did the fact that Nauiokas and Park didn't rely on the traditional limited partner (LP) model to raise capital (typically, LPs provide the capital while general partners (GPs) serve as fund managers responsible for investment decisions).

Instead, Nauiokas initially built Anthemis Group as a platform and a holding company, with no initial intention of venturing into asset management. "However, we found ourselves ahead of the industry," she said.

"Affording us several years during which we could secure capital intermittently, invest our funds, and nurture emerging companies." At that time, "fintech" was still relatively scarce; "you could count the number of companies described as such on two hands," Nauiokas recalled. Anthemis made early investments in some of the most influential fintechs to emerge from the 2008 crisis, including Betterment, eToro, Currency Cloud, The Climate Corporation, Carta, and Happy Money.

As an early investor in these companies that shape the fintech landscape so powerfully today, Anthemis was able to be more agile in its capital raising and deployment efforts, leading to the development of its full-platform asset management business. In 2016, Anthemis Asset Management was established and has since built, seeded, and scaled more than 200 financial services companies.[20] With $1.2 billion in assets under management, its approach to asset management – "sector-focused, sector-backed, purpose-led" – is unique, Nauiokas said. The company has worked with entrepreneurs and institutions to support small businesses, make cash management more accessible, strengthen supply chains, develop new insurance products, and fund efforts to address climate change. In 2022, Nauiokas and her team established Anthemis Asset Management as a separate legal entity, making it a vital holding of the Anthemis Group that can operate independently and sustainably.

"We set a very high bar for our investments right from the start and leaned into virtuous-cycle companies," she said. "Today, that is now clearly defined as environmental, social, governance, or ESG, investing." However, for Anthemis, the outcome of that virtuous cycle was significant. Additionally, Nauiokas aimed to build a team and deploy capital with a much more diverse and inclusive approach than before in financial services. In September 2021, Anthemis and Barclays' Female Innovators Lab fund expanded beyond the US into the UK, Europe, and Canada. The fund size increased from $15 million to $50 million, making it the largest fund and studio dedicated solely to female founders in fintech. "We start at the venture studio level, exclusively supporting female founders, then progress to early-stage investments up to Series B," she explained. In December 2021, Anthemis Group raised more than $700 million to invest in pre-seed through Series B embedded finance start-ups and fund early-stage fintechs. Its first environmental, social, and governance-focused special purpose acquisition company (SPAC), Anthemis Digital Acquisitions – which debuted on Nasdaq in November 2021, closing at $230 million – was led by Nauiokas and an all-women management team, but they delisted in 2023. Still, Anthemis's work has helped move the needle to mint more women and diverse founders in fintech, which inherently improves the industry's pace of innovation. As we know, fintech's gender diversity problem leads to more financial services products built by men for men, stifling innovation and economic progress.

Fifty percent of Anthemis' portfolio companies are founded by women or Black, Indigenous, or people of color. Nauiokas makes it a point to deploy capital to support women and minorities actively, and it's not just the companies in Anthemis' portfolio; it's their team, too. "At Anthemis, more than half of our team is comprised of women and 32% are people of color," she said. "Additionally, 69% of our investment team is female, and we've been organically and consistently representing over 50% women since our inception."

FROM OVERLOOKED TO ON TREND

Looking back, it's been quite a journey – from being perceived as outsiders to becoming insiders authentically driving the initiatives everyone wants recognition for, Nauiokas recalled. When she thinks about her journey building the business in recent years, one of the most memorable periods for Nauiokas was 2020. It was when conversations previously met with skepticism or dismissal started gaining traction.

"If we rewind to 2008, I was fortunate to have been present at the inception of what has evolved into the fintech evolution," she said. "Even before that, my experience spans the nineties and the early 2000s, working at the intersection of finance and technology. Back then, I don't believe the pioneers in this space foresaw a burgeoning movement or the potential for transformative change within the system. For quite a while, our efforts felt solitary, and rallying excitement around our vision was often challenging."

While the concept of impact investing – using capital to create positive social or environmental change, while also generating attractive financial returns – is not new (the term was coined in the early 2000s),[21] Nauiokas helped to pioneer impact investing practices specifically into the fintech sector – it is a strategy that larger financial institutions are now catching up with – coincidentally after the social reckonings of the 2020 pandemic. For instance, in September 2020, Bank of America allocated $200 million to equity investments in funds with diverse managers.[22] The $500 million Citi Impact Fund was launched in 2020, born out of a recognition that early-stage venture impact investing can play a meaningful role in advancing social progress.[23] J.P. Morgan Private Bank launched the Global Impact Fund in 2020 with more than $150 million in capital.[24]

Nauiokas recognizes that the influx of new players has sparked a flurry of activity, presenting some notable challenges. "The entry of big players has caused a ripple effect in the industry, compressing early-stage investments," she said. "It's akin to dropping a massive boulder into a boiling pot of water, displacing many VC players who have been active in the field for some time." This dynamic has stirred up considerable noise and anxiety among otherwise rational founders, challenging navigation.

From Anthemis's perspective, however, Nauiokas has been overwhelmed and genuinely grateful. "We've managed to navigate this vortex remarkably well," she said. "We might have lost one opportunity to the big players, but we've also emerged victorious in several instances where our valuation wasn't the highest. This speaks volumes about our brand's strength, reputation, and distinctive style."

The period between 2021 and 2023 has been undeniably challenging for many in the fintech industry. It began with a record boom in fintech funding, reaching $210 billion across 5684 deals in 2021. However, 2022 brought economic challenges with rising interest rates and inflation. The year 2023 saw a banking crisis, with institutions like Silicon Valley Bank, Signature, and First Republic facing significant struggles. Moreover, fintech start-ups, particularly those offering consumer-facing services like digital banking and early wage access, have needed help with fundraising. Layoffs have become commonplace, with analysts scrutinizing business models reliant on interchange fee income.

"Reflecting on these challenges prompts a consideration of their implications for venture capitalists and our own company," she said. "The past two years, especially 2022, have been a period of reckoning." The era of easy money ended, placing immense pressure on private equity firms. The events of 2023, including the collapse of Silicon Valley Bank (SVB) and other notable occurrences in the industry, can be attributed to the exuberance and subsequent over exuberance of 2021 and 2022.

However, amidst these challenges lies an opportunity for introspection and recalibration. "As we enter a new era, there is a palpable sense of reset and reflection within the industry," she said. "What was once perceived as problems may represent the most significant opportunities as we navigate the next phase of the fintech evolution." It's a time of reshaping and reimagining, where lessons learned from the past pave the way for a more resilient and innovative future in fintech.

After three decades of running and building purpose-led organizations at the intersection of access, equity, and innovation, Nauiokas has dedicated her career to seeing around corners and leading teams to uncover what could be rather than accepting the status quo. She's also a media entrepreneur. Through her award-winning production company, Archer Gray, she's focused on bringing new, diverse, and innovative stories to life. She's also a founder of the Bubble Foundation, a New York City non-profit that partnered with public schools to expand access to healthy food. She's also been involved with Make-A-Wish International and the Worldwide Orphan Foundation. She wears many hats and is the founder of several companies.

Ultimately, her unique perspective on fintech sets her apart from most investors, bankers, and entrepreneurs, making her a key driver of change in the industry. Her investment thesis remains rooted in the same principles today as it did in the aftermath of the pandemic, which acted as an accelerator of the changes that began after the 2008 financial crisis. Embedded finance, the integration of banking and other financial services into nonfinancial apps and services, is at the center of this change.

With this thesis, Anthemis can allocate capital across various stages of the investment cycle to companies that are not only shaping traditional sectors like banking, asset management, capital markets, and insurance but also bolstering the infrastructure layer that supports diverse industries along these financial pathways. "Our approach is underpinned by a profound comprehension of the financial services ecosystem and its extensive connectivity," she said. "Many of us come from backgrounds in financial services, and this insider perspective guides our strategy, recognizing that meaningful evolution in this marketplace is driven by both insiders and outsiders alike."

At Anthemis, Nauiokas looks at financial services and the role of fintech in a different light. It's the transaction layer where you see many payment and consumer interface businesses. The finance layer is for the lending side, followed by the new risk management layer. "If, as an industry, we appreciate that it is the underpinning of the entire economy and that it's healthy, robust, and resiliently built for the digital age," she said, "then virtually any business model that looks to innovate in any industry that relies on any of those three areas is within scope for Anthemis as a fintech investment."

Nauiokas has seen many opportunities emerge by seeing what others don't traditionally look at as financial services – her thesis about using embedded finance to invest in a diverse range of founders has the potential to create a ripple effect.

INCREASE THE SWELL OF FEMALE FOUNDERS

Embedded finance allows female entrepreneurs without backgrounds in Wall Street or Silicon Valley to break into fintech, creating a new wave of founders who may have previously felt excluded from the sector. To address the dismal funding figures, venture capitalists must diversify both the founders they consider and the industries from which they source these start-up founders. Additionally, entrepreneurs should seek opportunities to innovate outdated industries through fintech solutions.

Fintech investor Katie Palencsar was 29 when she first met a female tech founder, a moment that revealed to her the possibility of becoming a founder herself. "I was like, 'oh, wow, I can do something like this,'" she recalled. This pivotal encounter exposed her to the intricacies of raising capital and the challenges of navigating the entrepreneurial landscape. After founding and successfully selling her own company, she gained valuable experience working for the acquiring firm. She then made a bold move into venture capital by joining Anthemis Group. Determined to invest in female founders in fintech, Palencsar drew on her own early struggles – securing funding and building a network in a male-dominated industry. These experiences honed her resilience and strategic thinking. "Those challenges shaped who I am today," she reflects, "and they fueled my commitment to supporting other women on their entrepreneurial journeys."

In 2021, when Anthemis Group raised more than $700 million to invest in pre-seed through Series B embedded finance start-ups and early-stage fintechs, Palencsar said she saw pitches from more than 2000 female fintech founders from diverse backgrounds. This influx of diverse pitches highlighted the potential and untapped talent in the fintech industry.

Palencsar, who served as managing director at Anthemis Group from 2019 to 2024 and now acts as a venture partner, emphasized that embedded finance has unlocked a cohort of founders with varied backgrounds, fostering a new cycle of female leaders who bring more women into the fintech workforce. The firm has reviewed pitches from female founders with backgrounds in sustainability, law, beauty, and mobility. "We can get more women involved in fintech," Palencsar noted. "But not everyone is going to look the same on paper."

Take Ami Kumordzie, founder of Sika Health, for example. In January 2023, she raised $6.2 million in a round led by Forerunner Ventures as a Black female founder physician with no technical experience.[25] Kumordzie developed a fintech platform to connect consumers with the Internal Revenue Service (IRS)–compliant merchants. Unlike financial services, healthcare is a largely female-dominated industry, with women holding 76% of all healthcare jobs, according to data from the US Census Bureau.[26] When women use fintech to innovate in adjacent industries like healthcare, they show other women in those spaces the potential to create more financial services solutions in their industry. Kumordzie's success underscores how expertise in one field can lead to innovation in another, breaking traditional industry barriers.

NETWORK EFFECT

By leveraging embedded finance to open the scope of fintech investments to entrepreneurs outside of finance and technology, investors widen their pool of potential start-up founders and increase the likelihood of more capital being raised by women. Palencsar observed this in her experience with Anthemis. "When we launched this fund, I noticed a pattern emerging, although it wasn't intentional," she said. "I analyzed the backgrounds of the founders we encountered, and a trend became apparent."

While Anthemis invests in fintech, its portfolio's founders rarely come from traditional finance backgrounds. "One of our founders came from an e-commerce background, having managed numerous physical product businesses and even appeared on *Shark Tank*," she said. "Despite lacking a conventional capital markets background, she integrated payment solutions into her products." Another co-founder, previously an engineer at Reddit, transitioned into the fintech space. And the list goes on. It became clear that many of the most innovative founders possessed unique and varied experiences across different sectors.

This realization highlighted a significant untapped opportunity, particularly when considering the networks of most investors, who often stick to familiar territories. "This epiphany led us to observe that we were attracting more women into fintech," she said. "Even those who hadn't initially envisioned themselves in the field. This, in turn, catalyzed a sort of network effect."

Some of the businesses Anthemis encountered surprised investors who had never considered them. For example, a venture in the beauty industry seamlessly integrated payment solutions, prompting a reevaluation of sector boundaries. Not everyone fits the conventional mold on paper, but this diversity is precisely what makes the industry thrive.

"Founders with less traditional finance or tech backgrounds were also hiring more women who didn't necessarily think they would be in fintech," Palencsar said.

When women lead start-ups, there's a better chance of attracting female talent. Businesses with female founders build teams with 2.5 times more women, and companies with a female founder and executive hire

6 times more women than those led by men.[27] Plus, women founders with diverse experiences and backgrounds are well-suited to build outside fintech's oversaturated marketplace. This is critical to embedded finance as more business sectors look to expand their presence and grow market share.

Embedded finance allows businesses to differentiate their offerings and tap into a broader customer base. In 2021, embedded finance already reached $20 billion in revenues in the United States alone, according to McKinsey & Company.[28] This figure is expected to grow significantly in the coming years as more companies realize the potential of this form of finance and consumers' expectations for digital financial tools increase.

By leveraging embedded finance, companies can create innovative products and services that provide customers with greater convenience and value. It also enables them to maintain a competitive advantage over other fintechs in the market.

However, capitalizing on the growth of embedded finance will require companies to diversify their workforces. That requires women leadership as researchers found that male-founded start-ups have less diverse teams compared to women founders. In that light, investors and businesses have a significant incentive to ensure embedded finance unlocks funding for female founders.

Ultimately, misconceptions around fintech and biases within venture capital perpetuate cycles of exclusion for investors and female founders. To evolve, venture capitalists must look beyond traditional finance and technology and focus on investing in more women and diverse founders in adjacent industries.

By exploring solutions to the financial services pitfalls in different industries, female business leaders can have a hand in pushing the fintech industry forward. With the proper support, we'll keep seeing a swell of female entrepreneurs become powerful forces in the fintech space.

TAPPING INTO LATINA-OWNED BUSINESSES

Laura Moreno Lucas, a founder and investor, has dedicated her career to transforming her community. As the former Managing Director of the Nasdaq Stock Exchange, Lucas led high-profile initial public offerings (IPOs) for companies like Lyft, Beyond Meat, The RealReal, and Airbnb. Despite her success, she rarely saw herself reflected in the founders whose companies she helped take public.

This experience underscored the underrepresentation of people of color in business leadership and revealed the significant, overlooked potential of Latina(o)-owned businesses (LOBs), she told me. If investors funded LOBs equitably with non-Latino white-owned businesses (WOBs), they could generate $1.4 trillion in additional revenue today and $3.3 trillion by 2030.[29] For context, the total economic output of US Latinos was $2.7 trillion in 2019, making them the equivalent of the seventh-largest economy in the world.

Yet, systemic barriers persist. Less than 1% of funds from top venture capital and private equity (PE) investors reach LOBs. LOBs must secure twice as many investors as WOBs to achieve the same level of funding. This discrepancy becomes most apparent when LOBs near the $1 million revenue mark, where they struggle with profitability and cash flow. However, those that surpass this hurdle and reach $5 million grow nearly twice as fast as WOBs. Latinas, in particular, are one of the fastest-growing groups of business owners in the US, with more than 1.5 million founders generating $78.7 billion in revenue, according to the National Women's Business Council.

Despite this, Latina(o) founders receive only 2% of VC funding, a trend consistent for companies founded by women. Lucas, now a general partner at L'Attitude Ventures – a fund investing in Latina(o)-led start-ups – has witnessed this firsthand. After leaving Nasdaq in 2020, Lucas sought to better support founders in her community and found her answer in venture capital. By early 2022, she joined L'Attitude Ventures as a partner, helping close its first institutional fund, raising more than $100 million from major financial firms like JPMorgan Chase and Bank of America.

L'Attitude Ventures focuses on early-stage companies founded or run by US-based Latina(o) entrepreneurs, with significant investments in fintech and other tech industries such as PropTech, HealthTech, and EdTech. "It's about enabling our community to build wealth," Lucas said. "What better way to do that than by investing in founders who can employ a diverse cohort?"

Lucas's journey into early-stage capital was driven by the need to provide more capital to Latina(o) entrepreneurs at the earliest stages, helping them grow quickly and retain wealth, she says. As a two-time founder with an exit from Ladada, a fashion subscription service for women, and a mentor at 500 Startups, Lucas understands the challenges faced by Latina(o) business owners, drawing from her own experience immigrating from Mexico to the US.

In her role at L'Attitude Ventures, Lucas leads investor and external relations, expanding the ecosystem for founders and investors, recognizing the $2.7 trillion economic output of US Latinos. L'Attitude has already backed fintech companies such as Listo, Flow, and Camino Financial, with average check sizes ranging from $750 000 to $1.5 million.[30]

In 2024, Lucas took her dedication to investing in her community a step further by founding Libra Leaders, a platform with $1.2 billion investment capital, which launched with an inaugural cohort of Latina women leaders across the entrepreneurship ecosystem. Libra Leaders aims to support founders by providing access to influential women at every level of the capital markets, growth opportunities, and capital. The first cohort includes venture capitalists, fintech professionals, technology executives, and industry experts like Sandra Campos, former CEO of Diane von Furstenberg;

Betsabe Botaitis, CFO of Hedera; and Lisha Bell, head of economic opportunity at PayPal.[31]

Through these initiatives, Lucas hopes to mentor and invest in women-led companies ready to scale, multiplying the impact of L'Attitude and its flagship event, which brings capital, sponsorship, and investment opportunities to Latino-led companies.

Women are not only investing in female-founded fintech companies, but they are also working toward a future where women have enough wealth to become investors themselves.

BIRTH OF A SUPER ANGEL

Asya Bradley was born in a small village devoid of water and electricity. Her birth was never officially registered. She's among the countless victims of the United Nation's project to register girl children who were overlooked. "My family deemed the small registration fee unnecessary," she told me, "viewing my birth as a cause for sorrow rather than a celebration, given the societal devaluation of female children in South Asia." Even if Bradley managed to survive infancy, the prospects were bleak: marriage, not education or employment, awaited her. However, the trajectory of her life changed when her family decided to immigrate to the West.

Landing in a neighborhood called Rexdale in Toronto, Canada, her parents, driven by the necessity to accommodate their large family of five children, settled there without awareness of its reputation as one of the toughest areas to live in North America. Growing up was a challenge. Bradley's household was plagued by physical violence, creating a pervasive atmosphere of domestic abuse. Surviving in such conditions felt like a constant struggle for escape and survival. "Both of my parents worked tirelessly to make ends meet," she said. "My father took the day shift while my mother worked nights, leaving us as kids, often alone in the house."

After years of saving pennies, her father ended up being able to move their family to one of the wealthiest neighborhoods in the area, Oakville. It didn't matter because Bradley's mind was set. All she wanted to do was escape. Before she knew it, she was off to college.

Her first job out of school was with Cisco Systems in Amsterdam. Bradley thrived in the Netherlands; she loved the straightforward business style that was direct and efficient. The salaries were great, but something wasn't sitting right inside her. "I kept getting this feeling like I'm seeing all of this turmoil in the world," she shared. "It's not okay for me to just stay in Amsterdam and make a lot of money."

So, she started volunteering for Amnesty International, a grassroots human rights organization, working on the production of a film called *Against My Will*, a documentary that shed light on honor killings. In this violent crime, women are murdered by their families under the belief the woman behaved dishonorably. With a small crew comprising the director, videographer, and Bradley, she traveled to Pakistan to collaborate with a courageous human rights lawyer who had established a women's shelter. Her motivation stemmed from the grim truth that her clients were often murdered by their own families before they could seek justice in court. To address this injustice, she created a sanctuary for these vulnerable women. Their journey took Bradley to the clandestine location of this safe house, where they documented the stories of resilience and tragedy.

"Witnessing such atrocities firsthand made me question my comfort and privilege back in Amsterdam," Bradley said. "How could I turn a blind eye to the brutal reality faced by women simply because they defied societal norms or fought for their autonomy?" This experience spurred Bradley to delve deeper into the emancipation of women, leading her to work on another documentary focused on women's liberation in the Netherlands.

Contrary to her expectations, even in a country known for its progressiveness, women still grappled with systemic oppression, including childhood sexual abuse and gender-based violence. It was a stark reminder that the struggle for gender equality transcends geographical boundaries. "It doesn't matter," Bradley said. "You can be in a so-called 'third world country,' you can be in a liberated Western country, and as a woman, you are still not equal." She wanted to take more action. So, she went to Egypt to the Netherlands-Flemish Institute in Cairo, an academic center providing services for scholars and students from the supporting universities. She began working on various UN projects in the Middle East. "Based in Cairo, I collaborated on initiatives with organizations like United Nations Children's Fund (UNICEF), United Nations Programme on HIV and AIDS (UNAIDS), United Nations Development Fund for Women (UNIFEM), and the World Food Program," she recalled. "My fluency in English and dedication to learning Arabic upon arrival made me a valuable asset in this diverse setting." To sustain herself financially while pursuing her humanitarian work with the UN, she took on jobs helping launch major multinational brands in the Middle East, such as L'Oreal, H&M, and Starbucks. She anticipated staying and working in Cairo for a few months. She lived there for a few years.

After that, Bradley immigrated again, but this time to the US. As a Canadian citizen who immigrated on an investor visa, she wasn't allowed to work, thus pushing her directly into entrepreneurship. "To remain in the USA, I had to establish a company, so I founded a Wellness Center in the suburbs of Chicago. Spanning 20,000 square feet, our facility offers a comprehensive range of services," she said. "While I thoroughly enjoyed the experience, I yearned for greater scalability and a broader impact in my work." With prior experience working in tech, Bradley soon met the founders of future tech giant Synapse. They reached out to Bradley because they were building their founding team and asked her to lead as their Chief Revenue Officer.

"I eagerly joined the endeavor because I was captivated by its potential for tech scalability. Financial inclusion held profound personal significance for me; upon relocating to the USA, I encountered barriers in accessing basic financial services," she said. "Despite being a successful businesswoman with credit cards and bank accounts in Europe and the Middle East, I faced obstacles in opening a bank account in the US, which affected my ability to pay rent and utilities or even obtain a cell phone. This experience fueled my commitment to addressing financial inclusion challenges."

When the founders of San Francisco-based Synapse pitched their idea to Bradley, she saw its immense value in directly supporting initiatives for financial inclusion. Through this role, she helped pioneer the first banking as a service (BaaS) API provider, laying the groundwork for empowering other founders with similar aspirations. To recap from Chapter 1, BaaS is a financial technology solution that enables non-bank companies, such as platforms and marketplaces, to offer banking services that were previously only available to licensed banks. These services include bank accounts, cards, and loans. BaaS providers help with the setup process by providing the necessary technology stack and licenses required to offer banking services. They integrate these services into a business's core offering, brand, and existing interface. Additionally, they take care of compliance, risk, and know-your-customer (KYC) requirements.

In February 2019, Bradley left Synapse, and by December 2019, *Bloomberg* reported that she, along with three other women, sued Synapse Financial Technologies Inc. and its chief executive officer, Sankaet Pathak, for what they allege was a pattern of harassment and discrimination by Pathak at the fintech company.[32]

After leaving Synapse, the pandemic and the subsequent social reckoning following the murder of George Floyd radicalized the idea of Bradley's next start-up in fintech. "Two of my biological children are Black," Bradley said. "So, when George Floyd was lying on the pavement, calling out to his mom, it was like a kick in the gut for me." At the same time, Bradley had been a relentless advocate for financial inclusion and saw nothing was changing, so she thought, "I need to do something."

In 2020, she founded Kinly, a neobank focused on improving the financial outcomes of Black Americans and allies through financial education, saving, and wealth building tools such as managing day-to-day finances by offering early access to direct deposit funds, cash-back rewards, and overdraft protections. After three years of Kinly and raising $20 million in funding from investors like Forerunner Ventures, Point72 Ventures, Anthemis, and Kapor Capital, the company was acquired by Greenwood, the digital banking platform for Black and Latino individuals and businesses, bringing the two largest fintechs focused on the Black community together as one company.

My observations of entrepreneurs like Bradley and the many others profiled in this book are that they often draw strength from their history and heritage. Their cultural background and family traditions give them a unique perspective on challenges and obstacles in their business ventures. They can overcome adversity and move forward with confidence and determination by tapping into their ancestors' wisdom and resilience. We saw a similar characteristic in Sheila Lirio Marcelo in Chapter 2. This connection to their roots gives them a sense of purpose and identity that fuels their passion and drive to succeed. As an immigrant, Bradley is constantly drawn to the pull of giving back to her community. Money wasn't – and still isn't – enough. This key motivation fueled her ascent from a small village to the top of the tech industry.

As a fintech founder, Bradley was asked to speak at many industry events and would look to the left and right and see that nobody looked like her. "The majority were men: white men, Indian men," she said. "And if there were any women, there would be white women, but a handful. I had rarely seen a brown woman or a Black woman. This really got to me."

After experiencing a successful exit with Kinly, Bradley realized it was time to back her convictions with action. "I had the choice," she shared. "I could use my funds to buy a lavish house or invest in the change I wanted to see." As a Canadian, Bradley had been conditioned to pursue the "$2 million plan": buying a million-dollar house and saving the rest. While that was an option, she decided to take a different path. She asked herself, "Why wait for someone else to do it?" It was the same motivation behind starting Kinly – a personal obligation to fill the gap she saw in the market. "Similarly, with start-ups, I questioned why I should wait for someone else to fund them when I could do it myself?" So, she wrote the check because "paying women starts with women," she said.

Bradley began writing investor checks, primarily focusing on pre-seed and seed-stage companies. These are the stages where founders need the most support and assurance. As a result, Bradley has built a portfolio of nearly 40 companies that she has either directly invested in or serves as an advisor or board director. "The majority of these founders share similar backgrounds or are working on projects aimed at positively impacting the world," she said.

Bradley's actions exemplify angel investing, where successful entrepreneurs or high-net-worth individuals invest their money directly in emerging businesses – typically start-ups they believe in. When a start-up raises smaller rounds of funding before securing larger sums from venture capital firms, the founder may approach angel investors to bridge the gap between the initial "friends and family" rounds and the subsequent larger rounds from VCs interested in investing once the start-up has gained traction. Securities and Exchange Commission (SEC) rules require accredited investors to make at least $200 000 or have $1 million in assets, and these angel investors can often seek higher returns than traditional investments offer. They scout for promising start-ups and contribute their capital to foster their growth.

In Chapter 2, we went over systemic barriers that have delayed women from participating in investing, which is why women have historically made up a small percentage of active US angels. This lack of diversity in investing has major consequences, as early-stage investors decide which products and services get built and which founders gain prominence.

However, in recent years, angel investing has seen a remarkable transformation, creating more opportunities for female entrepreneurs in fintech. In 2023, women made up 46.7% of the angel investor market, a jump from 39.5% in 2022. This surge in female angel investors coincided with an increase in women-owned ventures seeking angel capital, which grew year over year to 46.3% in 2023 from 37.1% in 2022.[33]

Even more encouraging is the yield rate – the percentage of companies seeking funding that actually receive it – which rose to 28.8% for women in 2023, up from 25.6% in 2022. These data points, also reported by the Center for Venture Research, suggest that the increase in female angel investors is encouraging more women entrepreneurs to pursue high-risk angel capital. The high percentage of women presenting for funding and the above-market yield rate for women-led deals indicates the high quality of these ventures.

This progress is more than just a numbers game; it's a significant step toward parity in the seed and early-stage market. The fintech sector has benefited, with 12.9% of angel investments directed toward fintech, making it the most popular sector behind healthcare and software.

The rise in female angel investors is giving a refresh to the start-up economy, providing more opportunities for women to lead and innovate in fintech. This increased female participation in both entrepreneurship and investment paves the way for more inclusive and dynamic fintech start-ups to emerge.

The business landscape is significantly transforming, too, aided by cultural shifts gradually eroding long-standing barriers. Since the COVID-19 pandemic, start-ups and investing are now part of the mainstream national consciousness in a way they never were before. Social media platforms like TikTok have emerged as a rich source of business information, with founders and creators with experience in venture capital frequently sharing insights about their start-ups or expertise. In addition, popular shows like *Shark Tank*, featuring high-profile angel investors such as Mark Cuban and

Barbara Corcoran, have captured the public imagination since their debut on television in 2009. Even universities are stepping up their game with the introduction of entrepreneurship programs and classes about venture capital.

Throughout history, networks have been the foundation that has supported the growth and development of various asset classes. Early-stage investing with access to the cap tables of promising start-ups was dependent on privileges like who you know – perhaps a friend or colleague that will let you in – rather than your skillsets or experiences. The cycle began in the 1970s and 1980s, when executives and founders who had established successful companies during the transition from mainframe to personal computing sought to expand the new ecosystem by investing in other companies.[34] Since the leaders and creators of these successful companies were mostly men, they perpetuated gender inequality by mainly investing in start-ups founded by people they knew, who were also predominantly men.

In the 1990s, more formal syndicates (the legal structure that allows co-investors to bundle their money, expertise, and connections to make a joint investment) emerged, making it easier for anyone with a large bank account to get involved. Despite increased access, male founders already benefited from a funding cycle that disproportionately favored their start-ups over those of female founders. As a result, most angel investors were predominantly male, since they typically emerge after profiting from successful company exits via acquisition or IPO.

Still, women like Bradley are entering this space to diversify the types of founders and companies that get funded. This kickstarts a new cycle of female founders who can accumulate wealth after an exit or IPO and reinvest as angel investors. For example, Bradley is an investor in the fintech start-up Ansa, led by co-founder and CEO Sophia Goldberg. The company announced a $14 million Series A funding round in May 2024. What sets this funding round apart is its size and the fact that female investors contributed 95.6% of the capital.[35] That's the power of women investing in women. Bradley is also an LP at Cowboy Ventures, founded by Aileen Lee, the woman who coined the term "unicorn."

Bradley's advice for readers interested in getting into angel investing is to get involved with emerging fund managers. Similarly, joining early-stage companies offers high-risk, high-reward opportunities. Today, Bradley is a "super angel" investor. *Fast Company* reports that super angels "raise funds like venture capitalists but invest early like angels and in sums between the two, on average from $250,000 to $500,000."[36]

Rising from nothing to becoming a super angel in the tech industry, Bradley's success has enabled her to invest in female-founded start-ups that aim to improve the world. What sets Bradley apart is her unique ability to harness her personal story to drive success in her professional life. Unlike what most of us are taught, Bradley doesn't shy away from her vulnerabilities or personal experiences, which are often perceived as weaknesses. Instead, she leverages them to her advantage, and her openness and authenticity are why she has achieved great success. "I believe in maintaining a balance between the personal and the professional because, as individuals, we carry our entire selves into every facet of our lives," she said. Historically, we've been conditioned by systems not designed with our best interests in mind – systems that often sought to exclude us. "These systems encouraged us to compartmentalize our identities, but I refuse to conform to that notion," she said.

Bradley's candid sharing of her upbringing has proven to be a repository of invaluable lessons in entrepreneurship. Her formative years were characterized by scarcity, which taught her the significance of resourcefulness and resilience. However, what truly etched itself into her heart was the spirit of generosity and community that saturated her environment. She holds dear the memories of her childhood home being a sanctuary of hospitality where her mother always had a pot of food ready for anyone in need. Regardless of their financial status, all who stepped into their home were welcomed with open arms and left with a full belly and new job opportunities. This sense of community and generosity has guided Bradley's life, shaping her perspective and, as she says, steering her toward success.

An abundance mindset is grounded in principles fundamentally different from those of a scarcity mindset. Unlike the latter, which emphasizes the idea of dominance, hoarding, and competition, an abundance mindset is all about believing there are enough resources in the world for everyone – which aligns with the values of equity and inclusivity. It's about creating a level playing field for everyone, where equal access and rights are guaranteed to all. This mindset also involves being genuinely happy for others' achievements and recognizing that success is not a zero-sum game. There is enough space for everyone to share and succeed, and this belief is at the heart of the culture of sharing and support that characterizes communities with an abundance mindset.

Reflecting on this, Bradley couldn't help but wonder why we aren't doing more to uplift each other as educated and empowered women in fintech. Why do we perpetuate a mindset of scarcity rather than abundance? When we secure positions of influence or success, why do we not extend a hand to pull other women up alongside us? Why do we need to be the sole beneficiaries of our achievements?

Digging into these questions, I discovered that the systemic barriers we face as women can compartmentalize and overwhelm us with scarcity mindset, which can be highly detrimental to entrepreneurship. Scarcity mindset is a psychological perspective characterized by a belief that there will never be enough resources, opportunities, or success. This mindset can be especially harmful to women in fintech or other male-dominated industries, as the statistics around women's leadership roles and funding dollars can make them believe that they have to gatekeep opportunities and cannot share them with other women. This can lead to a "mean girl" effect where women are pitted against each other, playing into the patriarchal structures that are intended to keep them down. On the other hand, an abundance mindset can fuel success, even in the face of obstacles. Operating from a mentality of scarcity requires so much mental energy that those operating in this headspace are likelier to make mistakes or bad decisions than those with abundance mindsets.

When I asked Bradley how she transitioned her mindset from scarcity to abundance, she told me about a recent interview she saw with a female CEO of a well-known financial incumbent. When asked about the challenges she faced as a woman in her position, her response left Bradley incredulous. She dismissed the notion of gender-based challenges, asserting that she worked hard to overcome obstacles. "Frankly, I thought, 'No, that's not the reality.' We can't ignore the systemic barriers imposed on us due to our gender," she said. "We didn't choose our biology or the limitations society imposes because of it. To anyone who denies the existence of these challenges, I say loudly and proudly, 'fuck you.'"

When we refuse to acknowledge the obstacles that women face, we rob them of the ability to truly overcome them. Instead, Bradley has found that actively working to change the dynamics of any room where she is the sole representative is much more effective than believing in the false ideology of a meritocracy. "If I find myself in a position where I am the only woman in a room, I make it a priority to change it," she said. "Moreover, if offered a seat in a space where I'd be the first or only woman, I ensure that plans are in place to rectify that and how quickly they'll be executed." Bradley knows success isn't individual achievement; it's about advancing humanity collectively. "I want to see my underrepresented brothers and sisters thrive, no longer confined to the margins," she said.

Bradley is the first to acknowledge that what she's teaching us isn't easy – it's far from it. For example, in her early twenties, she was working at a company and had the chance to be promoted, but she was planning to leave for travel. At the time, Bradley suggested a friend for the position, thinking it was a way of bringing another woman up. "Little did I know, she became my boss and made my life a living hell," she said. "It was a tough situation, and I've heard similar stories from other women about their experiences with female bosses." However, Bradley refuses to let one bad experience sour her outlook. "Let's face it, we've all had moments where we've been bitches."

It's essential not to let these types of negative experiences perpetuate a scarcity mindset. Instead, we should focus on supporting and uplifting each other. I've also had incredible women who have been there for me during difficult times, providing support and comfort when I needed it most. These experiences remind me of the strength and resilience of female solidarity.

In challenging situations, which I've also encountered, it's crucial to recognize that we may all be operating from a place of trauma or stress. However, taking it out on those in vulnerable positions only perpetuates the cycle of negativity. Instead, let's work together to uplift each other and create a more inclusive and supportive environment. This is the core of an abundance mindset.

How do you implement an abundance mindset within yourself and your business? Bradley's first piece of advice: give freely and generously. It's crucial to foster a mutual support and exchange culture between women. For example, "while some may see me as a mentor to many, I consider myself a mentee to my mentees – I learn from every conversation, and there's no hierarchy in our exchanges," she said. "It's about sharing knowledge and experiences, enriching each other's journeys." Next, make sure you're giving first. "If everyone were to give first – nobody would feel like they were being taken advantage of," she said.

When considering the effort it takes to transform one's mind from scarcity into abundance, navigating the language of fundraising and entrepreneurship becomes a delicate dance. It's essential to remain true to yourself while finding ways to communicate effectively within these realms. "When working with female or underrepresented founders," Bradley said, "I prioritize uncovering their authentic selves and helping them convey their vision in a way that resonates with their goals and surroundings."

According to Merriam-Webster, "authentic" became the word of the year in 2023.[37] I bring this up because the word of the year is like a snapshot of our collective consciousness. Authenticity is defined as being true to one's own personality, spirit, or character. When people connect with your values, asking for funding becomes easier. Authenticity is the currency of success, and it's how you can find a community of backers who genuinely resonate with your vision.

Achieving authenticity and finding someone who shares your values can be a challenging task, and it's often easier said than done. While it's important to stay true to your beliefs, it's equally crucial to learn the language of fundraising and company building. According to Bradley, understanding these concepts is essential for success in these areas.

"That doesn't mean become like someone else, be who you are," she said. "But there are moments where you have to translate yourself so that the person in front of you can understand you – remain authentic, though." To always act authentically, you must first discover your true self by identifying your values. Here's how: What matters more to you than money? Why? Write those answers down – those are your values. (Also see Liza Landsman's action items for your annual self-inventory in Chapter 2.)

When working with founders, Bradley starts by finding the piece of a founder's journey that needs to shine out of them. "Then, we also think about how we can communicate that in a way that makes sense to others," she said.

Without being true to ourselves, we may end up chasing the illusory "American Dream" where we believe that working hard for a certain number of years will guarantee us the lives we desire. However, this idea is misleading and results in prolonged hardship. Bradley told me a story about a successful female founder she knows who once told her she lived by the phrase, "Kiss ass now, to kick ass later." While the idea of that mantra may sound doable, for context, this woman is 65 years old. "Are you going to be kicking ass from your grave?" Bradley said. "When do you start kicking ass? When does that happen? So start kicking ass today. Because if there are enough of us kicking ass now, then those of us that are kicking ass won't be out on a limb." Being the only one in the room, whether it's because of your gender, race, or being an outsider, can be lonely and challenging. I'm sure many of you who picked up this book can relate.

Bradley, recalling advice she received from her friend and fellow fintech leader, Michelle Tran, advises that you build your own "executive board" from your network to combat this feeling. "Find those four or five women who embody where you want to go and get them in your circumference so that these people are in your orbit," she said. "These are the people that you can call and quickly brainstorm an idea. I can't tell you how many women I know who have left money on the table because they didn't have that personal board of advisors."

This is especially important for female founders who must surround themselves with other women who lead by example and inspire them to be better versions of themselves. Collaborating and learning from each other's experiences is the number one tool for success in this field.

INVESTING IN WOMEN'S HEALTH

In April 2024, I asked Bradley what was at the top of her mind as an investor and where she was looking to write more checks. "I make it a point to emphasize this in every discussion," she shared. "I firmly believe that women's health, and by extension, the vagina, is incredibly significant. Investing in women's health is a priority for me."

In the VC landscape, Bradley said she is noticing a growing interest in the convergence of technology, artificial intelligence, and women's health. "I'm particularly drawn to the reproductive health sector," she said. "Being part of the queer community, it's vital to me that everyone has the opportunity to build the family they desire. We're born into families we don't choose, and while we may have complex feelings about them, today, we can create our own families."

That's where Swadl, the start-up in stealth mode she's involved with, comes in. Swadl is dedicated to reproductive rights, focusing on accessibility to in vitro fertilization (IVF) and fertility treatments. "We explore various aspects of feminine technologies, including diagnostics," she said. However, one glaring gap remains: accurately predicting labor onset. "It baffles me that in this age of advanced science, we still rely on the arbitrary 40-week marker," she said. "We need to invest more in research and stop viewing women's bodies and menstrual cycles as divine punishment." Much of the medical research in this area has been neglected due to antiquated beliefs, perpetuating the idea that women are meant to endure monthly suffering.

She's witnessed loved ones struggle with undiagnosed conditions like endometriosis or polycystic ovarian syndrome, only to be dismissed with generic solutions like birth control and painkillers. "This is an issue I'm deeply passionate about addressing," she said. "Fortunately, I'm witnessing a shift in the VC community's interest towards investing in women's health and advancing this crucial intersection of science and financial empowerment."

When it comes to our health as founders, investors, innovators, and women, Bradley doesn't want others to experience the adversity she's faced before they learn the lessons of sharing, community, and supporting one another. "It's crucial to change the narrative in our heads about being a burden," she said. "We need to remind ourselves that we're worthy of support and that helping each other ultimately benefits everyone."

If there's one key takeaway from Bradley's journey, it's that your success is my success – as it all contributes to the collective success. Thinking about how our achievements can enable us to give back to our community can be a motivating factor, and extremely lucrative. "Knowing that my success means I can write more angel checks helps me overcome the hesitation to accept help," she said. "I'm still a work in progress but committed to improving in this aspect of my life."

NOTES

1. PitchBook. "The VC Female Founders Dashboard." PitchBook News, accessed May 20, 2024. https://pitchbook.com/news/articles/the-vc-female-founders-dashboard.
2. Anthemis Group. Equity in Entrepreneurship: A Global Perspective. November 2023. Accessed May 20, 2024. https://www.anthemis.com/insights/equity-in-entrepreneurship-report/.
3. Anthemis. "Female Founders in Fintech: Global Fundraise Deep Dive." Accessed May 20, 2024. https://www.anthemis.com/insights/female-founders-in-fintech-global-fundraise-deep-dive/.
4. Boston Consulting Group. "Why Women-Owned Startups Are a Better Bet." May 2018. Accessed May 20, 2024. https://web-assets.bcg.com/img-src/BCG-Why-Women-Owned-Startups-Are-a-Better-Bet-May-2018-NL_tcm9-193585.pdf.
5. McKinsey & Company. "Underestimated Start-up Founders: The Untapped Opportunity." Featured Insights, accessed May 20, 2024. https://www.mckinsey.com/featured-insights/diversity-and-inclusion/underestimated-start-up-founders-the-untapped-opportunity.
6. University of North Carolina Pembroke. "Diversity and Inclusion: Good for Business." Accessed May 20, 2024. https://online.uncp.edu/degrees/business/mba/general/diversity-and-inclusion-good-for-business.
7. PR Newswire. "PitchBook Report on Women in VC Ecosystem Highlights Resilience and Strong Performance of Female Founders Amid Market Headwinds." Accessed May 20, 2024. https://www.prnewswire.com/news-releases/pitchbook-report-on-women-in-vc-ecosystem-highlights-resilience-and-strong-performance-of-female-founders-amid-market-headwinds-301667083.html.

8. Deloitte. "2023 Human Capital Survey Report." Accessed May 20, 2024. https://www2.deloitte.com/content/dam/Deloitte/us/Documents/audit/us-audit-human-capital-survey-report-2023.pdf.

9. IMD. "Gender Lens Investing Cuts Risk and Boosts Returns." Accessed May 20, 2024. https://www.imd.org/ibyimd/finance/gender-lens-investing-cuts-risk-and-boosts-returns.

10. Kauflin, Jeff. "These 12 New Billionaires Are Riding Fintech's Rising Tide." *Forbes*, April 8, 2021. Accessed May 20, 2024. https://www.forbes.com/sites/jeffkauflin/2021/04/08/these-12-new-billionaires-are-riding-fintechs-rising-tide/?sh=1d5ce76ca53c.

11. U.S. House Committee on Financial Services. "Testimony of Jenny Abramson." June 30, 2022. Accessed May 20, 2024. https://democrats-financialservices.house.gov/uploadedfiles/hhrg-117-ba00-wstate-abramsonj-20220630.pdf.

12. Wyman, Oliver. "Women in Healthcare Make 80% of Purchasing Decisions, Yet 13% of Executives." January 2019. Accessed May 20, 2024. https://www.oliverwyman.com/our-expertise/perspectives/health/2019/jan/women-in-healthcare-make-80-of-purchasing-decisions-yet-13-of.html.

13. TechCrunch. "Funding for Black Founders Down in 2023." January 17, 2024. Accessed May 20, 2024. https://techcrunch.com/2024/01/17/funding-black-founders-down-in-2023.

14. McKinsey & Company. "Underestimated Start-up Founders: The Untapped Opportunity." Featured Insights, accessed May 20, 2024. https://www.mckinsey.com/featured-insights/diversity-and-inclusion/underestimated-start-up-founders-the-untapped-opportunity.

15. MIT Technology Review. "Tech Fix: The Gender Problem." August 11, 2022. Accessed May 20, 2024. https://www.technologyreview.com/2022/08/11/1056917/tech-fix-gender-problem.

16. All Raise. "All Raise x Crunchbase VC Checkwriter Dashboard." Accessed May 20, 2024. https://www.allraise.org/all-raise-x-crunchbase-vc-checkwriter-dashboard.

17. Reuters. "New California Law Requires Diversity Reporting in Venture Capital, Private Equity." November 27, 2023. Accessed May 20, 2024. https://www.reuters.com/legal/legalindustry/new-california-law-requires-diversity-reporting-venture-capital-private-equity-2023-11-27.

18. U.S. House Committee on Financial Services. "Hearing on Combatting Tech Bro Culture: Understanding Obstacles to Investments in Diverse-Owned Fintechs." Accessed May 20, 2024. https://democrats-financialservices.house.gov/uploadedfiles/chrg-117hhrg48336.pdf.

19. U.S. House Committee on Financial Services. "Testimony of Sallie Krawcheck." June 30, 2022. Accessed May 20, 2024. https://democrats-financialservices .house.gov/uploadedfiles/hhrg-117-ba00-wstate-krawchecks-20220630.pdf.

20. Anthemis Group. "The Evolution of Anthemis Group and New Leadership for Anthemis Asset Management." Accessed May 20, 2024. https://www.anthemis .com/the-evolution-of-anthemis-group-and-new-leadership-for-anthemis-asset-management.

21. Scholars of Finance. "A Brief History of Impact Investing in the United States." Accessed May 20, 2024. https://scholarsoffinance.org/a-brief-history-of-impact-investing-in-the-united-states.

22. Bank of America. "Investing in Minority and Women-Led Funds." Accessed May 20, 2024. https://about.bankofamerica.com/en/making-an-impact/ investing-in-minority-and-women-led-funds.

23. Citigroup. "Citi Impact Fund." Accessed May 20, 2024. https://www.citigroup .com/global/our-impact/strengthening-community/citi-impact-fund.

24. Tideline. "Advancing Sustainability and Diversity Through Investment." Accessed May 20, 2024. https://tideline.com/wp-content/uploads/2022/11/JPM-Case-Study_Advancing-sustainability-and-diversity-through-investment.pdf.

25. Stengel, Geri. "A Black Female Fintech Founder Leaned into Her Differences to Raise $62 Million." *Forbes*, January 11, 2023. Accessed May 20, 2024. https:// www.forbes.com/sites/geristengel/2023/01/11/a-black-female-fintech-founder-leaned-into-her-differences-to-raise-62-million/?sh=3583521d5acb.

26. United States Census Bureau. "Your Health Care in Women's Hands." August 2019. Accessed May 20, 2024. https://www.census.gov/library/stories/2019/08/ your-health-care-in-womens-hands.html.

27. Gompers, Paul, and Sophie Calder-Wang. "Women-Led Startups Received Just 2.3% of VC Funding in 2020." *Harvard Business Review*, February 2021. Accessed May 20, 2024. https://hbr.org/2021/02/women-led-startups-received-just-2-3-of-vc-funding-in-2020.

28. McKinsey & Company. "Embedded Finance: Who Will Lead the Next Payments Revolution?" Accessed May 20, 2024. https://www.mckinsey.com/ industries/financial-services/our-insights/embedded-finance-who-will-lead-the-next-payments-revolution.

29. Bain & Company. "Closing the Capital Gap: Fueling the Promise of Latino-Owned Businesses." Accessed May 20, 2024. https://www.bain.com/insights/ closing-the-capital-gap-fueling-the-promise-of-latino-owned-businesses.

30. Azevedo, Mary Ann. "L'Attitude Ventures Closes on $100M Fund to Back Latino-Owned Early-Stage Companies." *TechCrunch*, August 3, 2022. Accessed

May 20, 2024. https://techcrunch.com/2022/08/03/lattitude-ventures-closes-on-100m-fund-to-back-latinao-owned-early-stage-companies/.

31. Alfaro, Lyanne. "This Platform with a $12B Investment Capital Helps Close the Latina Founder Investing Gap." *Forbes*, March 8, 2024. Accessed May 20, 2024. https://www.forbes.com/sites/lyannealfaro/2024/03/08/this-platform-with-a-12b-investment-capital-helps-close-the-latina-founder-investing-gap/?sh=4d0362ff5abe.

32. Bloomberg. "Three Women Allege Harassment at Tech Startup." December 18, 2019. Accessed May 20, 2024. https://www.bloomberg.com/news/articles/2019-12-18/-we-need-to-break-her-down-three-women-allege-harassment-at-tech-startup?embedded-checkout=true.

33. Sohl, Jeffrey. "The Angel Market in 2023: An Inflection Point for Women Angels?" Center for Venture Research, June 20, 2024. https://paulcollege.unh.edu/sites/default/files/media/2024-07/2023-full-year-analysis-report-final.pdf.

34. Boyd, E.B. "Why Millennial Women Are Embracing Angel Investing." *Fast Company*, June 28, 2023. Accessed May 20, 2024. https://www.fastcompany.com/90995239/why-millennial-women-are-embracing-angel-investing.

35. PR Newswire. "Ansa Raises $14 Million Series A Funding to Redefine Merchant Transaction Solutions." Accessed May 20, 2024. https://www.prnewswire.com/news-releases/ansa-raises-14-million-series-a-funding-to-redefine-merchant-transaction-solutions-302131675.html.

36. Fast Company. "How Super Angel Investors Are Reinventing Startup Economy." Accessed May 20, 2024. https://www.fastcompany.com/1715105/how-super-angel-investors-are-reinventing-startup-economy.

37. Merriam-Webster. "Word of the Year." Accessed May 20, 2024. https://www.merriam-webster.com/wordplay/word-of-the-year.

CHAPTER FOUR

FINANCIAL HEALTH IS HEALTH

D ani Fava became a single mom at 19 while still in college. She landed a job immediately after graduating, offering trade support at an investment manager on Wall Street. Every morning, she had to drop her daughter off at daycare, take the express bus into Manhattan, and be at work by 8:30 a.m. to run trading reports for all the traders. "At the time, I printed the reports, stapled them together, and put them on everyone's desk before the market opened at 9 a.m.," she shared. "So you can imagine my mornings being very stressful."

Realizing there had to be a better way to manage these tasks, she thought, "Can I automate this?" Using a somewhat open technology platform that allowed for custom commands, Fava figured out how to schedule and run the reports, then send them directly to the printer – all through her own coding. "I called it a hack because I essentially hacked into the platform to write my own code and automate these tasks," she said. This innovation saved her an extra 20 minutes each morning, which, as any mom would know, was invaluable.

One day, she received a phone call from the technology company behind the platform she was coding into. Fearing the worst, she thought she was getting fired. Instead, the company, impressed with her idea and ability to write code, offered her a job. She accepted, and that's how her journey into fintech began. "Since then, I've been innovating and solving problems," she shared.

NECESSITY IS THE GREATEST CATALYST FOR INNOVATION

Fava is one of the less than 4% of women globally who have worked leading innovation at a fintech company during her time at Envestnet, a wealth tech with more than $5.8 trillion in platform assets.[1] What's interesting about working in innovation at major financial institutions, Fava told me, is that these roles didn't exist, so she had to pitch the job she created for herself.

Reflecting on her career choices while recording an episode of my podcast together, Fava pondered the factors that led her to the path of innovation. Was it her innate passion for problem-solving and creating new revenue streams? Or was it the need for more representation she observed in traditional core business roles? "My digital finance journey began in the early 2000s," she said. "It was obvious no one looked like me," she said as a Hispanic, LGBTQ+ woman in leadership positions in sales, operations, or product departments.

Before Envestnet, Fava climbed the ranks in corporate America while working for TD Ameritrade. She convinced her supportive boss to let her become the Director of Innovation. She pitched the idea of pursuing new revenue and opportunities through innovative projects. In April 2024, Fava started her latest role as Chief Strategy Officer at Carson Group.

Throughout the pivots in her career, Fava is determined to represent that women like her can embark on entrepreneurial journeys within corporate spaces. "We shouldn't have to leave financial services to carve our own paths," she said. An alternative route is to ask for and advocate for the job title or role we want. By doing so, we could also increase the number of diverse leaders entering the C-suite, she says.

"There are two main strategies for creating change, as discussed in critical race theory," she said. "Building new structures outside the current system or staying within to reform it." Fava advocates for both approaches, but with Latinas making up 1.7% of chief executive positions and 4.4% of managerial positions in corporate America, Fava chose the path of reforming from within.[2]

HIDING THE VEGETABLES

Chapter 3 discussed how investors Amy Nauiokas and Katie Palenscar use embedded finance to help more women and diverse leaders join and grow in fintech. Fava is motivated to put the right financial tools in the right places – through embedded finance – to address major issues like the retirement crisis in America. Half of Americans have no savings in retirement accounts, according to the Federal Reserve's 2022 Survey of Consumer Finances.[3] Fava sees embedded finance as the solution to this crisis, which will also help address the health crisis. *(Yes, fintech connects to everything.)*

Embedded finance means putting financial products into non-financial customer experiences, journeys, or platforms. It's been around for a while, like private-label credit cards from retail chains, supermarkets, and airlines. But now, it's changing the game thanks to our smartphones. Typically, banks reached new customers by brick and motor interactions like going to a dealership to get a loan when buying a car, or financing appliances.

Today, transactions are integrated into the digital interfaces that people use on a daily basis. For instance, customer loyalty apps, digital wallets, accounting software, and shopping cart platforms all provide access to financial services. This means that for both consumers and businesses, accessing financial services has become a natural part of everyday activities. Embedded finance can be used for major life purchases, too. Thanks to the emergence of fintech companies like Carvana and Morty, consumers can even finance a car or a house without leaving their homes. During my time as an editor at *Auto Finance News*, I remember reporting on Carvana in its early stages. The company, founded in 2012, aimed to digitize the car buying experience from shopping and financing to delivery. No one was certain it would take off, but Carvana's business model centered around the experience of purchasing a car from the comfort of your smartphone without ever engaging with a human gained prominence as society changed. In the first quarter of 2024, the company, now publicly traded on the NYSE, reported auto originations of $1.8 billion.[4]

In recent years, the US has seen significant growth in embedded finance – the market was valued at $58 billion in 2022 and is expected to grow to $730.5 billion by 2032 – due to fundamental changes in commerce, consumer behavior, and technology.[5] Plus, companies that are successfully employing embedded finance already start with a significant customer base, a key factor since customer acquisition is a fintech company's greatest cost.

Fava tells me about a compelling example of embedded finance in everyday life that we have all encountered: the checkout line. "Have you ever noticed that items are always available while waiting in line?" she said. "This is intentional, as it serves as a way to encourage impulse buys, and it is effective." On average, Americans spend $151 on impulse purchases each month.[6]

"Imagine redirecting this amount into retirement accounts that are professionally managed, aligned with individual goals, time horizons, and risk appetites," she said. This, she asserts, could effectively solve the retirement crisis. The technology to implement such solutions already exists, allowing for micro-investments at every financial interaction – whether it's rounding up a purchase to contribute to a retirement account or saving a portion of funds received through payment apps like Venmo or Zelle.

"Imagine a future where every financial micro-moment contributes to long-term financial health and security," she said. This perspective aligns with the principles of behavioral finance championed by psychologists, focusing on understanding and influencing human behavior through technology solutions. This approach leverages existing technology and addresses the root of financial behaviors, making it a powerful tool for social and economic change.

In October 2023, Fava was proud to see the work she's been doing at Envestnet come to life when the company announced its embedded investing solution, providing a digitized process for banks, credit unions, and financial advisors to offer investing solutions within their own apps and websites to customers within their existing banking experience.[7]

According to Fava's explanation, Envestnet's technology embeds investment solutions within consumer apps, allowing users to see and manage their investments alongside their regular financial activities. This visibility encourages users to make frequent small investments, such as moving an extra $10 into their investment account whenever they get paid or think about their money.

Fava refers to this approach as "hiding the vegetables" – providing something enjoyable and engaging while ensuring it is beneficial. By meeting their target market where they are and offering more than just a passive ETF portfolio, Envestnet creates investment options that resonate personally with users, helping them stay committed through market volatility.

This innovative approach, blending behavioral insights with financial technology, represents a new approach to opening access to financial markets for more people.

It is also more likely to bring about healthy financial habits compared to other fintech tools that have become popular – like the widespread use of "Buy Now, Pay Later" (BNPL) services, which allow users to split purchases into a series of interest-free installments. More than a third of American shoppers have used BNPL because of its proximity – the ease and accessibility of the option right next to the checkout button.[8] This mirrors brick-and-mortar stores' strategy, which place impulse-buy items near the checkout to capitalize on the psychological principle of proximity. Imagine if we leveraged technology to guide consumers toward healthier financial habits instead of driving them into more debt.

"There's a critical difference between standalone financial apps and embedded investing features within apps people already use," she said. "Instead of downloading a separate app with great features and remembering to engage with it daily, an embedded investing feature within commonly used apps – such as those for bill payments, savings, or budgeting – leverages proximity to encourage consistent use."

As we shift to having fintech start-ups focus from merely capturing attention to promoting financial wellness, embedded finance opens the door, but understanding behavioral finance will take embedded finance to the next level.

UNDERSTANDING FINANCIAL BEHAVIORS

Working as a reporter gave me the chance to engage with some of the brightest minds in financial advice and wealth management. One standout is Dr. Daniel Crosby. I first encountered behavioral finance through his presentations at industry events and later through his bestselling books like the New York Times bestseller *Personal Benchmark: Integrating Behavioral Finance and Investment Management* and *The Laws of Wealth: Psychology and the Secret to Investing Success.* As a psychologist and behavioral finance expert, Dr. Crosby explores the intricacies of human experiences and decisions, focusing not just on what people do, but why they do it and how it influences their financial situations. I've also learned about my own money psychology through experts like Amy Schultz, the co-founder of Bolder Money. Through her personal finance coaching and workshops, she helps people uncover their financial resilience and understand their behavioral relationship with money. It's essential for entrepreneurs and executives to understand their complex relationship with finances and actively develop it.

From my research and experiences, along with years of interviews with behavioral finance scientists, I've learned that our relationship with money is complex and deeply influenced by our psychological and emotional makeup. Our financial decisions – spending habits, saving behaviors, and investment choices – are shaped by our money psychology. Many people's financial literacy is rooted in their upbringing and the financial habits they observed in their parents or guardians. Without access to financial tools and resources, developing strong financial literacy skills can be challenging. This presents a massive market opportunity for fintech.

Fintech addresses money psychology by offering digital financial services tailored to individual needs, preferences, and behaviors. Budgeting and financial planning apps use behavioral economics to nudge individuals toward financial education and healthy financial behaviors, as seen with fintech platforms like Stash, Ellevest, and Envestnet. These behavioral-finance-backed platforms help consumers avoid common pitfalls such as:

- **Tunnel Vision:** Fixating on a specific idea or plan and struggling to deviate from it.

- **Overconfidence Bias:** Believing we are immune to biases and overestimating our knowledge.
- **Describing Happiness:** Struggling to articulate what makes us happy and understanding what brings us joy.

The goal is to help consumers better understand their values. When people understand their values, they can set meaningful purposes. This is especially relevant when considering how finance intersects with our identities. By promoting empathy and understanding during financial decisions, fintech can help resolve identity crises.

Humans make significant financial decisions – like accepting a new job or buying a house – with their hearts as much as their heads. These decisions significantly impact who we become and how we spend our money, which is a physical representation of what we choose to care about.

THE MEGAPHONE OF IDENTITY

There's a saying that failing to plan means planning to fail, and Shruti Joshi jumped into fintech to help more people access financial planning. "I have always been captivated by how finances shape our identities," she told me in an interview. "Financial decisions are just another form of self-expression and exploration." Today, as the Chief Operating Officer at Facet, a registered investment advisor founded in 2016, she helps make financial planning more inclusive with a tech-driven approach, a flat monthly fee, and certified financial planners focused on human wellness. Joshi was an early investor in Facet before joining the company full time. Today, she sits at the intersection of financial planning, behavioral finance, and fintech, aiming to empower clients to make informed financial choices and align their financial decisions with their values and aspirations. It's an important job, given that our finances directly influence our sense of self.

Financial decisions are rarely based on logic alone. Nobel Prize-winning psychologist Daniel Kahneman found that 90% of financial decisions are driven by emotion, while only 10% are based on logic.[9] Considering that money is a leading cause of divorce in America and a significant source of stress for 90% of Americans, it's essential to understand how financial decisions shape our lives. Women are more likely than men to cite personal finances as their biggest source of stress in everyday life, with 65% of women and 60% of men reporting this.[10] This is partly because women are already set up at a disadvantage. We earn 16% less than men on average and have only 32 cents for every dollar of wealth owned by men.[11] At this rate, financial planning is a non-negotiable form of self-care. "Self-help is about living your best life," Joshi said. "How can financial decisions and choices shape who you are and how you choose to live?"

In November 2023, Facet launched a Financial Wellness Score that evaluates various aspects of an individual's finances, including emotions and money behaviors, and provides a unique score from 1 to 100. This score, used alongside Facet's certified financial professionals, helps create a personalized financial plan, offering a more holistic view of financial wellness than just the numbers in an investment account. According to Joshi, tools like these enable Facet to stand out in a sea of traditional RIAs by incorporating technology and behavioral finance into financial planning, which has remained antiquated since its inception in the 1960s.

Joshi, a former consumer tech founder and Fortune 15 executive, was drawn to the industry largely because of her upbringing, which made her question different ways of life and traditions. Her parents, originally from India, moved 7 times around the world before she turned 14, living in places like Brussels, New York City, Philadelphia, Switzerland, and Los Angeles.

This adventurous lifestyle fostered her love for exploration and showed her there isn't just one way to approach life. "My parents were unique in instilling a sense of curiosity and questioning why things are done a certain way," she reflects. Growing up exposed to diverse ways of doing things, Joshi naturally gravitated toward challenging the status quo. This inclination deeply resonates with her work at Facet, where she constantly seeks to innovate and improve financial planning, a business segment that is just starting to incorporate financial wellness into wealth management. "There is no holistic wellness without financial wellness," Joshi said.

EXERCISE DAILY

Money is one of the most emotionally charged topics, yet it remains taboo, even among families and loved ones. Financial freedom is about liberating your mind. It's the first step toward financial independence, acknowledging your relationship with the economy without letting it control your life. Let's focus on our values and mindset rather than letting tax systems and interest rates dictate how we live.

Erin Papworth, a behavioral finance expert and money coach, is the co-founder and CEO of Nav.it, a start-up dedicated to improving financial wellness. Nav.it is a great example of a fintech platform that uses behavioral finance to embed financial wellness into the one place most of us spend a lot of our time – our workplace.

This approach highlights a crucial aspect of total employee wellness that employers can't afford to overlook: financial well-being. In fact, a 2023 study on financial wellness in the workplace by PNC found that 80% of surveyed employees would stay with an employer that offers financial wellness benefits.[12] This underscores the significant role that financial wellness plays in employee retention and satisfaction.

On a broader scale, financial wellness is also the foundation for public health, as it helps protect and improve community lifestyles. In fact, Papworth's inspiration to become a fintech founder is largely driven by her background in public health sciences and her extensive experience working in sub-Saharan Africa, which gave her firsthand insight into how inadequate financial services lead to public health disparities. This is mirrored in America, where a study in California found that every $1 invested in public health yields up to $88 in improved health status and benefits to society, proving the adage that an ounce of prevention is worth a pound of cure.[13]

Founded in 2016 by Papworth and her co-founder Maia Monell, Nav.it aims to assist employees in building financial health, wealth, and confidence through their workplace, providing employees with personalized tools for automated savings, expense organization, community discussion groups, and financial coaching. Nav.it's platform is crucial in the movement to improve the financial well-being of the 79 million women in the US workforce by integrating financial health into workplace benefits, simplifying the management of finances and work-related stress.

In my conversation with Papworth, she emphasized the platform focuses on financially empowering its 65% female user base, encouraging women to reinvest in their communities. "Women are more likely to have a social mission built into their companies and serve under-represented populations," Papworth explains. "This creates a unique business opportunity to innovate on top of the fintech infrastructure we've seen boom in the last seven years." Up to 90% of a woman's income typically goes back into her community, highlighting the positive impact of financial wellness on society.

Integrating behavioral science into their core technology framework presents a unique challenge, but Papworth tackles it by breaking down behaviors into manageable daily habits, making the platform's approach more accessible. On the app, users check in daily on their mindset, assess their stress levels and emotions, and engage in an activity reminiscent of dating apps. They swipe left, right, or remain neutral on their expenses from the past 24–48 hours.

This exercise leverages the concept of mental accounting, making it easier for users to recall recent spending decisions and evaluate their impact. Over time, this process helps users develop a deeper understanding of their financial choices and prompts them to make more mindful decisions. These daily habits save users time, energy, and money over time, and serve as the foundation of Nav.it's approach, empowering users to cultivate healthier financial behaviors incrementally.

"Our society is evolving," Papworth said. "With technology, we can assist people in making informed financial choices, reducing stress, and helping them navigate the complexities of modern life."

A key issue is the lack of financial education. Financial planning and advice have typically been reserved for the ultra-wealthy, creating an industry focused on profit over education and humanity. Technology is changing this, and many consumers want more from fintech, particularly in helping them make better financial decisions. Nearly 7 out of 10 say it'd be helpful if fintechs did more to educate them or provide services specifically for times of high inflation, according to Plaid's 2023 Fintech Effect report. Half of the consumers (51%) are asking fintechs to do more to help them stay disciplined and reach their financial goals faster. Papworth saw the trend of financial health coming long before the internet did and built her platform to capitalize on the trend through an innovative B2B approach.

Much like physical exercise, the benefits of fintech are best realized through consistent, daily use. However, this can be particularly challenging in our modern world, where numerous distractions constantly vie for our attention. Yet, those who commit to integrating fintech into their daily routines will find themselves reaping significant rewards, gaining greater control and insight into their financial well-being.

MAKING PERSONAL FINANCE APPS – PERSONAL

It's common for individuals to feel ashamed and embarrassed when it comes to personal debt, a societal stigma that continues to persist. Whether it's due to credit cards, mortgages, student loans, or even the national debt, it's undeniable that the amount of money Americans owe continues to grow at an alarming rate. As of the beginning of 2024, US household debt has reached an all-time high of $17.5 trillion, as the Federal Reserve Bank of New York reported.[14] However, there has been a recent shift in how personal finance experts approach this topic by leveraging content and community as a channel for growth – sharing their relatable experiences with accruing debt and their practical tips for paying it off.

When Carmen Perez began her career in financial services, it didn't take long to realize that the financial industry wasn't quite as technologically advanced as she had imagined. She had been hired by a 200-year-old private bank in 2015. Despite the common perception that Wall Street was a hub of cutting-edge technology driving the way stocks and money movements happened, Perez soon found out that the industry was antiquated in more ways than one. She made a mental note of this observation and saved it for later. Simultaneously, Perez was struggling with debt, a fact that she kept hidden from the outside world. Despite her six-figure salary and her employment at a top-notch Wall Street firm, her credit score was abysmal. In fact, one of her early job offers from Goldman Sachs was rescinded when her credit report was examined closely.

In 2016, Perez faced one of the toughest challenges of her life when she was sued for defaulting on her student loans. This shocked her. As a full-time student, she received notices from her private student loan provider but ignored them, assuming it was a mistake. She believed that her loan repayment would begin only after she graduated. Unfortunately, she ignored the notices until it was too late and was eventually sued for $30 000.

Growing up with her two siblings under the care of a single mother, Perez was always aware of her family's financial struggles and saw what financial resilience looked like firsthand. Her mother's determination taught her to overcome financial obstacles. "Reflecting on my mom's journey, I realize she was a true hustler, juggling multiple jobs to make ends meet," she said. "Even now, she's hustling to catch up on her retirement savings after dedicating herself to raising us." That resilience left a profound impression on Perez – she learned that she could always find a way, no matter the circumstances.

In 2018, when personal branding and personal finance on social media had not yet taken off, Perez publicly shared her journey of paying off her debts and dealing with her lawsuit. By documenting her experience, she felt accountable and responsible for paying down her debt. Despite the vulnerability of airing her "dirty laundry," she was willing to take the risk to help others facing similar financial struggles. "I had started documenting because personal finance is hard for me to do, and I studied this formally and worked in banking," she shared, "I can't imagine what this is like for other people."

She created a blog called Make Real Cents, which eventually became an educational platform. On her blog, she shared her personal experiences dealing with the financial system, including being sued for her student loan, her mother's inability to co-sign the promissory note due to her poor credit score due to a divorce, and the common systemic issues in financial services. She also talked about defaulting on her loan while being a full-time student. However, what she found most frustrating was how lenders would shift blame onto her and continue to offer predatory products when she was already struggling with debt.

"My lawyer believed we could contest the lawsuit, as the lender breached their terms," she said. "However, the stress of potential job loss led me to settle. I paid what I owed, acknowledging my responsibility, but the ordeal had already caused significant harm, affecting my job and credit." Determined to break free of the debt cycle, she devised a system that worked for her and shared this system on her blog. She settled on using a cash envelope method for budgeting and the debt snowball method for paying off debt. The cash envelope method involves putting her credit cards away and transitioning to cash-only spending. At the beginning of each month, Perez determines how much she needs to spend, including all bills and expenses. She'd withdraw the cash at the bank and allocate it to different envelopes she'd label for other costs. Before heading to the grocery store, she'd open her "grocery" envelope and take out what she'd need for the trip. The cash envelope method is highly effective because it forces her to be thoughtful about how she spends her money. Debit cards, credit cards, and other digital forms of payment were designed to make spending money too easy, in her opinion. Paying with cash adds a layer of friction, giving her time to consider whether she wants to spend her last $5 on candy or lunch for the week. "Holding the cash in your fingers makes it feel more real," she said. More importantly, the cash envelope system forced Perez to stay within her budget and helped her understand how she was spending her money. This process worked, and she cleared her debt – eventually paying off $57 000 in two years and nine months.

So, she set out to learn how to turn her methods into a fintech application. At first, she used Excel to create spreadsheets and shared her unique formula for saving and paying down her debt. She sold hundreds of these spreadsheets and realized the market desperately needed a solution. However, she still needed to save more money before leaving her Wall Street job to become a full-time entrepreneur. So, she continued to work but put a strategy in place to quit after saving a certain amount of money while pursuing her passion – a fintech start-up. "Throughout that time, I kept a calendar on my desk, a secret tracker of sorts, marking each milestone towards my goal of quitting," she said. "With every extra amount I saved, I made a note on that calendar, visualizing my progress towards freedom."

She eventually saved enough money to quit her job and went all in on her vision of creating a fintech app. She enrolled in coding school at General Assembly, learning the ropes of programming. Simultaneously, she started crafting a basic version of her web app, Budget Better, in 2020. She took up a job to keep paying her bills while she built the app, but her journey hit a snag when the start-up where she had a software engineering role shuttered due to the pandemic's impact. "Still, I continued refining my app, even as I faced rejections from Y Combinator and TechStars during pitches."

The pressure mounted by the end of 2020 as she needed a stable income. So, she landed a role at Alloy, a pivotal move that marked her proper entry into fintech. "This opportunity allowed me to marry my compliance skills from traditional banking with Alloy's offerings, addressing a pain point I had encountered throughout my years in compliance at larger institutions," she said. And then, toward the end of her first year at Alloy, she finally got a call from TechStars, a pre-seed investor that provides access to capital, mentorship, and other support for early-stage entrepreneurs, asking her to apply again. "Third time the charm," she said. Her growing personal brand and the challenging economic environment for consumers due to the pandemic with rising inflation, interest rates, and consumer debt turned out to be the perfect storm for her personal finance start-up; the market was ready.

So, she left Alloy and launched Budget Better – a web app – in 2022, eventually renaming the app Much and launching the web app on mobile. Perez created Much to bridge the gap between what was missing in the personal finance market and the software needed to learn how to manage finances properly. Much also adds a community aspect that invites people to no longer consider money conversations taboo but helpful and empowering. "At Much, we believe in a highly personalized, zero-based budgeting framework," Perez explained. "When users join our platform and connect their bank accounts, we analyze 12 months of transaction data to determine their financial baseline. This approach ensures that our users' financial plans are tailored to their unique circumstances and goals." Much then works with users and their baseline to determine small interval percentages to slowly tighten budgets in a way that helps reduce spending without depriving users of experiences or setting unrealistic budgeting goals. The platform also offers webinars and workshops by people in the personal finance space and certified financial planners who have lived experience and are experts within their particular fields of knowledge. It also provides community challenges where users can connect with individuals and celebrate other people's wins.

By March 2023, Perez inked partnerships for Much, including with Secret deodorant, officially launched at the New York Stock Exchange, embarking on a financial wellness initiative to assist one million young women on their financial journeys. "Our partnership with Secret was a game-changer, aligning with a massive brand that opened up numerous opportunities," she said.

Perez unlocked a major founder hack when she uncovered vulnerability on social media while educating others and building up her personal brand (which now has nearly 75 000 followers on Instagram as of May 2024). Leveraging her brand has allowed her to scale and grow Much without relying heavily on VC dollars. "While having VC funding could accelerate progress, the doors opened by my personal brand have been invaluable," she said. "From appearances on the *Today Show* to collaborations with Public and Verizon In The Know Media, my brand has served as a pipeline for distribution, amplifying the reach of my app." This is an essential strategic approach for women in fintech, especially given the harsh funding environment. By building up our brands and leveraging connections, we can find new ways to grow and build outside the systemic biases that come from the grind of acquiring VC dollars.

Personal branding has become increasingly important in recent years. In the US, 78% of consumers believe a CEO or founder are responsible for driving a brand's purpose, according to a 2020 study commissioned by New York-based Zeno Group.[15] However, entrepreneurs often face difficulties establishing recognition in an overcrowded market, where consumer loyalty is hard-won due to ever-changing algorithms. This is where personal branding comes in. It involves defining and promoting what you stand for as an individual and demonstrating authenticity, trustworthiness, and credibility to your audience. Doing so can open the door to your purpose for building your business, building trust with your target audience, and encouraging them to take action, such as purchasing a membership or buying a product. Personal branding is not about tricking people into liking you. Instead, it's about leveraging the power of content and community to attract and retain customers and even corporate partnerships through value alignment.

Looking back, Perez realizes that having a personal finance brand and an established market fit significantly aided her entry into TechStars as well as provided a solid distribution channel and bolstered her credibility. Still, she acknowledges as a Black and Hispanic female founder in fintech, she faces skepticism. "Despite being technically proficient, I've often found myself having to assert my role as the technical lead, facing skepticism simply because of the way I look," she said. "It's frustrating to still encounter such biases, but I remain steadfast in challenging these misconceptions and proving that women can excel in technical roles."

By sharing her struggles openly, Perez connected with her audience and established a solid personal brand that propelled her ventures forward. Her success highlights the power of resilience, determination, and the ability to identify market gaps overlooked by others. Moreover, Perez's strategic approach to partnerships and her emphasis on community and personal brand building offers a roadmap for women in fintech to thrive despite systemic biases and funding challenges.

In June 2024, Perez announced on LinkedIn that Much closed its doors after two and a half years of operation.[16] As a first-time founder, she described the journey as one of the most "challenging, stressful, equally fulfilling, and growth-filled experiences." She admitted that achieving product–market fit with their available runway was difficult, ultimately making it hard to sustain long-term healthy unit economics.

While closing operations might initially seem like a negative, it's important to remember that it's not. Perez's efforts helped customers eliminate credit card debt, with some users even building fully funded emergency funds – all because of her work at Much.

In a world where success is often measured by dollar signs, especially for entrepreneurs, it's crucial to recognize other metrics of success. Perez significantly impacted many lives, influencing their financial decisions and fostering healthy financial habits. By this measure, Perez is a success many times over.

FEARLESSLY FUNDING FEMALES

When I see a brilliant female fintech founder with a working product, I can't help but think of the disproportionate amount of venture capital that goes to male founders with just an idea. Data from First Round Capital in 2015 shows that companies with a female founder perform 63% better on average than all-male founding teams.[17] Despite their potential for higher returns, women, particularly women of color, are historically underfunded.

The disparity between the rising number of Black female entrepreneurs and the minimal venture capital they receive is a major issue in the fintech ecosystem. Some investors are working to bridge this gap. For example, Fearless Fund, led by CEO and founding partner Arian Simone, invests in women-of-color-led businesses seeking pre-seed, seed, or Series A financing.

One of Fearless Fund's initiatives, the Strivers Grant program, supports early-stage Black-woman-owned businesses with grants ranging from $10000 to $20000. However, this program faced a lawsuit from the American Alliance for Equal Rights (AAER) in August 2023, led by founder and affirmative action foe Edward Blum. The lawsuit argued that the program discriminates against non-Black women founders.[18]

Fearless Fund fought the lawsuit for nearly a year, but in June 2024, a US federal appeals court ruling enjoined the grant program, barring grants to Black women entrepreneurs. Fearless Fund is considering its next steps, including possibly going to trial.[19]

In response to the ruling, Simone took to social media to ask for an immediate Executive Order by the President of the United States to protect DEI and the right to fund specific marginalized groups if and when racial disparities exist. She also asked for Congress to issue the Fearless Freedom Economic Civil Rights Act, an Act that supports this executive order.

The lawsuit against Fearless Fund is part of a broader and troubling trend of attacks against diversity, equity, and inclusion initiatives. Fearless Fund has been a crucial supporter of Black female-founded fintech companies, including Capway, led by founder and CEO Sheena Allen. On LinkedIn, Allen praised Fearless Fund, and specifically Arian Simone and Ayana Parsons, for their unwavering support during times when many others dismissed her efforts, saying, "You're too early. Come back when you've reached...xyz."[20]

Allen also highlighted the scarcity of Black founders in the fintech space, and the additional challenges faced by Black women. She emphasized that

Fearless Fund isn't just about funding; the leaders and the entire team add value beyond money and are committed to their success.

The legal efforts to dismantle workplace diversity programs have faced some setbacks, reflecting polarized opinions among judges. For example, a federal district judge in Ohio dismissed a lawsuit against Progressive and fintech platform Hello Alice. The lawsuit, filed by America First Legal, challenged a program offering $25 000 grants to Black small-business owners, claiming it was unconstitutional. Despite this, Hello Alice announced the lawsuit's dismissal on 28 May 2024, reaffirming its commitment to providing equitable access to capital for underrepresented entrepreneurs.[21]

As the fintech sector increasingly recognizes the importance of diversity in driving innovation and growing market share, we must organize and maintain this momentum by supporting, funding, and paying women of color what they deserve to grow and scale their businesses. Investors and start-ups must navigate the challenges of backlash against diversity initiatives with awareness of their implications for the industry's future growth, profitability, and capacity for positive change.

Instead of getting distracted by the bullshit, we must unite as a community, support each other intentionally, and innovate against the status quo. There are always steps we can take as individuals to change systems. For example, we can organize for policy changes, such as California Governor Gavin Newsom's signing of Senate Bill 54, the Fair Investment Practices by Investment Advisers (New Diversity Reporting Law). As shared in Chapter 3, this law requires VC companies with ties to California to annually report the demographic information of the "founding team members" at their invested companies. We need this law nationwide, and ultimately, we need policies that extend civil rights protections to venture capital investments.

By focusing on sustainable, inclusive growth and demanding regulation and systemic changes as a community, we can ensure the fintech industry's success and resilience, even in the face of challenges and setbacks that stifle innovation.

MENTAL HEALTH MEETS FINTECH

In Chapter 3, Asya Bradley talks about overcoming a scarcity mindset, especially for women building businesses. This mindset can affect many parts of our lives, especially our finances. Kelsey Willock Jones designed a fintech app to tackle this mindset head-on.

A 2024 report by the TIAA Institute and High Lantern Group found that financial struggles like debt worries, economic instability, and not meeting basic needs can trigger stress and reduce resilience against mental health challenges. High amounts of debt are often linked to anxiety, depression, and anger, while ongoing financial difficulties may lead to hopelessness and despair, potentially causing depression. The report noted that 42% of US adults say money negatively impacts their mental health.[22] This financial stress results in a 34% increase in absenteeism and tardiness, with financially stressed employees being five times more likely to be distracted by their finances at work. This lost productivity costs employers billions of dollars every year.

Willock Jones, who studied entrepreneurship and English at Wake Forest University, worked for various start-ups, including an edtech company, a fintech company and Rent the Runway. She loved the entrepreneurial spirit and the sense of being in control of her own destiny.

During her sophomore year in college, her parents' business failed, thrusting her into significant student debt and financial anxiety. She graduated college with $150000 in student debt, prompting her to get a job at Goldman Sachs, believing it was the best place to learn about money. Despite entering the finance industry, she felt unprepared and anxious until she met her manager-turned-financial coach, Amy, who gave her the confidence and guidance to start playing the financial game. With Amy's help, Willock Jones refinanced her debt, started investing, and improved her relationship with money. She realized not everyone has an Amy, which is why she founded her fintech company, Aura – to ensure no one starts their financial journey alone.

This experience marked the beginning of her journey to make money work for her rather than letting it control her. She spent six years at Goldman Sachs, working in the global markets division and on a project called Launch With GS, which aimed to build an ecosystem of entrepreneurs, highlighting the need to get more underrepresented voices invested.

While building Aura while at On Deck, an entrepreneurship program, she also started writing a weekly blog called "Not Your Partner's Investment Advice," where she used humor and storytelling to educate her audience about personal finance and investing. She also met her now co-founder, Courtney Cardin, who was working at Duolingo for financial literacy. Together, they realized the core issue with finances was one they faced themselves their entire lives – it was an emotional and behavioral issue. So, they founded Aura, a mindful money management platform aimed at addressing these challenges.

Willock Jones didn't set out to join fintech specifically. But she did recognize a widespread problem that needed addressing: many people have similar stories of financial anxiety but avoided discussing finances, leaving their financial decisions to partners or parents.

Willock Jones and Cardin designed Aura not to eliminate financial worries but to support individuals on their journey, much like a therapist supports clients through anxiety. At the start of her journey, Willock Jones was extremely anxious about her financial situation and felt embarrassed to discuss it. However, when she started having conversations, she realized she wasn't alone.

"Financial anxiety is a behavioral problem," she said. "Anxiety fuels irrational decisions, leading to poor financial outcomes, and the cycle of stress repeats. The problem worsens for individuals from lower-income communities who lack access to resources." That's why Aura is designed as a psychology-based financial wellness platform, helping individuals change their relationship with money by combining behavioral coaching with wealth management for a holistic experience.

While at Techstars, Aura has shifted its model to work with corporate partners with learning and development (L&D) budgets. These partners approve Aura as an L&D expense in exchange for hosting a free workshop, converting employees into Aura users in real-time for just $249 per member. Aura has hosted workshops with partners like Amplitude, Stripe, Clari, Peloton, and more. "The reception has been phenomenal," Willock Jones said. "With 100% of attendees saying they would recommend the workshop to a friend, 70% feeling more confident investing after just 40 minutes, and 33% already subscribing live. To date, Aura works with 16 corporate partners. About 70% of the platform's users are women."

The key is to keep the conversation going. Financial issues aren't about making something bad into something good; they simply are what they are. "We all experience financial turbulence, and it's not a straight path upward," she said. Even as a founder, she still faces financial anxiety, especially after quitting her job and losing a steady income.

Behavioral economics, crucial yet often overlooked in finance, is central to Aura's mission. Money is closely tied to people's values and helps shape their identity. Willock Jones aims to help people understand that money isn't just about clearing debt or achieving a certain status – it's a continuous journey. Managing finances is a constant practice that becomes part of your routine, like therapy or any long-term commitment.

PRODUCT INCLUSION – IN REALITY

In her book *Invisible Women: Data Bias in a World Designed for Men*, Caroline Criado Perez highlights how our world is engineered with men in mind, often ignoring women's needs. One vivid example she gives is the design of public bathrooms. At concerts, movies, or events, you'll notice that women's bathroom lines are usually longer than men's. This isn't just by chance – it's due to male-biased design. Most designers allocate equal floor space to both men's and women's restrooms, considering it fair. However, this approach doesn't account for the different ways women use bathrooms compared to men.[23]

This bias isn't limited to architecture. Financial institutions, dominated by male leadership, show the same skew in their products. Top product executives have developed precise frameworks to make inclusion a reality. Anaid Chacón, who has led product teams at Dropbox, NuvoCargo, and Argyle before developing her startup DiscernFit, emphasizes the importance of always asking, "Who else?" when building products. This approach shifts from merely giving historically underrepresented consumers a "seat at the table" to engaging in co-creation and full collaboration. "This ensures better outcomes, higher innovation, and increased market share," she said.

Chacón's journey from Chihuahua, Mexico, to the United States for graduate school illustrates her commitment. "Moving to a new country presented significant challenges, particularly in understanding financial systems like credit scores and housing," she said. "I had an engineering degree, but navigating the financial landscape was overwhelming." This experience fueled her passion for fintech, driving her to demystify financial products and make them more transparent and approachable for people like her.

Product inclusion means intentionally designing financial tools that make people feel seen by considering different aspects of their identity during the design and development process. This involves recognizing the diverse races, genders, and behaviors of users worldwide and understanding how these dimensions intersect when interacting with a product. Chacón joined fintech to help solve the problems she faced when she moved to the US. The lack of diverse viewpoints in designing products for the majority of fintech users was glaring. "In fintech, the focus is on simplifying complex financial systems while emphasizing thoughtful consideration," Chacón said. "There is also a crucial service layer that involves integrating human interaction to add differentiated value."

Chacón advocates for a holistic and intersectional view of target users when building products. "Money represents the tangible result of how people spend their time, making it incredibly valuable," she said. "Everyone wants to feel that their financial activities are purposeful and align with their values."

One area where fintech could help increase product inclusion is with traditional underwriting models that cater primarily to segments with greater access to financial products. "For example, the workforce has dramatically transformed over the last decade," Chacón said. "Especially with the rise of gig work."

More people now engage in freelance or gig work, either as their primary income or to supplement existing income. Financial institutions and banks have yet to fully integrate signals from this changing workforce, creating a product inclusion gap. This gap presents an opportunity to offer products to individuals who would greatly benefit and to open up fintech to larger and more diverse customer bases.

When we build for the margins, we get the center for free. This is the underlying truth of the "curb-cut effect" which exemplifies product inclusion.[24] For example, while originally created for wheelchair users, curb cuts are now used by everyone, including people with skateboards, suitcases, or shopping carts, proving that building for historically marginalized groups leads to better outcomes for all. Another example is closed captioning, which benefits a wide range of users beyond those who are deaf or hard of hearing.

Creating inclusive products has clear economic benefits, but Chacón recognizes that implementing this vision can be challenging. Business leaders must understand how to capture a larger market share by creating more inclusive products for people of color, women, and other underrepresented groups. There's a simple way to make it less complicated: Proactively hiring diverse perspectives to design, engineer, product manage, and conduct user research is crucial.

Tracking progress toward product inclusion and equity at the company level is also essential. Customer satisfaction, sentiment, and daily active users are important metrics, says Chacón. Companies must also intentionally review data to avoid overlooking historically underrepresented groups. When assessing product-market fit, consider whether feedback was gathered from appropriate demographics, as different groups can have unique needs.

"Each interaction must be thoughtfully designed to ensure it effectively brings about positive change," Chacón said.

FINTECH FOR THE FEMALE GAZE

Vrinda Gupta decided to work in financial services after seeing her overly confident Indian immigrant mother lose her fire when managing her family's finances. Despite building a successful career in a new country and having substantial earning power, she needed help understanding financial matters and knowing which questions to ask when dealing with her financial services providers. "I remember countless instances where she would defer to my dad during phone calls with the bank," Gupta told me in an interview. Her mother was utterly disempowered by her lack of knowledge of the financial system despite making a good living. "Looking back," she said. "Her concerns were valid."

After Gupta finished college, she started her career as a product manager, building the Chase Sapphire Reserve at Visa. She figured – what better way to learn about finances than to be inside the financial system creating these products? She was responsible for crafting nationwide regulations for the construction of credit products. This involved determining how Visa credit cards should be structured, defining reward programs, and identifying target demographics. "I felt confident in my understanding because I was directly involved in shaping these products and ensuring adherence to regulations," she said. Gupta was so giddy when the Chase Sapphire Reserve card launched, tailored for young millennials living in urban areas – a demographic she identified with, being based in San Francisco with a well-paying job. She eagerly applied for the card, but they rejected her application. Despite her heavy hand in launching the credit card, Gupta was denied due to her lack of credit history.

Her initial reaction was to wonder what she had done wrong. "It felt like I was taking an important test for which no one had taught me how to prepare," she said. So she did her research. Gupta learned that because the credit card she used was her father's (she was an authorized user), she wasn't responsible for paying the balance, which meant she was not building her credit history. "I didn't realize I was building his credit, not mine," she recalled. Despite her efforts to work in finance and bridge her financial education gap, she realized that even working in the system leaves knowledge gaps. "Had I known better, I would have taken steps to build my credit independently," she said. "However, my lack of awareness prevented me from taking these actions, leading to a vicious cycle." Rejection from credit applications further damaged her credit score, exacerbating her initial disadvantage.

She started to research more, obsessing over how many other women faced the same problem. It turns out credit cards disproportionately reject women – while also giving women lower credit limits and receiving higher interest rates despite the evidence that women achieve similar credit scores to men.

Ironically, women have the world's greatest purchasing power, controlling 85% of all consumer purchases in the US. Yet, as women shoulder more household burdens worldwide, they feel less financially secure. "I saw in Visa data that 70% of women's spend is on noncredit building products, like debit cards and credit cards in other people's names," she said. "It's leaving valuable rewards on the table and, ultimately, affecting our ability to access credit fairly and equitably because we aren't building credit histories."

So, she researched even more and soon began to recognize systemic biases within the financial services industry, which often excluded women and communities of color. This realization fueled her determination to address these systemic issues, as she understood that the problem wasn't her – but the inherent flaws in the financial system.

She discovered even more deeply troubling facts. Until 50 years ago, in 1974, women could be legally rejected from bank accounts and credit cards without a male cosigner. Until 1988, women could be required to have a male cosigner to obtain a business loan – a reality that persisted until just two years before Gupta's birth. "It's sobering to realize that these historical injustices are not as distant as they may seem," she said. Even during the recent pandemic, women and people of color faced disparities in accessing PPP loans for their businesses, highlighting the enduring legacy of inequality in the financial industry.

Adding fuel to the fire, financial services companies spend more money advertising their services to male-centric audiences than female-centric ones. Only 1% of financial content is directed toward women. In 2018, financial services companies invested 13 times more money on advertising banking, investment, and retirement products and services in male-skewed magazines than in female-skewed ones. This lack of representation leaves many women feeling alienated, giving them the impression that financial organizations do not consider female customers as a demographic they care about. Research by Merrill Lynch in 2020 found that "out of 839 articles in 17 women's magazines, only one had anything to do with personal finance and money."[24]

Determined to close the credit – and knowledge – gap for women, Gupta decided to pursue entrepreneurship. Before striking out alone,

Gupta felt she needed to learn about starting a business. She left Visa and went to the Haas School of Business at the University of California, Berkeley, where she did her MBA summer internship at IDEO.

In 2019, Gupta founded Sequin Financial, the first debit card that builds credit geared toward women, risk-free with no credit history required. At first, Gupta built Sequin as a credit building tool but in 2024 announced a pivot to cashback rewards, instead. "Typically debit cards do not earn rewards, credit cards do," she said. "But credit cards disproportionately leave women in cycles of high interest debt." Women pay more in credit card fees and have higher credit card interest rates. Even the best credit cards are not designed to reward women-focused spending, and instead provide most rewards on dining and travel.

In Gupta's nature, she did a ton of research before designing the product. Her analysis revealed dissatisfaction among women with credit card rewards programs, built based on what men want rather than what women want. She uncovered that women typically use their credit cards to make retail, beauty, charitable contributions, and household purchases.

Addressing these disparities requires a nuanced understanding of women's needs and lifestyles. It goes beyond merely targeting women; it involves recognizing and addressing hidden costs such as the Pink Tax, healthcare expenses, career interruptions for caregiving, and student debt. These factors significantly impact financial decision-making and must be considered when designing products and services for women.

With this knowledge, Gupta designed Sequin Financial as the first debit card in US history to reward women where they spend and fight the Pink Tax, with up to 6% cashback on beauty and drugstore hauls, gyms, local salons, and more. The Pink Tax costs the average woman $188 000 or more over her lifetime on purchases of necessary personal care products.[25] This figure doesn't even include period products (estimated to cost $9000 over our lifetimes and still taxed as a luxury good in 21 states). Women also pay hundreds of thousands more in healthcare costs, whether it's monthly pills, vitamins, and supplements or the hidden costs of a healthcare system designed for men. What's more, none of the above costs include the impacts of the gender wage gap, which causes a $1.6 trillion hole in the US economy every year.[26] Gupta decided it was time to act and build a debit card to fight the costs of womanhood – for the first time in US history.

The product was absolutely solid – addressing a massively underserved market with a unique approach no one else was taking. Still, as a woman, a person of color, a first-generation immigrant, and a first-time founder in the male-dominated fintech industry, the chances of Gupta raising venture capital for Sequin were slim. Against the odds, she raised a pre-seed round, which Gupta said she navigated through that process herself.

Gupta pitched to both male and female investors. It was crucial to her that Sequin's investors understood the company's mission, which women were more likely to do. Those who invested recognized that Sequin targeted a large, lucrative, and grossly underserved market. Gupta spent more time on fundraising to attract investors who shared her values. With that approach, she could close a pre-seed round of $700 000.

Nearly all of Sequin's earliest investors are women representing consumer tech, financial services, and design industries. Investors included Carrie Schwab (chair and president of the Schwab Foundation), Kevin Weil (former head of product at Instagram), Deb Liu (CEO at Ancestry), Dorothy Jean Chang (president at Kode with Klossy), and several women from IDEO.

In 2021, Gupta successfully closed her second funding round, a $5 million seed financing round, bringing the total amount raised to $5.7 million. Investors include Y Combinator, Matrix Partners, Scribble Ventures, IDEO, Thomvest, and Commerce V.C. She recognized the advantages of participating in a Y Combinator accelerator program. In one example, Gupta shared that when she was being conservative in talking about her projections, mentors in the program called her out. As a first-generation immigrant, she was taught to be humble. But if you're going to impress investors, you must have – and articulate – a big vision.

"Being around other people questioning the status quo is inspiring," said Gupta. "It's shown me the power of my vision, and it's given me the encouragement to continue to bet on myself daily." While more voices like Gupta are now speaking up about these disparities, particularly in the financial realm, much remains to be done. We must dissect how financial products are constructed, examine access issues, and scrutinize how the financial products we use daily are structured. Most products are geared toward male users because the products are designed by men, thus creating a perpetual financial education and wealth gap between women and men.

Education is at the core of addressing these issues. "I've observed that while there are resources discussing topics like general finances, savings accounts, and emergency funds, there remains a significant gap in credit education," Gupta said. "Many resources fail to consider women's unique spending patterns and financial needs, as they often manage households and face different economic challenges." As builders in fintech, we must consider the hidden costs and systemic biases they face.

It's also important to illuminate how factors like the gender wage gap can impact credit calculations and offer insights into navigating the system more effectively. Despite legal provisions against gender discrimination, societal biases still influence algorithms, underscoring the importance of understanding and addressing these issues.

As they say, money is power, and when you combine knowledge with financial resources, you can confidently navigate life's decisions. Education is indeed crucial, allowing individuals to make informed choices without judgment. While our society typically idolizes individualism, there's immense value in fostering a sense of community, especially for women, when it comes to finance.

In some cultures, including some areas of the US, finances are approached more communally, with lending and support networks among community members. A more community-focused approach to finance provides practical support and fosters a sense of belonging and shared responsibility.

NOTES

1. Envestnet. "About Envestnet." Accessed May 20, 2024. https://investor.envestnet.com/about.
2. Ibanez, Fernanda, "Latinas in Leadership Positions in the United States: Theories, Characteristics, and Recommendations" (2023). College of Science and Health Theses and Dissertations. 482. https://via.library.depaul.edu/csh_etd/482.
3. Yahoo Finance. "Here's How Much Americans Have Saved for Retirement." Accessed May 20, 2024. https://finance.yahoo.com/news/heres-much-americans-saved-retirement-104600457.html.
4. Carvana. "Carvana Reports First Quarter 2024 Financial Results." May 1, 2024. Accessed May 20, 2024. https://investors.carvana.com/news-releases/2024/05-01-2024.
5. Payments Cards and Mobile. "Embedded Finance Market to Reach $730.5 Billion by 2032." Accessed May 20, 2024. https://www.paymentscardsandmobile.com/embedded-finance-market-to-reach-730-5-billion-by-2032.
6. PR Newswire. "Americans Are Spending Less on Impulse Purchases in 2023 Than in Prior Years, According to Annual Survey Commissioned by Slickdeals." Accessed May 20, 2024. https://www.prnewswire.com/news-releases/americans-are-spending-less-on-impulse-purchases-in-2023-than-in-prior-years-according-to-annual-survey-commissioned-by-slickdeals-301886019.html.
7. PR Newswire. "Envestnet Launches Embedded Investing Solution, Helping Financial Institutions Meet the Demand for Banking Apps That Address More Components of a Customer's Financial Life." Accessed May 20, 2024. https://www.prnewswire.com/news-releases/envestnet-launches-embedded-investing-solution-helping-financial-institutions-meet-the-demand-for-banking-apps-that-address-more-components-of-a-customers-financial-life-301964424.html.

8. Bankrate. "Buy Now, Pay Later Survey." Accessed May 20, 2024. https://www
.bankrate.com/loans/personal-loans/buy-now-pay-later-survey/.

9. City National Bank. "Emotions and Financial Decisions." Accessed May 20,
2024. https://www.cnb.com/personal-banking/insights/emotions-and-financial-
decisions.html.

10. Laurel Road. "Financial Survey: Annual Survey on Women's Personal
Finances." Accessed May 20, 2024. https://www.laurelroad.com/resources/
financial-survey-annual-survey-womens-personal-finances/.

11. Ellevest. "Closing the Gender Wealth Gap." Accessed May 20, 2024. https://
www.ellevest.com/magazine/disrupt-money/closing-the-gender-wealth-gap.

12. PNC. "Financial Wellness in the Workplace: What Employees Want and
Need." Accessed May 20, 2024. https://www.pnc.com/insights/corporate-
institutional/gain-market-insight/financial-wellness-in-the-workplace-what-
employees-want-and-need.html.

13. Center for American Progress. "How Investing in Public Health Will Strengthen
America's Health." Accessed May 20, 2024. https://www.americanprogress.org/
article/how-investing-in-public-health-will-strengthen-americas-health/.

14. Federal Reserve Bank of New York. "Household Debt and Credit Report."
Accessed May 20, 2024. https://www.newyorkfed.org/microeconomics/hhdc.

15. Zeno Group. "2020 Zeno Strength of Purpose Study." Accessed May 20, 2024.
https://www.zenogroup.com/insights/2020-zeno-strength-purpose.

16. Perez, Carmen A. "I can't believe I'm saying this, but I share. . ." LinkedIn,
June 30, 2023. Accessed May 20, 2024. https://www.linkedin.com/
posts/carmen-a-perez-i-cant-believe-im-saying-this-but-i-share-activity-
7205937168752504832-Fc-b.

17. First Round. "10 Years of First Round." Accessed May 20, 2024. https://10years
.firstround.com/.

18. Reuters. "US Court Decision Casts Shadow on Diversity in Venture Capital
Funding." July 2, 2024. Accessed May 20, 2024. https://www.reuters.com/
legal/us-court-decision-casts-shadow-diversity-venture-capital-funding-
2024-07-02/.

19. Davis, Dominic-Madori. "An Appeals Court Rules That VC Fearless Fund
Cannot Issue Grants to Black Women, but the Fight Continues." TechCrunch,
June 3, 2024. Accessed May 20, 2024. https://techcrunch.com/2024/06/03/
an-appeals-court-rules-that-vc-fearless-fund-cannot-issue-grants-to-black-
women-but-the-fight-continues/.

20. Allen, Sheena. "Fearless Fund Faces Lawsuit with Far-Reaching Implications." LinkedIn. Accessed May 20, 2024. https://www.linkedin.com/posts/sheenaallen_fearless-fund-faces-lawsuit-with-far-reaching-activity-7095062704935026689-nMnJ.

21. PR Newswire. "A Win for Hello Alice in Lawsuit Marking a Significant Boost for the Small Business Community." Accessed May 20, 2024. https://www.prnewswire.com/news-releases/a-win-for-hello-alice-in-lawsuit-marking-a-significant-boost-for-the-small-business-community-302155566.html.

22. TIAA Institute. "TIAA Institute Report Finds Ties Between Financial Stress and Mental Health." Accessed May 20, 2024. https://www.tiaa.org/public/institute/about/news/tiaa-institute-report-finds-ties-between-financial-stress-and-mental-health.

23. Criado Perez, Caroline. Invisible Women: Data Bias in a World Designed for Men. New York: Abrams Press, 2019.

24. Investra Financial Services. "Key Influences on Women's Life Journeys and the Retirement Preparedness Gap." May 6, 2021. Accessed May 20, 2024. https://investrafinancial.com/2021/05/06/key-influences-on-womens-life-journeys-and-the-retirement-preparedness-gap/.

25. Bankrate. "Pink Tax: How Women Pay More." Accessed May 20, 2024. https://www.bankrate.com/personal-finance/pink-tax-how-women-pay-more/#key-insights.

26. Star Tribune. "Pink Tax and Gender Pay Gap: Financial Tips for Women and LGBTQ." Accessed May 20, 2024. https://www.startribune.com/pink-tax-gender-pay-gap-financial-tips-women-lgbtq/600353813.

CHAPTER FIVE

COMMUNITY IS YOUR COMPETITIVE ADVANTAGE

B uilding a fintech company in today's crowded market isn't just about promising wealth anymore. It's about creating an experience that deeply resonates with consumers, giving them a greater sense of purpose and connection. That's why investing in community building is crucial for any fintech company. When done right, it can unlock market share, and it's exactly what the next generation of wealth builders crave.

Take Gen Y and Gen Z, for example. They make up 47% of the US population and inherit $541 billion annually, which is about 30% of the wealth transferred today. This percentage is only expected to grow, according to a 2022 Fidelity report.[1] Gen Z, the most diverse generation yet, with 48% of 7- to 22-year-olds identifying as non-white, is passionate about making money and making a positive difference in the world. They are coming together as a community to drive change, and digital financial services are one of their most effective tools. By embracing fintech, Gen Z can coordinate, collaborate, and take action more innovatively and efficiently.

INVESTING IN GEN Z

A great example of a fintech start-up using "community" as a core pillar is Alinea Invest, a fintech app offering investing and wealth management aimed at Gen Z women. From my observations, Alinea taps into all six hallmarks of its target user: diversity, life path, values, FOMO, mental health, and technology. Community is at the heart of their value proposition. Instead of traditional marketing, they share their story through content creation on TikTok and host events that bring their target consumers together regularly.

And it's working. Alinea Invest's community has grown rapidly despite being only a few years old. Between Instagram and TikTok alone, they have more than 200 000 followers. Their platform hosts 500 000+ investors, with 92.7% being female, 72% first-time investors, and 70% Gen Z. Founded amid the COVID-19 pandemic in December 2020 by Anam Lakhani and Eve Halimi, along with Chief Technology Officer Daniel Nissenbaum, Alinea began as a school project and quickly grew into a full-fledged fintech. They raised $2.1 million from Y Combinator and strategic investors in 2021, followed by another $3.4 million in January 2024.

"As women, we are constantly marketed everything from beauty products to designer clothes to hair products," said Halimi. "But we are never marketed how to make money." When they spoke with investors early on, they were often turned down, being told that women didn't care about investing. But hundreds of daily messages on TikTok and via email proved otherwise, as women expressed a desire to invest but didn't know how to start.

Michael Seibel from Y Combinator was the first to believe in them. During their 10-minute interview, he grasped what they were trying to build and why it was so significant. However, it was incredibly difficult to get other investors to see the vision, the founders told me. As women building a female-centric finance app, the founders admit it took hundreds of interviews before Alinea was finally accepted into the Y Combinator incubator program.

Despite the challenges, they persevered. Investing was not accessible to Gen Z women, and they aimed to change that by creating a platform free from predatory behaviors. Their goal is to elevate the voices of regular people who want to build intergenerational wealth. Personal experiences highlighted the importance of ensuring every aspect of their platform remains non-predatory, a commitment fundamental to their mission.

The key to their success is authenticity, which has fostered a strong community based on trust. Gen Zers prefer to learn about finance from friends and peers, making authenticity and community invaluable. Rather than making grand claims about making millions, Lakhani and Halimi built a marketing foundation on their personal finance stories, something no other fintech can duplicate. They share their stories on TikTok, including how it felt for them to get started investing, engaging with their community directly.

By staying in constant communication with their users, Lakhani and Halimi know precisely what features to build next. Alinea Invest is now working on launching auto-managed investing and educational content around the fund they're managing for an annual fee. Storytelling is central to their strategy. It's not just about crafting compelling narratives but also about resonating deeply with others and inspiring them. The founders of

Alinea are refreshingly candid about their motivation. While working on Wall Street, they observed a significant disparity: men invested their money far more than women. Determined to change this, they didn't just talk about the problem – they became the change they wished to see. Since then, they have leveraged their social media following and their growing fintech platform to empower users to invest with purpose. Through Alinea, users can now organize and invest in causes they care about, turning financial growth into a tool for social change.

For example, when Roe v. Wade was overturned in 2022, Alinea's community immediately responded by creating a pro-abortion-rights playlist – a basket of stocks supporting companies that stood for reproductive health care. This demonstrated that investors want to use their money to support companies that share their values, and Alinea was right there as a fintech tool for users to take action.

Building a community around trust, transparency, and shared values is essential. It works for Alinea, which generates a revenue run rate of $1.8 million, operating profitably with its lean six-person team, as of January 2024.[2] According to Halimi, the investing app's winning themes include:

1. Empowerment: Breaking free from traditional finance bros.
2. Education: Filling the gaps schools leave behind.
3. Relatability: Sharing real stories to build trust.
4. Action: Making investing easy and a habit.
5. Change: Encouraging women to own their financial decisions.

Consumers want to feel part of something bigger than themselves. Providing resources that enable them to learn about financial topics and engage with industry experts gives your community a greater sense of purpose and connection. Demonstrate how your company is making a positive impact by investing in social causes that resonate with your customers. Show them that you're not just a digital financial tool but an active participant in creating a better future for all.

When your intentions are clear and customers can see how you're making a difference, they will likely remain loyal and engaged with your brand. Community building works best when it's truly about making an impact, inspiring change, and bringing people together. If you're only focused on profit, your impact will be minimal, and community-focused fintechs will take over your market share.

RETHINKING RETIREMENT SAVINGS

Small businesses are an integral part of the United States economy. There are 33.3 million small businesses in the US, which employ about 61.6 million workers, according to 2023 data by the Small Business Administration.[3] On top of that, small businesses generate 44% of the country's economic activity. Of these small businesses, a large swath are owned by immigrants. Notably, a 2022 study by the American Economic Association revealed that immigrants are 80% more likely to initiate business ventures than individuals born in the US.[4] Immigrant Americans play a critical role in the small business economy as they have a higher inclination toward entrepreneurship than the general population. This tendency may stem from relocating to another country's inherent adventurous and risky nature. Moreover, obstacles with work visas often lead immigrants to pursue entrepreneurship as an alternative to securing corporate employment. Data from the New American Economy, a bipartisan research and immigration advocacy organization, shows that about 3.2 million immigrants ran their own businesses, making up one in every five entrepreneurs in the country. Immigrant-owned businesses employed almost 8 million American workers and generated $1.3 trillion in total sales.[5] These statistics demonstrate immigrant entrepreneurs' vital role in job creation for all Americans.

As a child of Korean immigrants growing up in Los Angeles, Jean Smart was constantly exposed to the world of small businesses and entrepreneurship. Her parents owned various small businesses, including restaurants, dry cleaning services, and grocery stores – all in pursuit of the American Dream. Despite their numerous challenges, including language barriers, long work hours, and juggling multiple responsibilities, her parents persevered and worked tirelessly to make ends meet. However, a lack of financial education and guidance resulted in her parents having no retirement savings or plan after a lifetime of work. "For my parents, their retirement plan was centered around their children – a cultural norm, perhaps," she said. "They lacked awareness of 401(k) plans, retirement savings, or even the stock market basics." Growing up, the *Wall Street Journal* wasn't part of her household reading material; these concepts were foreign to her family. "While my parents wore smiles working every day, privately, they hoped for us kids to pursue higher education and stable corporate careers – to become doctors, lawyers, or professionals."

As expected of her, Smart went off to college, attending the University of California, Berkeley, followed by stints at well-known financial institutions like Charles Schwab, Citi, and UBS. "It wasn't until my first job after college that I was introduced to retirement savings plans," she admitted. By the time she reached her early 40s, Smart wanted to do something more. She liked that her work in financial services provided a steady career and a good paycheck, allowing her to support her parents and have her own family. But she also felt restless and wanted to feel good about her work.

And then COVID happened, followed by George Floyd's murder and the increased violence against Asian Americans (hate crimes against Asians spiked 164% in the first quarter of 2021).[6] Plus, the struggles faced by small businesses shuttering throughout the pandemic – particularly those owned by marginalized communities – underscored the urgent need for change. Scared and angry, Smart decided she was tired of being beholden to others. She wanted to make a change and have a direct hand in making life better for average Americans. As an Asian woman who's spent her whole life navigating rooms where she's the first and only, she had a clear vision of the kind of company she wanted to build – she would ensure more people like her parents had better access to retirement savings plans, which enable employees to build wealth through regular contributions and investments gradually. She decided she would use the power of advanced technology to do it.

Smart had been saving diligently for years and accumulated enough money to support her transition from corporate America to entrepreneurship. Plus, the pandemic afforded her time to reflect on how she wanted to bring her idea to the market. To begin with, she contemplated the issues that exist in the market. While some businesses adapt to modern technology by migrating to cloud-based platforms, Smart knew from her time on Wall Street that most existing players still rely on outdated systems. Major hurdles exist in the form of intermediaries and hidden fees, which negatively impact both employers and employees. Fees charged as a percentage of assets under management, however small, can add up to significant deductions from paychecks over time. Despite a 401(k) retirement plan being a way to take care of employees' financial wellness and provide a tax benefit to companies and their employees, most legacy 401(k) providers avoid marketing to the smallest businesses because the market isn't very profitable. It's a missed opportunity, given that a vast majority of companies have fewer than 20 employees.

As the pandemic fallout continued, businesses struggled to stay afloat, and the government intervened to provide aid. Then, Smart had an idea – a fintech platform designed for small companies – specifically microenterprises. She identified the need to target businesses with at most 20 employees, which constituted most small businesses needing help. She knew many of these businesses were owned by women, minorities, and immigrants. Using fintech, Smart decided to build a self-serve business model, making it affordable for small businesses to provide retirement benefits. With this approach, the momentum behind her start-up began to build.

Smart ultimately designed a retirement savings platform for small businesses and entrepreneurs that offers a turnkey solution that automates employee investing, streamlines cost and paperwork, and provides employee learning tools. In a world where 401(k) plans have long been considered a perk exclusive to large corporations, Smart's platform aims to humanize retirement planning, simplifying the complexities of 401(k) and making financial wellness accessible to all. "By stripping away the unnecessary complexities and adopting a user-friendly approach, we aspire to create a solution that resonates with everyone, regardless of their financial literacy or background," she said. The product is specifically designed for Americans earning less than $100 000 annually, individuals who diligently contribute to their savings over 30–40 years. "Even saving just one basis point over this timeframe can lead to substantial wealth accumulation," she said, "enabling them to pass on generational wealth to their children and future generations."

She launched the platform in January 2022, and named it Penelope, after her daughter. "I want her to be able to build on the generational wealth I'm handing down to her," she said. "I don't want her to be my retirement plan." Through a low-cost subscription model, Penelope's technology platform provides practical savings tools for employees, and offers the choice of Pooled Employer Plans (PEP), traditional 401(k)s, and Solo 401(k)s. It's a cloud-based 401(k) platform. There are no 30-to-40 page documents with complicated jargon, and the content is brief, to the point, and uses plain English. People have different learning styles, so content is provided as text and videos.

One of the biggest misconceptions is the belief that 401(k) plans are prohibitively expensive. While the cost can be a concern, Penelope leverages government incentives and offers a streamlined approach to make it affordable. Smart points to the Secure 1 and Secure 2.0 legislation, which provides tax credits of up to $16500 for businesses getting started with retirement plans.[7] While many providers employ assets under management pricing, Penelope opts for fair, flat pricing. They charge for the general expense ratios of maintaining and administering the fund, eliminating the costly asset-based pricing accumulating over time. This approach saves employees hundreds of thousands of dollars over their working lives.

Another common myth is about the perceived complexity of investment choices. With more than 6000 funds available, choosing the right ones can be daunting. Penelope takes a straightforward approach by offering index funds based on an employee's birth date, known as target date funds. These funds are managed by a world-class asset manager, ensuring a balanced and safe investment strategy that adjusts with age.

Smart also built the platform to simplify the entire process. Instead of drowning in a sea of questions and options, small business owners only need to answer a few essential questions to get started. "Instead of making you answer 130 questions, we just ask a few questions around eligibility," she said. A big portion of Penelope's plans are what she calls a "safe harbor," which has a matching component. "We do that because that will save small business owners a significant amount of time in administrating and going through auditing and compliance testing down the road," she said. Smart also recognizes the unique challenges faced by immigrant entrepreneurs and built the platform to offer multilingual support while striving to eliminate financial jargon. Ultimately, the goal is to ensure every employee, even at the smallest of companies, has a chance to accumulate a retirement fund.

Smart's passion is to also emphasize the importance of retirement planning for women and women of color who tend to earn less, live longer, and take on primary caregiving roles. It is crucial to start planning early to ensure financial security by making financial planning less intimidating.

While employer-sponsored retirement plans are largely voluntary across much of the country, that reality is changing in some places. In the absence of federal laws requiring employers to offer retirement plans, many states are passing legislation mandating that businesses provide these types of employee benefits. While the number of states that already have such programs in place remains small, at 16, it's important to note that over the past decade, some 47 states have been proactive, either taking steps toward adopting a mandated retirement program or introducing related legislation. This is a significant stride, according to Georgetown University's McCourt School of Public Policy Center for Retirement Initiatives (CRI).[8]

"I'm optimistic that state mandates will provide much-needed support and comfort not only to small, family-run businesses like my parents' but also to start-ups and new ventures," she said. "As the saying goes, the best time to start saving was 20 years ago, the second-best time is today, and the third is tomorrow. There's nothing else."

Penelope has successfully raised $2.1 million in pre-seed fundraising led by Slauson & Co. Additional investors include Amplify LA, Black Jays, and executives from Wells Fargo, Citigroup, and US Bank. But even Smart had to put aside thinking too deeply about how rarely venture capital funding went to female founders to raise her capital.

"If I thought about those numbers, the weight would have stopped me in my tracks," Smart said. Instead, she put in the extra labor required to secure financing: "I took it as a math problem – if I need to have 100 meetings, that's five meetings every day, and I've got to do the LinkedIn search, figure out who knows them, who the decision-maker is," she said. "I thought of it like flipping burgers and told myself to keep flipping them."

As an Asian woman and child of immigrants, it's worth noting how vital Smart's representation is in climbing the corporate ladder and her breakout as a fintech founder who has raised venture capital. Asian women in corporate America typically face the "bamboo ceiling," coined by Asian American career coach Jane Hyun in her 2005 book *Breaking the Bamboo Ceiling: Career Strategies for Asians*. The term is a metaphor for the cultural, organizational, and individual systemic barriers that keep Asian

Americans from attaining career progress and leadership positions. More than 80% of Asian American and Pacific Islander (AAPI) women say the bamboo ceiling effect is real, according to a 2022 study published by the Association of Asian American Investment Managers and co-authored by Backstop Solutions. Additionally, 65% of AAPI women disagree that opportunities for advancement are equitable regardless of race or gender.[9]

To circumvent these barriers, Smart leverages the community's and her network's power to open doors. She's a founding member of Chief and frequents networking events and community gatherings in New York City, where she's based. "You have to get off your computer and meet people in person," she said.

In the next three years, Smart aims to impact our economy by assisting hundreds of thousands of small businesses and empowering a million individuals who have never ventured into the world of stocks or bonds to participate in the capital market space. "Over two decades, I've witnessed the transformative power of investing, even in small increments," she said. "Contrary to popular belief, wealth accumulation isn't merely a stroke of luck or the result of striking it rich in entrepreneurship or cryptocurrency. It's a gradual process that unfolds over generations."

In 2024, Smart announced Penelope was expanding into the third-party administrator space with white-label retirement plans, in an effort to reach even more small businesses. The platform is also expanding into recordkeeping – a further effort to disrupt the outdated retirement plan industry. Legacy recordkeeping platforms are clunky and expensive, and this corner of the retirement industry has been woefully slow to evolve. Penelope is looking to reinvent retirement recordkeeping the same way they have reinvented 401(k) plans – with an eye toward ease and accessibility through fintech.

At the heart of it all, her vision is about reducing financial, psychological, and emotional human suffering. Money can evoke strong emotions, and navigating the complexities of business and finance can be daunting.

Yet, by implementing sound financial practices, individuals can alleviate these burdens and progress toward their goals. It's about empowering individuals to take control of their financial futures, one step at a time.

BRIDGES AND TUNNELS

Sofiat Abdulrazaaq believes that technology can be a game-changer for communities financially. Her drive comes partly from witnessing her father's struggles as a Nigerian immigrant whose business faced overwhelming complexities. "Running a business takes complex staffing and management that small businesses often don't have the time and resources for," she says.

Inspired by her parents' immigrant experiences coupled with her passion for the way food brings together cultural experiences, Abdulrazaaq identified a significant market opportunity for a fintech solution: food trucks. "There aren't always many African or Caribbean food options in restaurants," she noted. "But there are many authentic cuisines in the food-truck communities." Immigrants largely run the food truck industry; in fact, they make up 51% of food truck vendors, according to a 2015 report by the Institute for Justice.[10] Food trucks also have lower start-up costs than brick-and-mortar restaurants, offer flexibility to move to different locations, and have lower operational risks to help mitigate financial risks. Ultimately, they provide a platform for immigrants to start businesses and share their culinary heritage with a diverse audience by introducing unique, authentic dishes from their home countries, creating a niche market with consumers interested in diverse food experiences. It's hard work, but the market size of the US food truck industry was reportedly $1.4 billion in 2023.[11]

Abdulrazaaq had a hunch that food trucks were a goldmine for fintech. But before venturing into entrepreneurship, she learned the importance of resilience and perseverance from the strong women in her life.

"In life, there are situations, places, and moments that will accelerate your career," she told me. "These are bridges. And there are things, businesses, and moments you have to struggle and persevere through – these are tunnels. On the other side of both lies opportunity."

Abdulrazaaq's first tunnel was in college, where she graduated with double majors in Political Science and Psychology from Virginia Tech and met her future co-founders, Lemaire Stewart and Kyle Miller.

In 2007, while at Virginia Tech, Abdulrazaaq endured the trauma of a mass school shooting, losing friends and classmates and grappling with survivor's guilt. "It gave me a thirst for life, a passion for life," she said on my podcast *Humans of Fintech*. Traumatic experiences like that "fuel you to start feeling like, hey, maybe I'm here because of a responsibility to share the stories of those I lost," she said.

Despite this tragedy, Abdulrazaaq pressed forward, graduating from Virginia Tech, earning a Master's Degree in Global Affairs from the University of Denver, and a Juris Doctorate from American University Washington College of Law. *(What, like it's hard?)*

After school, she lived a comfortable life as a corporate girlie for a few years before becoming a fintech start-up founder. She landed a job at Wells Fargo, working under another woman as her executive assistant. Although Abdulrazaaq was hired as an EA, her boss never treated her like one. Instead, she took Abdulrazaaq on business trips, involved her in business deals, and enrolled her in managerial classes. Eventually, the woman executive gave Abdulrazaaq her first management job. One day, Abdulrazaaq asked, "Why are you doing all this?" Her boss replied that she felt a responsibility to invest in her as a successful woman in finance and to pay it forward. She wanted to pour energy and effort into the next generation of female leaders.

Working at Wells Fargo was a bridge. So, when the fintech industry came calling, and a friend pitched the idea of combining finance with social impact, it meant leaving the comfortable life she had grown accustomed to in order to become something more for others.

In January 2019, she jumped into entrepreneurship by launching Goodfynd as CEO, alongside her co-founders. The start-up began from their love of good food and a passion for tackling the challenge of keeping track of their favorite food trucks. Initially building an app for this purpose, Abdulrazaaq soon realized food trucks needed broader support, particularly a tech stack tailored for their financial needs. So, she developed Goodfynd as a payments platform and marketplace for food trucks and mobile vendors, addressing the most critical component of the small business: payments. Through fintech, she provides mobile small business owners with essential financial tools via an easy-to-use payments platform that helps them scale. After launching, Goodfynd quickly gained traction.

Then, COVID-19 struck. The food market where they operated had to close due to CDC guidelines. "We went home and thought our business was over," Abdulrazaaq told *Forbes*.[12] "People weren't even going out to get takeout. We just wasted six months developing something that now has no merit."

However, new guidelines for consumer-facing businesses soon emerged. Food trucks, able to operate within these guidelines, saw business quickly ramp up as they became one of the few safe dining options. Food trucks could take advantage of lower overheads and the ability to be mobile in response to the increased demand for ready-made food. What could've been a fatal blow to their business turned into an opportunity – yet they needed capital.

In a landscape where Black founders in the US raised only 0.48% of all venture dollars in 2023,[13] Abdulrazaaq and her partners faced not only the pandemic but systemic oppression on top of the usual start-up hurdles. Despite the odds, they succeeded in raising $1.8 million in a round led by Diana Murakhovskaya of The Artemis Fund. Abdulrazaaq recalled feeling unprepared for the investor call, thinking it was an informal introduction. "She asked the toughest questions," Abdulrazaaq said. "I felt unprepared and thought I had blown it. But there was a great vibe, and at the end of the conversation, [Diana] said she would talk to her partners." The rest, as they say, is history.

As CEO, Abdulrazaaq leverages technology to help women, people of color, and immigrants – who often face language barriers and unique obstacles – succeed in the food-truck industry. Goodfynd's user base is notably diverse: 34% are Latinx, 31% are Black, 20% are Asian and Pacific Islander, and 15% are white immigrants.[14]

Food trucks are a powerful catalyst for economic growth in cities across the US, with community engagement being a cornerstone of the industry's success. These mobile eateries frequently source their ingredients from local producers and suppliers, providing essential support to local agriculture and businesses. This practice not only bolsters the local economy but also strengthens the bond between food truck operators and the community, fostering a sense of shared purpose and mutual benefit.[15]

Goodfynd offers comprehensive support through various software-as-a-service tools, aiding payment processing, operations management, supply-chain security, and inventory control. For instance, its inventory-management feature prevents overselling by linking sales to stock quantities. This technology addresses specific needs of mobile entrepreneurs, including food preparation, supply procurement, tax management, language barriers, and industry insights. Goodfynd goes the extra mile by providing one-on-one support, offering tools and assistance in both English and Spanish, and plans to expand to other languages.

Food-truck owners also face the challenge of frequent menu updates. Abdulrazaaq designed Goodfynd's menu feature to enable easy electronic uploads and changes, enabling vendors to adapt swiftly to trends or events. One day a food truck might cater to taco enthusiasts at an art festival, and the next, serve burgers at a corporate affair.

Goodfynd also delivers data on customer behaviors, trends, event schedules, and other foot traffic-related metrics. This helps food-truck owners make informed decisions about parking and operating hours, crucial for sales performance. A 2022 study by Elsevier highlighted location as a key challenge for food-truck owners, impacting customer targeting, exposure, and financial sustainability.[16] However, today owners can use technology to attract hungry people. The integration of QR codes and automated emails enhances customer relationships and fosters loyalty to drive the foot traffic needed to turn a profit. QR codes facilitate payments, while email updates inform customers about upcoming locations and menu changes.

As Abdulrazaaq continues to grow and carve her lane in fintech, her journey is a testament to turning life's "tunnels" into "bridges" into opportunity. As for the future of women in fintech? She confidently states, "I have never met a badass woman in my life who squanders opportunity."

GROWING OUT OF BUSINESS

In the fall of 2010, Lara Hodgson received word that any small business owner would be elated to hear – a global retailer wanted to buy 1500 units of the product she and her business partner, Stacey Abrams, invented to help busy parents feed their babies. Their company, Nourish, manufactures spill-proof baby bottles filled with pre-measured purified water, making it easy to mix formula. The deal would take Nourish, their scrappy small business, to the next level.[17]

However, they ran into a major problem when they finally realized they would need a significant capital investment to make this deal happen. To manufacture that much product, 20 times their typical order, they would need to automate equipment and pay their suppliers – expenses they couldn't afford without payment upfront from the retailer. It was the first time Hodgson had learned that more prominent buyers could take advantage of their status and take longer to pay. The retailer wanted a net 30 payment term, meaning it wouldn't have to pay Nourish until 30 days after they shipped the 1500 bottles. They tried everything, including negotiating with suppliers, vendors, and investors. The Great Recession was still in the background then, and getting a high-interest bank loan wasn't the answer.

By May 2011, Hodgson and Abrams decided to let the opportunity go and ultimately shuttered Nourish a few years later. The duo officially *grew out of business*, Hodgson told me in an interview for my podcast. It's the harsh reality for small businesses. There are those bleak statistics that "90% of start-ups fail," and as women and minority-led businesses, securing the capital needed is exceedingly difficult. Diverse-owned firms are more likely to be denied bank loans and to pay higher interest rates for credit. Women-owned ventures account for just 16% of conventional small-business loans and 17% of SBA loans, even though female-owned firms make up a third of all small companies in the US.[18]

Hodgson had more questions, too. Why was this the status quo? Why did no one seem to think it was a big deal? And why was no one bothered to create a better solution in a country that calls small businesses the backbone of the economy?

Small businesses with 500 employees or fewer make up 99.9% of all US businesses and 99.7% of firms with paid employees, according to the US Small Business Association (SBA).[19] Of the new jobs created between 1995 and 2020, small businesses accounted for 62% – 12.7 million compared to 7.9 million by large enterprises. A 2019 SBA report found that small businesses accounted for 44% of US economic activity.[20] The American economy and workforce would be essentially nonexistent without small businesses.

To solve their pain as small business owners who had to close their growing business due to capital constraints, Hodgson and Abrams co-founded Now Corp. This business-to-business financing solution lets small business owners get paid for invoices immediately, with low, flat-rate fees while building up their credit and outsourcing the time-consuming task of tracking down payments. Since its inception in 2010, Now has fast-tracked almost $1 billion in costs for nearly 1000 businesses and doubled in growth in the past two years.

This level of innovation comes from a longstanding partnership with Hodgson and Abrams, who met in 2004 during a leadership program in Atlanta. During a workshop, the facilitator had researched the attendees beforehand and aimed to target their insecurities, Hodgson told me. The goal was to prompt deeper conversations about biases. Despite being an extrovert who loves to talk, the facilitator did not allow her to speak.

"At the end of the weekend, he told me he needed me to know what it felt like to have no voice," she said. "I did *not* like that." This experience proved significant for her and impacted how she views the importance of giving a voice to those who may not have one. Abrams, an introvert, was constantly pressured to speak by the facilitator, who eventually asked her to share her greatest ambition. "She said she wanted to be president of the United States," Hodgson recalled. "I remember thinking, I always said that as a little girl, and girls don't say that out loud." Hodgson made a beeline for Abrams when they broke for lunch in the buffet line. They became friends, and a couple of years later, they founded a consulting company together, using Hodgson's business connections and Abrams's knowledge of local tax law. Then, they founded Nourish.

That brings us back to 2010 when Hodgson and Abrams identified a massive problem in financial services that only fintech could solve. As a small business owner, when you're suddenly asked to place a large sum of money upfront for production, you might struggle to find suitable options. Traditional bridge-funding solutions such as a bank loan or invoice factoring can be inaccessible or predatory. Small business owners with poor credit or those who are uncomfortable with personal guarantees may find it difficult to obtain bank loans. On the other hand, recourse-factoring companies that buy invoices from small businesses charge variable fees and additional accruing fees for late payments, which are often unpredictable and out of the businesses' control. Moreover, they usually use invasive tactics such as collecting money from the business's bank account daily or weekly. If a payment falls through, the small business is liable for the full payment plus late fees, which leaves a liability on its balance sheet for months. To both women, this situation just felt wrong. They knew they couldn't be the first entrepreneurs to find themselves suddenly growing out of business. So Hodgson and Abrams created something for small businesses that was even easier and less risky than being paid with a credit card.

This idea eventually became NowAccount (Now): Small businesses would apply to be Now's clients and pay an annual membership fee of $750.[21] When clients receive an invoice from a new buyer, Now would assess the buyer's risk, and if they approved, the client could start uploading invoices. Now would vet each invoice, then pay the client the total amount almost immediately, minus a flat fee based on the payment terms (ranging incrementally from 3% for a net 15 invoice to 8% for a net 120 invoice). And Now would be reimbursed when the payment is made. This would shrink the payment schedule from a few months to a few days.

In the case of Nourish, it would have looked something like this: If the global retailer placed an order of, say, $50 000 worth of goods from Nourish, with 30-day payment terms, Nourish would take that invoice to NowAccount, who would confirm its validity with the retailer, and then pay Nourish $50 000 right away (minus the 7% fee for a net 30 invoice). Then, Now would be reimbursed whenever the retailer paid.

For a small business owner, this setup has numerous advantages: No added interest for late payments you can't control, no liability on your balance sheet, no unforgiving credit checks or invasive debt collection strategies, and no personal guarantees. Unlike factoring companies, which hold you responsible if a payment falls through, NowAccount absorbs the risk of every invoice it accepts. In this way, Now acts as a kind of insurance for their clients. Hodgson knew this concept was groundbreaking.

But it wasn't quite resonating with investors at the start. There was also some confusion about why this was even a problem from the finance side. What's stopping any small business owner from going to their local bank to get a loan at a lower annual interest rate or negotiating better terms with their factoring company or buyer?

Financial institutions often overlook the countless variable barriers for small business owners. Many are becoming entrepreneurs for the first time, figuring it out as they go without much financial education or resources. Plus, a large portion of small business owners are women and people of color, who regularly are denied loans based on algorithmic biases. Slowly but surely, investors began to hear Hodgson and Abrams's message. First came credit unions, then equity investors, and finally, Goldman Sachs.

Then, in 2020, the George Floyd protests happened, and corporations nationwide started making public pledges to spend more with minority-owned businesses. At that point, Hodgson realized they were sitting on a goldmine of data. Sure, plenty of business databases are out there – but only Now has years' worth of invoice data, giving them visibility into which suppliers can deliver at what level. What if they created a curated platform that helped big businesses find diverse suppliers to meet their needs? Small businesses would be free to join, while big companies would pay a membership fee. And that's how the next Now product – NowNetwork – was born. This network aims to bridge the gap for small and underrepresented business owners, connecting them with customers they may not have had access to otherwise. "Our vision is to leverage the expansive network we've built through NowAccount to facilitate these connections, curating meaningful interactions between businesses and consumers," Hodgson said. "By facilitating these connections, we not only expedite payment processes but also open doors for growth and expansion." Hodgson believes that by supporting the development of small businesses, we can foster generational wealth and create lasting value for our communities. "That's the ultimate goal driving our efforts," she said.

A lot has happened since Hodgson and Abrams founded Now in 2010. Abrams kept working at NowAccount during her tenure in the Georgia House of Representatives but left the company in 2016 to pursue those two runs for governor. After that, she and Hodgson decided that NowAccount and NowNetwork should be separate companies acting as partners with service agreements. Hodgson runs NowAccount, and Abrams runs NowNetwork.

AN OUTSIDER'S FRESH PERSPECTIVE

Hodgson attributes much of her success to her outsider perspective as an entrepreneur without a finance background. "I don't come from fintech – I accidentally got into it – but that brings such a beautifully diverse set of perspectives," she said, reflecting on her journey. "Some empathy comes from realizing that innovation always comes from the demand side of a problem, not the supply side."

Hodgson's path to fintech was one of having a problem that no one could solve. Approaching an industry from the perspective of someone who has suffered from that same problem builds empathy, which is the ability to put yourself in the other party's shoes and understand what they're going through viscerally.

Hodgson's path started as an engineer. She's an aerospace engineer by training, but she quickly realized that while she loved the problem-solving aspect of engineering, she is ultimately a people person. "The idea of spending the rest of my life in a lab designing wings did not fit my personality," she said.

When Hodgson and Abrams started NowAccount, people would look at the two and scratch their heads. Neither of the entrepreneurs are bankers, so there was always the question of how they got into fintech. That level of doubt became the fuel Hodgson needed to realize that our differences are a superpower. As an entrepreneur, having two diverse perspectives as founders outside of industry norms proved to other female entrepreneurs that it's not about what you know; it's about what you notice. As business partners, Hodgson shares that Abrams brings her a ton of balance, and vice versa.

"There are times when something will go wrong," she said. "Having a partner allows you to see your blind side; I wouldn't have noticed if she hadn't been there. If she hadn't brought it up, I wouldn't have noticed. And so having that partner that can sort listening while you're talking to say, I noticed this, we need to address it. You can't put a price tag on that. It's invaluable."

Finding the right business partner can be challenging, but building a network is the only way to do it. "I believe your network is your net worth," Hodgson told me. "A lot of people, unfortunately, think, "Well, I'm not born into a network. I wasn't born with a network; I don't have parents that worked in influential positions." But Abrams wasn't born with a network either. So, they both had to start from scratch. What do they do best? Lean on each other's strengths. Hodgson is the talker – she just loves to meet people. And Abrams is the best listener you've ever met; she can sit in a room, listen to other conversations, and extract invaluable insights from it. "So together, we are unbeatable," Hodgson said. "So, just having the ability to be curious about people and not judge their value based on their title or where you know them from," Hodgson said. "Every person you meet in a day can add value to your network; you just have to give them a chance."

That type of opportunity makes Hodgson so excited to build in fintech. It's the only industry that touches every single person. "The world of finance doesn't touch everybody," Hodgson said. "Nobody wakes up Monday morning and says, I'll get a loan for fun." But fintech includes things like payments; payments touch every single person, whether you like it or not; you buy things, sell things, and engage in some form of a payment transaction. And because it's so prolific, it democratizes the movement of money. From that perspective, fintech, especially in the payment space, has the potential to be a great equalizer. It can give every person on this planet who buys and sells anything equal access to those types of transactions. "But the only way to do that is to unthink how we used to think about it," she said.

It's how Hodgson came up with the idea of NowAccount. Because she and Abrams weren't in finance, they asked simple questions like, "Why can't we just get paid faster?" That's how two non-finance people can build a fintech company by understanding the problem, being empathetic, and asking straightforward questions. "If you come from outside the industry, you have the greatest skill set you could ever have," Hodgson said. "Which is a fresh perspective." Don't do yourself a disservice by thinking that coming from the outside is a negative or a challenge to be overcome. Coming from the outside is what makes you valuable.

"So don't lose that outside perspective, that curiosity, that willingness to ask a question that you think everyone might think is stupid," Hodgson said. "It is the best question you could ever ask." Hodgson would say the challenge for the whole industry is that we have an unprecedented opportunity to be the great equalizer, to level the playing field for underrepresented businesses and underrepresented individuals, and to truly allow the economy to level up in a way that's inclusive of everyone. "We have that opportunity, and it's lucrative, so let's not kid ourselves," she said. "This is not an industry of nonprofits. We can make incredible value, but with opportunity comes responsibility."

As a fintech industry, we must feel the burden of driving inclusive innovation. And that's not easy. We often think we're being inclusive because we're including one group that wasn't included before. But if including one group means excluding another group, that's not innovation. So, we have to challenge our creativity. "I'll give you an example," Hodgson said. "When we first introduced NowAccount and engaged with leaders in the fintech sector, such as Intuit, we were initially fixated on showcasing the sophistication of our technology." However, other fintech companies found it genuinely remarkable that they could seamlessly integrate advanced technology with the option for customers to submit paper checks. "At first glance, this might not seem particularly high-tech; it might even evoke memories of traditional finance companies from decades past," Hodgson said. "However, our decision to offer this option was driven by a simple reality: not all small businesses can handle advanced electronic payment methods like automated clearing house (ACH), wire transfers, or electronic data interchange (EDI)." Ultimately, many small businesses still rely on paper-based processes, especially in environments like job sites where digital tools may not be readily accessible. Knowing this made Hodgson an even more formidable start-up founder. Some of the most significant innovations arise during times of crisis or in bear markets. When resources are scarce, creativity thrives, and individuals are compelled to find new and innovative solutions to overcome challenges. In contrast, having unlimited resources can often stifle creativity because there's less need to think outside the box to achieve success.

It's easy to overlook the opportunities presented by challenging times, but these are the moments when the playing field is leveled. During times of abundance, there's less urgency to innovate or adapt because things are already going smoothly. However, when faced with adversity, individuals and businesses are pushed to innovate and find ways to thrive despite the challenges.

Hodgson and Abrams co-authored and named their book *Level Up* with these principles and learning lessons in mind. "We firmly believe that true progress comes from lifting others, not pushing them down," Hodgson shared. "By empowering everyone to succeed and leveling the playing field, we can create a more equitable and prosperous society where everyone benefits."

When Hodgson and Abrams first launched Nourish, they faced challenges accessing capital because they didn't fit the mold of a typical high-tech start-up. Despite being in Atlanta, near the heart of the beverage industry, the duo encountered skepticism about their venture's potential. This narrow focus on specific sectors or types of companies as the epitome of entrepreneurship perpetuates a hierarchy where those outside the norm are marginalized. We need to dismantle this mindset and recognize the value in all types of entrepreneurs, whether following childhood dreams or starting of necessity. Whether it's a cookie company or a fintech start-up, entrepreneurship comes in many forms, and we must be inclusive of all ages, identities, and backgrounds.

Expanding our aperture to embrace diverse perspectives fosters a more equitable ecosystem and fuels market growth. "I challenge my own company to prioritize diversity and inclusion, both in hiring practices and everyday interactions," Hodgson said. "Surrounding ourselves with people who offer different viewpoints enriches our decision-making and strengthens our collective potential."

As leaders in the fintech industry, we are responsible for leveraging our influence for positive change. By advocating for inclusivity, we can shape a narrative that celebrates diversity and empowers all entrepreneurs to thrive. It's not just about doing what's right; it's about harnessing the full spectrum of talent and innovation for the benefit of everyone.

MONEY CIRCLES

Tapping into the power of community might seem like a new idea in American fintech, but many non-Western countries have been using community accountability to boost their financial well-being for centuries.

In various regions, these community systems have different names: "Tanda" in Mexico, "Susu" in Ghana, and "Chits" in India, fintech founder Nina Mohanty explained to me. They all operate on the same basic principle. Officially known as Rotating Savings and Credit Associations (ROSCAs), these groups agree to save a certain amount of money regularly, and each month, the pooled sum is given to a different member until everyone has received it once. ROSCAs are informal, democratic, and locally owned, aiming to strengthen community bonds and local economies.

The idea is to sidestep traditional banking systems. In both the US and the UK, many immigrants face barriers when accessing credit and financial services. These obstacles include discrimination, language barriers, limited credit history, and unfamiliarity with local banking systems.

The beauty of the ROSCA system is that it allows people to manage their finances with those they trust, whether based on ethnicity, nationality, or shared financial goals like buying a house. Mohanty's start-up, Bloom Money, aims to digitize this process.

ROSCAs unite communities by creating financial support networks where members save and lend among themselves. With Bloom Money, Mohanty is leveraging immigrants' natural inclination to seek community support to initiate cycles of building wealth with tools tailored to their specific needs.

Not all of us want to discuss money with a stranger to whom we pay a fee to make us more. Some of us would instead share the involuntarily high-profile role money plays in our lives with a community of others with shared experiences.

Growing up in Silicon Valley as the daughter of an Indian father and Taiwanese mother, Mohanty saw firsthand the struggles immigrants face in achieving financial stability. She experienced these challenges herself after moving to the UK, realizing just how tough it can be for immigrants to set up financially. Mohanty saw not just an economic justice issue but also a significant business opportunity in addressing these challenges.

In 2021, Mohanty founded her UK-based fintech start-up. By November 2023, the company had raised £1 million in funding, with a cap table nearly 70% women, almost 50% from minority backgrounds, and about half first or second-generation immigrants. Available on Google

Play and soon on the Apple Store, the Bloom Money app allows users to set up and manage savings clubs, or "Bloom Circles," directly from their phones. Users can invite up to 10 friends to join their clubs, all protected by secure anti-fraud measures. The app also offers educational resources on living in the UK, including explanations of credit scores.

Mohanty's journey into fintech began at companies like MasterCard, Starling Bank, and Klarna, where she noticed that products aimed at immigrants often focused on remittances. While remittances are vital – they represent the largest source of foreign income for many developing countries – they don't address the need for wealth-building opportunities within immigrant communities.[22] "My parents' experience highlighted this gap," Mohanty said, noting that her family's foresight in seeking financial advice helped them avoid student loan debt, a privilege not afforded to many immigrants.

Bloom Money emerged from the realization that while cultural practices vary, certain financial behaviors, such as group savings, are common across immigrant cultures. These practices, rooted in community ties, offer a chance for tailored financial solutions often overlooked by mainstream banks. "By digitizing group savings with Bloom Circles, we're not just meeting immediate needs but also paving the way for credit-building and potential lending products," she said.

Mohanty used to discuss Bloom Money's market potential in broad terms, focusing on the global migrant population, which makes up about 3.5% of the world's population.[23] "But I've realized that what really resonates about Bloom Money is its deeply personal nature," she said. For example, "growing up in Silicon Valley, I experienced a scarcity mindset and a sense of duty to send money back to India. This experience mirrors that of many others with similar backgrounds."

For Mohanty, the concept of "building your perfect customer" means recognizing that today's underserved immigrant communities are tomorrow's prime customers. This mindset opens up possibilities, from addressing specific needs like immigration or legal fees to supporting small businesses. The opportunity here is immense, far beyond the scope of traditional banking audiences. "I hope the incumbents are paying attention," she said. "We're coming for their immigrant customers."

Despite the financial system's significant flaws, Mohanty believes we are at a pivotal moment in fintech, where the potential to cater to specific communities has never been greater. Many fintech companies still use a "one-size-fits-all" approach, offering superficial customizations like niche cashback offers, but they often fail to address fundamental issues.

The real opportunity in fintech lies in understanding the unique behaviors and needs of underserved communities. Immigrants, for instance, face the daunting task of rebuilding their lives in foreign countries, leading to financial needs vastly different from those of native-born individuals. This gap remains largely unaddressed by traditional financial systems, but Mohanty is working on it.

Looking ahead, she hopes to see much more diversity in fintech, from the founders and operators to the economic problems being solved. "We don't want to cater solely to high-net-worth individuals; they're already well-served," she said. From her perspective, Bloom Money's strength, and resilience to handle changing markets as a start-up, comes from its diverse team – 71% from first- or second-generation immigrant backgrounds. "We even have a team member born in a refugee camp, whose insights have been invaluable," she said.

Innovation lies in the details and diversity of the data. In the early stages of building Bloom Money, the start-up's culturally diverse data scientists used their networks to reach their target customer. "Our data is authentic and representative, grounded in real experiences," she said. That's because the product's leadership team shares lived experiences with the user base they're targeting.

Mohanty has strong conviction in her start-up, focusing on diversity from all angles – from her team to her target audience to the product development. "Diversity brings fresh perspectives to our vision," she shared.

"It helps us identify issues and opportunities, guiding our product roadmap, commercial strategy, and core values." This diversity-driven growth is set to deliver superior products that resonate with a broader audience.

To maximize their reach further, fintech founders can expand their focus beyond America and Europe and explore opportunities in Asia, a market with the largest population of underserved consumers.

NOTES

1. Fidelity Investments. It's Time to Change Your Mind about Young Investors. Accessed May 20, 2024. https://clearingcustody.fidelity.com/app/proxy/content?literatureURL=/9907600.PDF.
2. Perez, Sarah. "Gen Z Investing App Alinea Raises $3.4M, Plans to Launch an AI Copilot." TechCrunch, January 24, 2024. Accessed May 20, 2024. https://techcrunch.com/2024/01/24/gen-z-investing-app-alinea-raises-3-4m-plans-to-launch-an-ai-copilot/.
3. U.S. Small Business Administration. "Frequently Asked Questions about Small Business 2023." March 7, 2023. Accessed May 20, 2024. https://advocacy.sba.gov/2023/03/07/frequently-asked-questions-about-small-business-2023.
4. American Economic Association. "2022 Study by the American Economic Association." Accessed May 20, 2024. https://www.aeaweb.org/articles?id=10.1257/aeri.20200588.
5. New American Economy. "New Data Shows Immigrant-Owned Businesses Employed 8 Million Americans, Immigrants Wield $1.1 Trillion in Spending Power." Accessed May 20, 2024. https://www.newamericaneconomy.org/uncategorized/new-data-shows-immigrant-owned-businesses-employed-8-million-americans-immigrants-wield-1-1-trillion-in-spending-power.
6. Center for the Study of Hate and Extremism. "Report to the Nation: Anti-Asian Hate." April 30, 2021. Accessed May 20, 2024. https://www.csusb.edu/sites/default/files/Report%20to%20the%20Nation%20-%20Anti-Asian%20Hate%202020%20Final%20Draft%20-%20As%20of%20Apr%2030%202021%206%20PM%20corrected.pdf.
7. Human Interest. "Secure Act 2.0: Understanding Proposed Legislation Securing a Strong Retirement Act." Accessed May 20, 2024. https://humaninterest.com/learn/articles/secure-act-2-understanding-proposed-legislation-securing-a-strong-retirement-act.

8. Georgetown University McCourt School of Public Policy Center for Retirement Initiatives. "States' Retirement Initiatives." Accessed May 20, 2024. https://cri.georgetown.edu/states.

9. Association of Asian American Investment Managers. "New AAAIM Study: 80% of AAPI Women Say Bamboo Ceiling Effect Is Real." Accessed May 20, 2024. https://aaaim.org/new-aaaim-study-80-of-aapi-women-say-bamboo-ceiling-effect-is-real/.

10. Institute for Justice. Upwardly Mobile: How Occupational Licensing Hinders Immigrant Entrepreneurs and What to Do About It. Accessed May 20, 2024. https://ij.org/report/upwardly-mobile/.

11. Zippia. "Food Truck Statistics." Accessed May 20, 2024. https://www.zippia.com/advice/food-truck-statistics/.

12. Stengel, Geri. "POC-Founded Fintech Raises $1.8M in VC to Help the Food Truck Industry." Forbes, January 26, 2022. Accessed May 20, 2024. https://www.forbes.com/sites/geristengel/2022/01/26/poc-founded-fintech-raise-18m-in-vc-to-help-the-food-truck-industry.

13. Davis, Dominic-Madori. "Stay Up-to-Date on the Amount of Venture Dollars Going to Underrepresented Founders." TechCrunch, March 1, 2024. Accessed May 20, 2024. https://techcrunch.com/2024/03/01/stay-up-to-date-on-the-amount-of-venture-dollars-going-to-underrepresented-founders/.

14. Business Insider. "How Cloud-Based POS Are Helping Marginalized Food Truck Owners." September 2023. Accessed May 20, 2024. https://www.businessinsider.com/how-cloud-based-pos-are-helping-marginalized-food-truck-owners-2023-9.

15. Food Truck Club. "The Food Truck Economy: Impact on Local Communities." Accessed May 20, 2024. https://foodtruckclub.com/the-food-truck-economy-impact-on-local-communities/.

16. Lichy, J., Dutot, V., & Kachour, M. (2022). When technology leads social business: Food truck innovation. Technological forecasting and social change, 181, 121775. https://doi.org/10.1016/j.techfore.2022.121775.

17. Abrams, Stacey, Lara Hodgson, and Heather Cabot. Level Up: Rise Above the Hidden Forces Holding Your Business Back. Hardcover. February 22, 2022.

18. U.S. Senate Committee on Small Business & Entrepreneurship. "21st Century Barriers to Women's Entrepreneurship." Accessed May 20, 2024. https://www.sbc.senate.gov/public/_cache/files/3/f/3f954386-f16b-48d2-86ad-698a75e33cc4/F74C2CA266014842F8A3D86C3AB619BA.21st-century-barriers-to-women-s-entrepreneurship-revised-ed.-v.1.pdf.

19. U.S. Small Business Administration. Frequently Asked Questions About Small Business: March 2023. Accessed May 20, 2024. https://advocacy.sba.gov/wp-content/uploads/2023/03/Frequently-Asked-Questions-About-Small-Business-March-2023-508c.pdf.

20. U.S. Small Business Administration. "Small Businesses Generate 44 Percent of U.S. Economic Activity." January 30, 2019. Accessed May 20, 2024. https://advocacy.sba.gov/2019/01/30/small-businesses-generate-44-percent-of-u-s-economic-activity.

21. Now Corp. "Now Corp." Accessed May 20, 2024. https://nowcorp.com.

22. International Monetary Fund. "Remittances." Finance & Development. Accessed May 20, 2024. https://www.imf.org/en/Publications/fandd/issues/Series/Back-to-Basics/Remittances.

23. World Economic Forum. "IOM Global Migration Report: International Migrants 2020." January 2020. Accessed May 20, 2024. https://www.weforum.org/agenda/2020/01/iom-global-migration-report-international-migrants-2020/.

CHAPTER SIX

MAKING FINANCE WORK WORLDWIDE

W hen I first arrived in New Delhi, India, the streets were filled with a chaotic mix of motorcycles, taxi cabs, overcrowded buses, and even the occasional wandering cow. Bicyclists and small businesses sold various goods, including chai tea, spices, jewelry, paintings, and fabrics. I noticed that many of these businesses were run by women, and they played a significant role in driving the local economy. However, even though money was changing hands right outside the doors of the banks, the vast majority of India's 104 million entrepreneurs, or approximately 11.5% of the adult population,[1] have difficulty accessing traditional financial services due to their inability to meet the criteria required by conventional banks. This paradox became increasingly apparent to me during my three-week travels across six different cities in India.

With a population of 1.4 billion, India is home to many individuals without bank accounts who rely solely on cash transactions.[2] The limited access to traditional banking services has left most people with no option but to operate in cash despite having access to mobile phones. However, this has also created an opportunity to tap into an overlooked customer base waiting to embrace digital financial services. Mobile payments have emerged as a proven way to boost financial inclusion for the unbanked and underbanked adults in India, as showcased by the popularity of fintech products like Paytm. Despite this, significant barriers still impede financial inclusion for the 22% of India's adult population who remain unbanked.[3]

According to research, the top issue is physical access – as one of the largest countries in the world, a significant portion of Indian adults, 43%, say that banks are situated too far away.[4] Even if they were closer to financial services, more than 70% of those unbanked in India expressed the need for guidance in utilizing financial services tools. Moreover, women who do not possess bank accounts are 10% more likely to have insufficient financial confidence than their male counterparts. To overcome these hurdles, fintech companies can play an essential role by leveraging digital banking and expanding their services to reach more locations. The industry can do it today largely thanks to a technology that is so pervasive that more than one billion users in India already have it: The mobile phone.

WHEN IN INDIA

To comprehend the global opportunity gap, it is crucial to understand that catering to the worldwide majority is not about their financial capacity to deposit money in a bank account or any other financial services. Instead, it is about the impact of having the right tools to manage their finances effectively, irrespective of their amount, and the ripple effect on our economy when more people have access to financial tools. Imagine the possibility of equipping low-income entrepreneurs in India with the necessary financial tools, such as savings accounts and insurance, to manage their income effectively. It is a fact that many of these entrepreneurs struggle to keep their businesses afloat due to financial constraints. However, if we can digitize their cash transactions and provide them with access to the appropriate digital financial services, like business loans and online payments, the potential for economic growth and empowerment is enormous. We could amplify small businesses' success by billions of people, leading to transformative change in their lives, communities, and the global GDP.

Established in 1979, Women's World Banking has pioneered the promotion of financial services and economic opportunities for women in developing countries like India and globally by leveraging data, research, and technology. The organization has been instrumental in advancing financial inclusion and gender diversity by offering services that enable women to step into their power and take control of their economic destinies. Initially, Women's World Banking focused on microfinance, but over time, it has expanded its scope to encompass financial inclusion, digital finance, and gender diversity within the financial sector. Speaking at TEDxWallStreet in 2013, Women's World Banking President and CEO Mary Ellen Iskenderian shared a UN research team's 11-year study of 600 households in Bangladesh that proved the power of a bank account. "There was a dramatically different outcome where the women had access to a combination of loans, a savings account in their own names, and financial education," Iskenderian said. "Both the women and their daughters vote regularly in local and national elections and even stand for election themselves to the village council." A bank account is, clearly, more than a tool to save money and budget. Banking ultimately enables women to speak up, represent themselves, and take responsibility for their advancement.[5]

In that light, Women's World Banking's mission is clear: to equip women with tools and resources to nurture their businesses, secure their futures, and invest in themselves and their families. Through its partnerships with

74 financial service providers in 34 countries, Women's World Banking has extended a lifeline of opportunity and empowerment to more than 50 million women, as of May 2024. The organization has discovered through its research that a digital footprint of women entrepreneurs can be a proxy for their lack of banking and credit histories and assets. By leveraging this new digital data, Women's World Banking has addressed the needs of women previously excluded from the financial mainstream, providing them access to financial services and opportunities that were once out of reach.

I met Iskenderian during the summer of 2022. At that time, I was actively pitching content to Money20/20, a prominent event in the fintech industry. I proposed a panel titled "Why Financial Inclusion is the Only Thing Keeping Fintech from Failing" to the conference producers. My objective behind this panel was to educate the audience on the crucial role of financial inclusion in promoting economic growth, particularly in developing countries that have been historically underserved. I highlighted the significance of tapping into these sectors of the economy, especially in the face of an impending economic downturn resulting from the pandemic's financial upheaval. Digital payments and contactless cash became invaluable during a global health crisis in these emerging economies. Therefore, engaging with these sectors and promoting financial infrastructure is vital as the time to act is now. The event producers loved it, and I invited Iskenderian to be one of my panelists on stage in Las Vegas.

By October 2022, I was interviewing her live in front of an enthusiastic audience eager to learn about innovative ways to enhance global financial inclusion. The following year, Iskenderian invited me to join the Women's World Banking team in Mumbai. I was thrilled to be a part of the team, where I had the opportunity to contribute to coverage for their flagship event, the Making Finance Work for Women Summit. This experience afforded me invaluable experience of seeing fintech impact a country like India while delving into the insights of the Women's World Banking team's market research expertise and their unwavering commitment to promoting financial inclusion. Working with the nonprofit, I learned that Iskenderian's contribution to the financial inclusion sector spans more than 18 years. Her exceptional leadership skills have driven the organization's mission to bring financial services to the underserved. Her unwavering dedication has made a tangible difference in the lives of millions of people worldwide.

Iskenderian shared with me an interesting data point from research by Oliver Wyman, which highlighted that the banking, insurance, and asset management sectors could generate an additional $700 billion in revenue by providing financial services to women at the same rate as men.[6] This underscores the staggering potential for economic growth through gender equality in the financial services industry. However, achieving this goal is not without its challenges. Globally, women face systemic barriers, as we've discussed, that limit their access to the same opportunities as men.

To help me understand how these systemic barriers are addressed, Iskenderian explained the significance of financial inclusion gaining prominence about a decade ago. At that time, financial inclusion wasn't just limited to microfinance; it encompassed various products and services. She explained that institutions like the International Monetary Fund were initially dismissive of concerns about fostering growth or expanding financial access. However, in recent years, they have recognized the indispensable role of financial inclusion as a macroeconomic driver and have begun emphasizing it as a critical factor in addressing income inequality. This has led to significant regulations and recommendations to governments, particularly around digital financial services.[7]

This is where fintech plays a crucial role for a leader like Iskenderian, who has been on the frontlines of the movement to invest in women's economic power. She told me she is excited about fintech's natural alignment with financial inclusion, particularly in surmounting the barriers that have traditionally excluded low-income entrepreneurs, particularly women, from the economic system. Fintech companies can use alternative data to circumvent these barriers and provide access to financial services to those who have been marginalized.

For example, she shared that in many developing economies, another significant obstacle for people experiencing poverty, especially women, is the lack of real estate or land to offer as collateral for traditional loans. Additionally, legal restrictions in some countries can prevent women from inheriting property or making decisions about property ownership or disposal in their names. Fintech is disrupting this traditional approach by using cash flow or business earnings to assess loan eligibility, empowering individuals who lack conventional assets. Similarly, digital insurance providers are transforming the industry by offering flexible insurance plans that can be replenished as required, similar to top-up a cell phone plan. This convenience and accessibility were previously unheard of, and fintech's innovative solutions are transforming the entire spectrum of financial services. By providing tailored alternatives to suit the unique requirements of the financially underserved, particularly women in impoverished communities, fintech is challenging the status quo and making a significant impact.

In emerging markets, one of the most significant challenges consumers face is the lack of an official form of identification. This issue particularly affects the unbanked and underserved population with limited access to essential financial services. To address this problem, Women's World Banking has amplified fintech start-ups like Paycode, lead by CEO Gabriel Ruhan, which use biometric identity to create affordable access to financial services for those without a physical ID.

Consider the case of a farmer living in Zambia who has never possessed or required a physical ID in her entire life. She earns less than $2 per day and is often robbed of her earnings because she has no secure place to store her money. Fintech start-up Paycode addresses this issue by offering a safe and internet-free way for the unbanked to store their cash using biometrics.

As a result, individuals like the farmer in Zambia can now access financial services for the first time, enabling them to secure their earnings, grow as entrepreneurs, and eventually invest in a more resilient and sustainable future with clean technologies, spearhead environmentally conscious initiatives, and bolster climate resilience. As research shows, when women have access to wealth, they are much more likely to use their wealth to support community associations they care about, invest in social goods, and have an interest in seeing the impact their resources can have. For example, educator Ruth Gottesman gifted $1 billion to the Albert Einstein College of Medicine to provide free tuition to medical students in the Bronx.[8] This indicates how women inheriting wealth can reshape society. However, we're stalled by low-income women not having financial services catered to them. "I've heard it countless times – women expressing that traditional banking isn't tailored to their needs, that it fails to understand them," Iskenderian said. Instead of pushing people out of their comfort zones, successful strategies often involve leveraging existing practices and adapting them to digital or alternative products.

"One particularly effective approach we've seen, notably in Indonesia, is rooted in a longstanding custom: when a woman becomes pregnant, she traditionally saves money with her midwife each month to cover delivery and postnatal care expenses," Iskenderian shared. "We've digitized this process, transforming the midwife into a banking agent within her village."

This provides an additional revenue stream for the midwife and creates a seamless, familiar way for rural women to engage with digital financial services. What's remarkable, Iskenderian said, is the sustained engagement they've observed – the women continue to save and utilize the digital platform long after giving birth. Women's World Banking has proven that we, as an industry, can foster greater inclusion and participation in financial services by meeting customers where they are, demonstrating a genuine understanding of their needs and circumstances, and offering adaptive digital solutions. It's about showing that we are genuinely invested in their lives and committed to making financial services accessible and relevant to them. Instead of forcing communities to retrofit their lives to financial institutions, we shape and mold fintech into their demands and needs.

This establishes something even more important than monetary compensation for underserved communities. It provides a sense of confidence, leading to healthy economic productivity and growth. Imagine having to conduct your life only in cash; it would likely make you feel insecure about investing in your future. How would you keep your money safe from being stolen? And how would you ever save toward longer-term goals such as your children's education, a down payment on a house, or retirement?

As the head of Women's World Banking, Iskenderian witnessed firsthand the transformative impact of access to and, more importantly, control over financial resources. For an individual woman and her family, it means wielding greater decision-making power within the household, potentially reducing vulnerability to domestic violence, increasing political participation, and even fostering leadership ambitions. The ripple effects are profound – empowerment, shifts in power dynamics, and enhanced relationships – simply by providing a secure avenue for savings, efficient money transfer options, fair borrowing opportunities, and comprehensive insurance coverage.

It's important to recognize women as consumers rather than charity cases. Doing so opens up a global market opportunity. Providing people experiencing poverty with the right tools to manage their finances, regardless of their little money, can be incredibly impactful. Currently, three billion people, 40% of the world's population, need access to reliable financial services. These individuals are often referred to as the "unbanked," with more than half of them being female entrepreneurs. There is absolutely nothing "micro" about a market that size, asserted Iskenderian.

When we provide the right tools for people experiencing poverty to manage their money, we offer more than just financial security. We also empower them to dream, plan, and hope for a better future for themselves, their families, and their communities. If we extend this access to the three billion people living in poverty worldwide, the world can look like a different place.

Without an intense focus on women's global financial inclusion, "Women will still be lagging behind men when your daughter's daughter's daughter is born," said Iskenderian. "I'm too impatient for that."

Women's World Banking actively supports financial inclusion by collaborating with fintech companies. There are three main ways in which the organization works with fintech companies to achieve its mission. Firstly, it helps fintech companies develop innovative financial products that cater to the needs of women worldwide. Secondly, it provides access to its network of financial service providers, with extensive experience working with women in different markets. By connecting fintech companies with these institutions, Women's World Banking enables them to build relationships with potential customers and gain valuable insights into women's needs and preferences. Lastly, Women's World Banking promotes gender diversity in the fintech industry, recognizing that women are underrepresented in technology and finance.

Fintech companies with diverse leadership focus on sustainable growth and financial inclusion, which have the potential to close gender gaps and support economic progress faster, particularly in challenging times like today. This is especially significant for women in low-income communities and emerging markets. In the past few years, we have seen a dramatic increase in women's adoption of digital financial services. Based on the 2021 Global Findex Report, for the first time in a decade, the gender gap has decreased from 9% to 6% in key emerging markets, thanks partly to an increased number of low-income women leveraging fintech.[9]

However, on the fintech founder side, the current state of capital providers shows a clear gap when it comes to funneling funds into the hands of women and diverse entrepreneurs actively working to solve the most pressing issues of our economy. This gap results from a disconnect between the pursuit of high returns and rapid business expansion on the one hand and the commitment to inclusion on the other hand. It is crucial to address the root cause of this disconnect. During a conversation with Iskenderian, I asked her how we can help capital providers recognize that promoting inclusivity is socially responsible and beneficial for scaling their businesses. In response, Iskenderian shared that she has encountered numerous fintech leaders and founders who embarked on entrepreneurial journeys driven by a desire for inclusion. They entered the industry to make products or services more accessible and affordable to underserved people. This ethos often resonates during the early fundraising stages, from seed capital to Series A or B rounds.

"But then somewhere when they get to a point where they're raising money that they've gotta scale the folks who are funding them in that part of their journey almost forced them into abandoning that inclusion mission," she said.

As start-ups progress and seek more significant investments to fuel growth, there's a tendency for investors to steer them away from their inclusion-centric narrative. There needs to be more clarity about the distinction between thinking that the return on investment and wanting to grow a business is separate from inclusion. "In later-stage rounds, such as Series B or early Series C, where we've taken the lead, I've been encouraged by the number of investors who share our commitment to gender diversity," she said. "We make it clear that, as Women's World Banking, our investment signifies a dedication to specific gender-focused goals." It's heartening to see investors recognize that while diversity is crucial, a vast untapped market awaits exploration.

Although pursuing inclusion may entail a slightly longer path to scale, Iskenderian is optimistic about the growing number of capital providers willing to embark on this journey. By aligning with investors who prioritize inclusivity, founders can maintain their original mission of inclusion without compromising on their growth trajectory.

Ultimately, organizations like Women's World Banking, which collaborates with fintech solutions, can bridge the gap in financial inclusion by offering innovative and tailored digital financial services to reach the unbanked and underbanked populations. Targeting efforts toward promoting financial inclusion, especially for women, can unlock significant economic potential and drive growth. Partnerships between fintech companies, microfinance institutions, and other financial service providers are crucial in expanding access to financial services.

Aligning with investors who prioritize inclusivity and understand the long-term value of financial inclusion efforts is essential for sustainable growth. Sharing stories of entrepreneurship and resilience can inspire others to pursue inclusive solutions and contribute to closing the gender gap in financial services. Achieving financial inclusion requires collaboration, innovation, and a steadfast commitment to empowering underserved communities, particularly women.

WHY WOMEN ARE THE BEST BORROWERS

In rural India, the daily routine for most women begins with preparing meals for their families using traditional mud *chulhas*. This process takes several hours and is repeated every day. In addition to consuming a significant amount of time, it also has a negative impact on the health of millions of women.

Born and raised in India, Mumbai-based engineer Neha Juneja set out to address these challenges by developing a clean cooking solution with her co-founders Ankit Mathur and Shoeb Kazi. Approximately

500 million people in India lack access to clean cooking options, according to a report by the Centre for Science and Environment (CSE).[10] Biomass fuels, relied upon by 41% of India's population, contribute significantly to carbon dioxide emissions. The smoke from burning these fuels for cooking and heating is a major cause of indoor air pollution in India. The World Health Organization (WHO) estimates that annually, 3.2 million people die prematurely due to illnesses linked to household air pollution from incomplete combustion of solid fuels and kerosene used for cooking.

Between 2010 and 2011, Juneja and her co-founders traveled to more than 30 villages in five Indian states: Punjab, Haryana, Madhya Pradesh, Maharashtra, and Rajasthan. They were on a mission to study and better understand the needs of the local communities and to develop an affordable and portable stove that would make cooking healthier and more efficient for those living in rural areas.

During their extensive research, Juneja and her team designed and tested more than 10 prototypes, taking into account valuable feedback from consumers. The result was the Greenway Smart Stove, a single-burner stove using various solid biomass fuels, including wood, dry dung, crop waste, coconut waste, and bamboo. The stove not only reduces cooking time but also offers the convenience of portability. Since its launch in 2012, Greenway has sold three million cookstoves.

To get those stoves into millions of villages in India, Juneja had to collaborate closely with microfinance operators. Through that experience, she uncovered something most banks or lending institutions overlook – the economic power of low-income female entrepreneurs.

"This collaboration led me to ponder two key questions," she recalled. "Firstly, why aren't more people, especially fintech companies, tapping into this market?" Women borrowers in India, particularly in the microfinance sector, exhibit remarkably low default rates, even lower than those seen in home mortgages. "Moreover, the interest rates generated from these models, averaging around 20–21%, far exceed the national average of 12–14%," she said. So, she questioned why women were subjected to some of the highest interest rates despite being among the most credit-worthy borrowers.

Microfinance loans serve nearly 150 million people living in poverty worldwide, with 80% being women. At the Grameen Bank, the world's largest microfinance institution, more than 90% of loan clients are women – showing that women tend to make payments more reliably than men, and loans in their hands have a greater potential to impact their lives positively.[11] When women have access to credit, the opportunities for their children and the prosperity of their communities increase. Despite facing challenges like lower incomes and occasional breaks in income due to childbearing, women consistently demonstrate their value as borrowers.

It shows that when women entrepreneurs succeed, it's despite the system, not because of it. Worldwide, there's a $1.7 trillion gap between the credit women need and what they can get.[12] Systemic transformation is necessary to close the gap and unlock as much as $6 trillion in global GDP if women entrepreneurs reached parity with men, which would be a monumental boon for the world and cannot be overlooked.[13] Many financial systems were not designed to meet the needs of small borrowers, especially women. Juneja was determined to find a way to capture this market opportunity.

To build her next business model, Juneja was inspired by the success of the microcredit models by the Grameen Bank, pioneered by Nobel laureate Muhammad Yunus. She told me that Grameen Bank created a movement demonstrating how women, often lacking traditional assets or credit history, could unite in joint liability groups. By vouching for each other, they became each other's collateral, enabling them to access capital and build small businesses. This model – which uses the power of the female collective voice – has empowered millions of low-income women by granting them access to affordable credit and capital they need to run their businesses. Through this initiative, women have gained confidence in handling finances and have been trained in responsible borrowing. This approach has been widely adopted in the Global South, benefiting billions of women.

So Juneja thought about how to replicate this model through a fintech start-up with a business model that would showcase women borrowers as having a higher return on investment compared to most traditional asset classes. The microcredit approach challenged the traditional logistics of conventional lending practices, particularly for small loans averaging $1000, which pose challenges for large Indian banks due to high processing fees. Additionally, the complex journey of capital from the bank to the borrower, often involving multiple intermediaries, presents another obstacle. Juneja decided to remove the intermediaries and, in October 2021, laid the foundation of IndiaP2P, a peer-to-peer lending platform to close the credit gap for women entrepreneurs in rural regions of India.

Juneja was confident in the business model because she saw firsthand the daily lives of these female borrowers. "These women typically have the burden of responsibility when it comes to other people's care and other people's money," she said. "This translates into a more prudent and disciplined approach to money matters." This sense of responsibility extends to managing their finances and those of their families.

Through IndiaP2P, investors can lend small amounts, as low as $60, to a handpicked group of borrowers sourced by the platform. Before being selected, these borrowers undergo a rigorous inspection process to verify their creditworthiness. With the help of technology, investors can diversify their investments across multiple borrowers, minimizing risk. The platform effectively manages the complexities of investment diversification and repayment management, making it accessible and cost-effective for investors. Previously, such diversification would have required significant capital, but IndiaP2P enables investors to achieve it with minimal investment. Through this model, IndiaP2P can demonstrate to traditional lenders that women in rural areas are an excellent asset class, capable of paying back loans on time, and are significant contributors to the economy.

When Juneja started raising venture capital for her company after successfully giving an exit to VCs who invested in her previous business, she faced a unique challenge while pitching to investors – convincing them that women borrowers are the best asset class to invest in. Initially, Juneja would begin her pitch by highlighting this fact, but it was not always well-received. To overcome this, she changed her approach and started showcasing data-driven slides that presented compelling statistics about the size of the asset class and the average returns – which in India alone amounts to $80 billion. She would then quiz investors about what they think is India's best asset class before revealing that it's women borrowers. This approach worked wonders in her favor. It turns out that presenting the data first and then unveiling the target customer as women helped investors see the vision more clearly (*go figure*). Despite raising one capital round, Juneja is still on the VC treadmill as an early-stage start-up.

IndiaP2P takes practical approaches to ensuring the creditworthiness of its borrowers. "For example, if someone claims to operate a grocery store, we physically inspect the store's condition and location, as well as assess its foot traffic, to ensure the credibility of their income source," she said. This is an additional step in due diligence that most traditional lenders don't bother to take.

The value of this diligence extends beyond immediate risk mitigation. By gaining insights into how people generate income, Juneja continuously enhances her understanding of various earning patterns and business dynamics. "This ongoing learning process enables us to refine our platform and better serve our users over time," she said.

Ultimately, Juneja's goal with IndiaP2P is to become a multibillion-dollar facilitator of capital for women entrepreneurs. Within the next four to five years, she aims to emerge as the largest facilitator of capital for women entrepreneurs, reaching nearly a quarter of all Indian households. That's a substantial number of families, accounting for about 80 million women, roughly 20% of all Indian households. As a veteran start-up founder, Juneja is confident in her approach. "Lending presents the most straightforward path to reach this ambitious target," she said. "Which is why the roadmap looks exceptionally clear."

That clear vision is helping IndiaP2P stand out from the competition. As a serial entrepreneur, Juneja understands that achieving scale isn't necessarily the biggest hurdle. What truly matters is delivering a differentiated product or service and executing it effectively. Unlike some industries where market size may limit growth, fintech sectors offer ample room for expansion. However, growing as fast as possible isn't a sign of success. Instead, success hinges on being genuinely innovative and executing flawlessly.

"It's worth noting that while it's relatively easy to conceive a fintech idea and even start a company, maintaining momentum and delivering on promises is where many falter," she said. "Execution is key in this fast-paced and competitive landscape. A misstep can quickly derail even the most promising ventures, underscoring the importance of strategic planning and meticulous execution in the sector."

Juneja's approach to IndiaP2P rests on two fundamental pillars. Firstly, she's identified an asset class that is either under-penetrated, underserved, or underfunded. This presents an opportunity for retail investors to earn attractive returns by investing in this asset class. Secondly, her success hinges on disciplined execution as both a lender and an investment facilitator.

"We operate in an environment where risks are inherent, and it's crucial to be forthright about potential drawbacks," she said. "Whether it's borrower defaults or lender losses, we believe in being upfront and transparent about the realities of our business."

This level of honesty requires a high degree of conviction in a founder's mission. Discipline is not just important; it's essential. However, maintaining this level of discipline is no easy feat. It requires unwavering dedication and a willingness to adhere to protocols, even when faced with challenges or temptations to deviate.

How to Stay Disciplined

"As a seasoned founder with previous ventures under my belt, I've had my fair share of experiences, including making mistakes and learning from them along the way," she said. "One of the key lessons I've gleaned is the importance of building a team that prioritizes accountability, transparency, and adherence to processes from the outset."

In forming her initial team for this venture, Juneja made a deliberate effort to bring on board two other co-founders who, like her, possess extensive industry experience and a commitment to their shared vision.

In contrast to her past start-ups, where hiring decisions were influenced by personal resonance, this time around, she's taken a more intentional approach. By being deliberate and cautious in her hiring process, she aims to cultivate a team that is not only capable of executing IndiaP2P's vision but also resilient in the face of challenges and committed to driving her organization forward.

Forming a cohesive team within a young and growing organization involves several vital principles; Juneja shared her blueprint for building successful teams for start-ups.

Firstly, transparency is crucial. Keeping information accessible and avoiding silos ensures that everyone is on the same page, particularly when facing challenges or competition. This fosters a sense of trust and alignment within the team.

Secondly, cultivating a culture of integrity and accountability is essential. This means avoiding shortcuts in all aspects of the business, including hiring practices and customer interactions. Leadership sets the tone, and if shortcuts are taken or wrong actions are condoned, it sets a detrimental example for the entire team.

Thirdly, fostering a healthy work culture is paramount. A relentless "hustle" mentality may seem appealing, but it's ultimately unsustainable and can lead to burnout and diminished productivity. Instead, prioritizing work-life balance and creating an environment where stress is managed effectively contributes to a more sustainable and productive organization.

Additionally, embracing diverse perspectives and feedback is critical for growth. Listening and learning from others is essential rather than becoming defensive in the face of differing opinions. This openness to feedback fosters a culture of continuous improvement and innovation. Juneja also shared that "Building a successful organization requires more than hard work," she said. "It requires a thoughtful approach to team dynamics, culture, and communication."

From addressing the pressing need for clean cooking solutions with Greenway to founding IndiaP2P, Juneja's observations about the potential of women borrowers in the microfinance sector have challenged traditional lending practices and inspired a new wave of financial inclusion.

Juneja's vision for IndiaP2P extends beyond just facilitating loans; it aims to empower millions of women entrepreneurs, close the credit gap, and unlock significant economic potential. Through meticulous execution and a commitment to transparency, Juneja is leading IndiaP2P toward becoming a multibillion-dollar force for positive change in India's financial landscape.

As she navigates the challenges of scaling her venture, Juneja's disciplined approach and dedication to building a solid team underscore her unwavering commitment to success. With IndiaP2P, Juneja is not just creating a business; she's pioneering a movement toward more significant financial equity and empowerment for women across India and changing the future for women worldwide.

SERVING THE GLOBAL MAJORITY

About 2.5 billion adults, half of adults worldwide, do not have a bank account in a formal financial institution. This means they lack essential financial resources like a safe place to save money or gain credit access.[14] In emerging markets, a staggering $2.5 trillion credit gap exists for micro, small, and medium-sized enterprises, which are crucial for the economic advancement of these markets.[15]

Several factors contribute to the exclusion of these entrepreneurs and small businesses, but a core issue is the need for alternative data. For instance, when a consumer or business owner applies for a loan, banks and other legacy financial institutions must check their identification to track their credit history and determine their creditworthiness to repay the loan. The problem with this approach is that nearly 850 million people worldwide lack formal records like an official identification as of the end of 2022.[16] Within low-income countries, 46% of adults cite documentary requirements, 44% mention the distance to registration points, and 40% highlight the prohibitive costs of obtaining an I.D. as reasons for not having one. Globally, approximately one in three adults without an I.D. face challenges in accessing financial services, receiving government financial support, applying for employment, or participating in electoral processes. Even if a small business owner has an I.D., most banks are skeptical of offering them loans because they lack a track record of employment.

However, with fintech, companies can develop alternative data metrics and partner with banks to make access to credit a reality for millions. This will give these individuals purchasing power to grow their businesses, spurring economic activity and increasing global GDP. In that case, it's a massive opportunity – and possible – to open access to millions of new customers to participate in the worldwide economy. Still, someone must step up, start the new cycle, and be willing to take the first risk.

More than 10 years ago, Shivani Siroya set out to tackle the greatest obstacle to global economic progress head-on – the inadequacies of the existing financial infrastructure, which failed to serve the needs of the world's global majority. Early in her career, Siroya took a job with the United Nations Population Fund in 2006, studying the impact of microcredit in sub-Saharan and West African countries and interviewing more than 3500 individuals and entrepreneurs in nine different countries. To fully understand their behaviors around money, she began gathering alternative data by following them to work and tallying their spending and savings habits. "I understood this customer and their daily life," she told me. "I walked in their shoes before lending to them myself."

Through that experience, she discovered how to calculate a new kind of credit score based on cell phone data, like how much someone pays for their cell phone bill or how many remittances they're receiving, among other alternative data points that a phone can acquire. This gives a good sense of consistency in cash inflows and outflows. By spending time with this consumer and fundamentally understanding their daily financial behavior, Siroya uncovered a way to use technology to unlock the potential of millions of credit-worthy borrowers.

So, she started building a fintech company in 2011, named it Tala, and formally launched it in 2014. She developed an Android app that instantly evaluates and understands customers using the data on their mobile devices and delivers personalized and customized financial services in minutes. Tala makes loans of $10 to $500 to customers with little or no formal borrowing history in the Philippines, Mexico, Kenya, and India. It offers a digital wallet in the Philippines, which lets more than one million customers pay bills through the Tala app. It aims to save them money by preventing them from having to cash out and incur fees. In 2023, Siroya and her team rebuilt Tala's data infrastructure to cut the time most customers take to get approved for a loan from two minutes to just a few seconds. Today, millions of people have used Tala products to start and expand small businesses, manage day-to-day needs, and pursue financial goals. The Santa Monica, California–based fintech company has delivered more than $4.5 billion in credit access, reached 9 million customers by the end of 2023, and raised nearly $500 million in debt and equity funding since its inception.

This success results from Siroya's unwavering faith in people and her unyielding focus on building radical trust with customers. "During my nearly five years living and working in emerging markets, I witnessed the immense potential within this segment," she said. "This belief in their purchasing power and untapped potential serves as a driving force for me and underscores what I believe will propel Tala to success."

To build trust, you need to lead with empathy. It's an approach that redefines innovation. While most lenders aren't willing to take the first risk, Siroya built Tala to reframe how financial services perceive risk and value. "Our success hinges on our commitment to building uniquely for this segment – a strategy that sets us apart from others," she said. "When I think about radical trust, I envision a future where we embrace saying 'yes' more often." This philosophy permeates every aspect of Tala's business, from its technology, decision-making processes, and interactions.

Since many of Tala's customers lack traditional data points typically found in credit bureaus or bank databases, such as employment records, Siroya had to devise innovative approaches to understand their financial behavior. "Drawing from my experience of interviewing over 3,500 individuals across nine different countries in emerging markets, I learned the importance of immersing oneself in their daily lives to predict risk accurately," she shared. "We sought to replicate this approach using technology." For example, by leveraging mobile data provided by customers and behavioral data gathered through interactions with customers, Siroya pieced together a comprehensive picture of their daily lives. "The way we assess creditworthiness revolves around tapping into a diverse array of data sources, all of which originate from the customer," she said. Rather than simply amassing data from its customers, Tala aims to provide them with tangible value in return for their data. It's about co-creating data and fostering a mutually beneficial relationship. "Our credit scoring model isn't static; it evolves based on the ongoing interactions and the value we deliver to our customers," she shared.

Instead of solely assessing risk, Siroya focuses on how Tala can continue to create value for every individual within these populations. For Siroya, it's about establishing a customer relationship based on trust rather than expecting it to be automatically granted from the top down.

Given the unique challenges presented by its customer base – such as the predominance of cash transactions in many emerging markets – Siroya had to adopt a multifaceted approach. This involved building various components of Tala from scratch, including KYC, identity verification, fraud detection, proprietary credit scoring models, and interoperable payment systems. The necessity to tackle these multifaceted challenges head-on underscored the importance of diversity in problem-solving and decision-making processes. The diverse perspectives at the company's table have been instrumental in shaping its sustainable business strategy. Ultimately, Siroya built Tala's supply chain and infrastructure to create an ecosystem that starts with telling customers, "We trust you," she said. "Trust is a feedback loop, but somebody has to start it."

It works. Tala's global repayment rate is 90% across first and repeat loans, and 95% of customers repeat and stay with Tala as they graduate to the next financial product offering to continue building their economic lives.

The financial services sector is struggling to establish trust and is ranked among the least trusted industries globally, according to the 2023 Edelman Trust Barometer.[17] The only sector that fares worse than finance in this regard is social media. In sharp contrast, the technology sector enjoys a high level of trust among consumers. However, fintech, which operates at the intersection of finance and technology, faces the challenge of bridging this trust gap. Empathy and human touch must be injected into a world often driven by transactions to achieve this. It is essential to follow the example of those who have realized that success hinges on caring for people. Leaders like Siroya display qualities that can help build trust in the fintech industry.

Women excel in most leadership skills, including taking initiative, resilience, self-development, driving results, and demonstrating high integrity and honesty, according to a 2019 research report in *Harvard Business Review*.[18] Women outperform men in 84% of these competencies measured, including inspiring and motivating others. Women in fintech exemplify this idea, proving that harnessing your purpose to drive innovation is the key to earning the coveted trust of customers.

For Siroya, her purpose in fintech is to do more than drive value from a transactional level. She is not interested in simply showing up for some time, moving the needle slightly, and leaving. That's not financial inclusion. Siroya's purpose is to fundamentally rethink the economic system. "As a mission-driven company working in technology and financial systems, we think about creating legitimacy and proving that this customer is creditworthy," she said. "Ultimately, we want to show that customers' financial health, confidence, and purchasing power increases over time with us."

Like any consumer product company, the more value Tala offers, the stronger the bond with the customer becomes. Therefore, it's incumbent upon the fintech company to provide increasingly tailored experiences, adding benefits and offers to incentivize customers to keep their money in their accounts. "This aspect is particularly thrilling because our initial results indicate that by delving deeper into these customized experiences, we're enhancing customer satisfaction and extending their lifetime value (LTV) with us," Siroya said. It's about creating a compelling business model that fosters long-term customer relationships.

Siroya's company and leadership style showcase how much success and fulfillment can come together when we move off the traditional status quo. If something has been done historically, it's an excellent opportunity to innovate and fill a gap in the market. Despite the numerous macroeconomic factors that have stifled growth for most fintech companies in a post-pandemic era, Tala continues to grow. For Siroya, the company's competitive advantage and resilience also come from how Tala generates revenue. Instead of only focusing on new customers, Siroya understands that the best way to gain scale, along with profits, lies in cementing repeat business with customers, which gives momentum to revenue and cuts down on customer acquisition costs. Tala's approach differs significantly in the realm of credit – the platform refrains from demanding any upfront payments. Under this model, users only pay for what they require, with payment deferred until the end of the term. Moreover, customers are offered clear terms, rates, and pricing aligned with their income with Tala's guidance at every step.

Siroya's commitment extends beyond merely providing credit as Tala strives to introduce a range of products that cater to the diverse needs of its customers. In recent years, the company has evolved to loan originations, bill pay, and other digital services facilitated across its platform. It collects a flat fee, making money off interchange- and transaction-based charges. Additionally, Siroya prioritizes sustainability in Tala's business model. She recognizes the pitfalls of overexpansion, which could jeopardize Tala's ability to serve its clientele effectively in the long run. "Unfortunately, this is a pitfall all too common in the development of financial products – a fintech company introduces innovative solutions only to find themselves unable to sustain them," Siroya told me.

Consequently, customers who have grown accustomed to these offerings are left without access when needed most. To innovate beyond these typical challenges, over the years, Tala can leverage its recurring business from loyal customers to build a treasure trove of data that can add more dimensions to the relationship. Tala uses machine learning and artificial intelligence to apply data across the financial services "supply chain" to personalize offers and fine-tune servicing.

Intentional Focus

On stage in May 2023, during an industry event called Fintech Nexus in New York City, I asked Siroya how Tala can maintain that sustainability when so many other fintech companies are struggling in the current environment. Her initial response was focus. Siroya exemplifies a leader with an intense focus and obsession with the problem she's working to solve. A misstep I often observe in founders I've interviewed is the desire to catch the next wave or shiny new tech tools they can build new products or ideas around. Siroya sticks to the fundamentals, consistently asking herself how to get more purchasing power and credit into the hands of consumers and business owners. "We stayed focused on that," she said. "We said the first thing we need to prove is that credit scoring this population using alternative data is possible."

Ultimately, she had to prove that the customer base was creditworthy and had purchasing power. "Along the way, we ended up creating a unique proprietary platform to deliver financial services to the global majority, and so, as a result, we developed our competitive advantages," she shared. "We now have one of the most interoperable payment systems across three continents. And it was because we stayed focused on the problem that we're solving that we created multiple competitive advantages that we can now build off of."

That's how Tala moved beyond credit to become a complete financial account for its millions of customers. But that transition had its challenges. When deciding to launch its product in the Philippines, Siroya learned a valuable lesson: meet customers where they are. "The Philippines marked a pivotal moment for us, transitioning from a typical

B2C company focused on credit scoring and access to credit to evolving into a platform," she said. "We realized the importance of meeting our customers where they are, necessitating an ecosystem approach." Whether customers were visiting remittance centers to accept money or paying bills elsewhere, Tala needed to be present. The company aimed to empower customers to manage, utilize, and grow their money effectively, requiring a flexible approach that accommodated their diverse needs and preferences. The Philippines' approach compelled Tala to reconsider how its model could adapt and thrive in any market worldwide, particularly those resembling the Philippines.

It's worth highlighting two key factors that contributed to Siroya's success. Firstly, proximity to the problem was crucial. Without intimate knowledge of the challenges faced by its target demographic and their aspirations, Siroya wouldn't have expertly expanded Tala across four countries, three continents, and various underserved segments. "Our global teams, complemented by local talent, immerse themselves in the same environment as our customers, allowing them to understand and address their needs effectively," she said. "This proximity isn't just a matter of team composition; it's ingrained in our leadership and organizational culture."

Secondly, recognizing market gaps and seizing opportunities is paramount. Instead of passively observing, Siroya takes pride in her team's active pursuit of solutions. She says, "The best way to predict the future is to create it." Therefore, Siroya encourages individuals and organizations to engage directly with the problems they aim to solve, embracing a proactive approach to innovation and impact.

Siroya's journey exemplifies a determination to challenge conventional wisdom and reimagine the possibilities for financial inclusion. By leveraging alternative data metrics and pioneering tailored financial products, she aims to empower individuals with the purchasing power and liquidity they need to participate fully in the economic marketplace. Yet, as Siroya herself would likely attest, the journey toward meaningful change requires vision and action – a willingness to step forward and be the catalyst for a new cycle of progress.

Siroya's innovative approach has changed the economic landscape for women worldwide. Tala's customer base is 58% female. "We're helping improve women's lives at the foundational level," Siroya said. "This creates cycles of improvements in families and other areas. When a woman finds value in our services, she's likely to share it with 10 others in her community."

Tala's community-based approach and word-of-mouth referrals are a source of the company's customer acquisition – a testament to the value customers see in the fintech company. This value creation is critical, considering that when we examine global financial inclusion, one stark reality is that women are 16% less likely than men to use the mobile internet. This translates to 264 million fewer women using the mobile internet globally, a significant gender gap that can be addressed when women's financial situations are improved.

Moreover, emerging markets have immense potential to leverage data to construct identities. Traditional identity verification methods may not be feasible for everyone, but by analyzing behavior and relationships, we can develop more inclusive and effective identity solutions. Ultimately, Tala found that 76% of its customers reported improved quality of life, with 80% reporting improved ability to face financial emergencies and increasing self-confidence, according to a 2022 third-party report on their customers commissioned by Tala.[19] That's a much higher percentage than statistics reported in the US, where most (57%) US adults cannot afford a $1000 emergency expense.[20] In addition, more than three in five working Americans feel anxious about their current financial situation, according to Harris Poll research.[21] With access to digital loans, 63% of Tala's customers in the same study reported reduced financial stress. Meanwhile, 58% of women borrowers experienced an increased influence on decision-making; of those, 67% talked about having more economic independence. It's a step in the right direction, proving that fintech solutions are helping women create pathways to wealth.

Women-led fintechs are changing the game by leveraging digital platforms to curate content and tools to deconstruct systemic issues that have made access to financial services typically inaccessible. With the right fintech tools, women can access the same playing field as their male counterparts, empowering them to reach their goals while increasing market share for fintech companies focused on serving them. By allowing more women to participate in financial services, fintech companies are helping create a more equitable world for everyone.

When I asked Siroya what changes in the industry she hopes to see more of, she said she believes we're beginning to see the potential to shape this system to serve everyone better. However, we must shift our focus toward mutual value creation; rather than merely offering more choices, we must empower consumers by placing greater power in their hands. Trusting their ability to navigate this system is vital, but siloed approaches between financial institutions still dominate, hindering progress. Therefore, Siroya is eager to see a surge in collaboration within the industry. That collaboration is how Siroya is stepping into the next phase of Tala's growth.

The key is fostering a partnership mindset. It's not about what "I" or "we" will earn individually, but rather what "we" as a partnership will achieve together. This collaborative approach sets the tone for a mutually beneficial relationship where both parties are invested in creating value and driving impact. It's about recognizing the shared goals and working hand in hand to realize them.

NOTES

1. Markinblog. "How Many Entrepreneurs?" Accessed May 20, 2024. https://www.markinblog.com/how-many-entrepreneurs/.

2. Pew Research Center. "Key Facts as India Surpasses China as the World's Most Populous Country." February 9, 2023. Accessed May 20, 2024. https://www.pewresearch.org/short-reads/2023/02/09/key-facts-as-india-surpasses-china-as-the-worlds-most-populous-country.

3. World Bank. "Financial Inclusion for the 22 Percent of India's Adult Population Who Remain Unbanked." 2021. Accessed May 20, 2024. https://thedocs.worldbank.org/en/doc/4c4fe6db0fd7a7521a70a39ac518d74b-0050062022/original/Findex2021-India-Country-Brief.pdf.

4. World Bank. "Indian Adults, 43 Percent, Say That Banks Are Situated Too Far Away." 2021. Accessed May 20, 2024. https://thedocs.worldbank.org/en/doc/4c4fe6db0fd7a7521a70a39ac518d74b-0050062022/original/Findex2021-India-Country-Brief.pdf.

5. TEDxWallStreet. "TEDxWallStreet 2013." YouTube video, 18:20. Accessed May 20, 2024. https://www.youtube.com/watch?v=bEPyv3JmRWg.

6. Oliver Wyman. "Women as Financial Services Customers." November 2019. Accessed May 20, 2024. https://www.oliverwyman.com/our-expertise/insights/2019/nov/women-as-financial-services-customers.html.

7. Humans of Fintech. "S3 Ep13: Live from Money 20/20: Financial Inclusion Is the Only Thing Keeping Fintech From Failing." Accessed May 20, 2024. https://podcasts.apple.com/us/podcast/s3-ep13-live-from-money-20-20-financial-inclusion-is/id1600731457?i=1000587248068.

8. Associated Press. "Ruth Gottesman Gifted $1 Billion." Accessed May 20, 2024. https://apnews.com/article/free-medical-school-tuition-ruth-gottesman-11eec429784776027161bcd1b6ea1905.

9. Women's World Banking. "Global Findex 2021: Women's World Banking Response." Accessed May 20, 2024. https://www.womensworldbanking.org/insights-and-impact/global-findex-2021-womens-world-banking-response.

10. Center for Science and Environment. "India's Transition to Electric Cooking." Accessed May 20, 2024. https://www.cseindia.org/india-s-transition-to-electric-cooking-12024.

11. Asia Society. "Microfinance and Women: Micro Mystique." Accessed May 20, 2024. https://asiasociety.org/education/microfinance-and-women-micro-mystique.

12. World Bank. "MSME Report: Bridging the Gap." Accessed May 20, 2024. https://documents1.worldbank.org/curated/en/653831510568517947/pdf/121264-WP-PUBLIC-MSMEReportFINAL.pdf.

13. Women's Entrepreneurs Finance Initiative. "The Case for Investment." Accessed May 20, 2024. https://we-fi.org/wp-content/uploads/2022/06/We-Fi-Case-for-Investment.pdf.
14. International Monetary Fund. "Financial Access Survey." Accessed May 20, 2024. https://www.imf.org/external/pubs/ft/fandd/2012/09/picture.htm.
15. World Bank. "MSME Report: Counting the Cost." Accessed May 20, 2024. https://documents1.worldbank.org/curated/en/386141468331458415/pdf/713150WP0Box370rillion0and0counting.pdf.
16. World Bank. "850 Million People Globally Don't Have ID: Why It Matters and What We Can Do About It." Accessed May 20, 2024. https://blogs.worldbank.org/en/digital-development/850-million-people-globally-dont-have-id-why-matters-and-what-we-can-do-about.
17. Edelman. "2023 Edelman Trust Barometer." Accessed May 20, 2024. https://www.edelman.com/trust/2023/trust-barometer.
18. Harvard Business Review. "Research: Women Score Higher Than Men in Most Leadership Skills." June 2019. Accessed May 20, 2024. https://hbr.org/2019/06/research-women-score-higher-than-men-in-most-leadership-skill.
19. Tala. "Global Impact Study." March 1, 2023. Accessed May 20, 2024. https://tala.co/blog/2023/03/01/global-impact-study.
20. Bankrate. "Annual Emergency Fund Report." Accessed May 20, 2024. https://www.bankrate.com/banking/savings/emergency-savings-report/#n3i.
21. PR Newswire. "More Than 3 in 5 Working Americans Feel Anxious About Their Current Financial Situation." Accessed May 20, 2024. https://www.prnewswire.com/news-releases/more-than-3-in-5-working-americans-feel-anxious-about-their-current-financial-situation-301754585.html.

CHAPTER SEVEN

ROOT
OF PROBLEMS

I n 2017, consumer credit rating giant Equifax suffered one of the country's largest and most headline-grabbing data breaches, exposing the personal information of 147 million US citizens, roughly 40% of the population, to hackers.[1] Since then, data breaches have been escalating for several years, a trend that shows no signs of slowing down. Year after year, as our society's digital footprints grow, we witnessed several incidents involving the theft of sensitive information. Companies and organizations across various industries and sizes have fallen victim to data breaches, resulting in millions of dollars in fraudulent damages for US businesses and consumers.

Another notable – and more recent – example is the widely publicized T-Mobile data breach in 2023.[2] Prominent tech companies like Dell and Dropbox have also suffered data breaches in 2024. Dell notified customers – including myself – via email on 9 May 2024, that 49 million records were hacked following an attack on its portal, while Dropbox informed users on 1 May 2024 in a blog post that its service had been accessed by a threat actor, potentially exposing data such as email addresses, phone numbers, and passwords.[3]

In late May 2024, Evolve Bank & Trust, a popular financial institution for fintech start-ups, announced a ransomware attack by the criminal organization LockBit, which gained access to their systems when an employee inadvertently clicked on a malicious internet link.[4] The data breach impacted a number of fintech companies including Affirm, Yieldstreet, Marqeta, and Mercury, to name a few.[5]

As a finance journalist, I have covered the impact of fraud and data breaches on the economy for nearly a decade. It is an ongoing issue in the financial services industry, given that major financial institutions hold some of consumers' most sensitive data. Despite being a crucial topic that impacts every company – from start-ups to banks, it is not always the sexiest topic to report unless you're covering a data breach as significant as Equifax. In fact, from my observations, fraud has become so pervasive that companies tend to put a Band-Aid on it, shrug at the headlines, and forget about it.

NO MORE BAND-AIDS

The fintech industry is growing exponentially as the world becomes increasingly digitized. However, with this growth comes the risk of cyber-attacks and data breaches that fintech companies are far from invulnerable to. Research shows that fintechs, on average, lose a staggering $51 million every year to fraud, which equates to a median of $400 000 or 1.7% of their annual revenue, according to a 2023 report by PYMNTS Intelligence.[6] This is why nearly half, or 47%, of fintech firms list the cost of fraud as the top challenge they face in doing business.

The situation is further exacerbated by the escalating sophistication of fraud schemes, mirroring the rapid evolution of technology. Criminal syndicates now offer "fraud as a service" on the dark web, making stolen information readily available for purchase. This has led to a 13% surge in fintech fraud in the past year alone.[7] Alarmingly, fintech companies were the most likely financial entities to report higher fraud losses, underscoring the urgent need for robust fraud prevention measures.

It's important to note that lost dollars are far from the only cost of fraud. Fraud schemes can pose significant threats to fintech companies' bottom lines through reputational risk, regulatory penalties, legal fees, or even the loss of business revenues. Fintech start-ups and financial institutions cannot afford to overlook fraud prevention as a crucial component of their long-term financial profitability strategies, especially when sustainable profitability is the focus of everyone's mind. One major solution could be leveraging the power – and advancements – in biometric identity technology to circumvent fraud at the source.

Frances Zelazny has long been fascinated by the concept of identity and its profound impact on shaping individuals. Raised in a household rich with stories of her parents' journeys, her father, a Holocaust survivor, and her mother, who fled Cuba at the rise of Fidel Castro's regime, Zelazny was exposed to the significance of preserving and honoring one's identity from an early age. She grew up in New York after her parents migrated from Israel, and her parents' narratives instilled a profound appreciation for diverse cultures and perspectives, igniting a passion within her for foreign policy and international relations. So, during college, she interned with the United Nations, where she actively contributed to a sustainable development initiative. "This formative experience underscored my conviction that global collaboration and mutual understanding must be necessary to foster a more harmonious world," she said.

Throughout her journey, several pivotal career moves eventually led Zelazny into a business sector perfect for someone so passionate about human identity and uncovering sustainable solutions: biometrics. In cybersecurity, the definition of biometrics refers to the use of unique biological features for digital authentication and access control. Biometrics are biological measurements – or physical or behavioral characteristics – that can be used to identify individuals. For example, fingerprint mapping, facial recognition, and iris scans are all forms of biometric technology, but these are just the most recognized options.

Zelazny tells me in an interview that her journey to biometrics would be far from linear. She was flipping through the *New York Times*, scanning for job opportunities after finishing her undergraduate degree in the 1990s. "The first listing, starting with an A, caught my eye," she recalled. "Without much thought, I applied and landed the position."

She worked at a receivables finance firm, a subsidiary of a larger publicly traded entity – it was her first entrance into finance. The company operated like a start-up, she said, within a larger framework. "My initial task was to assist with marketing despite my lack of formal training or education in the field," she said. "I hadn't attended business school or any business courses, so I was navigating uncharted waters."

While at her first job, Zelazny returned to school at night to receive her master's degree and subsequently found herself in the start-up world, this time in the hospitality industry, which she found unstimulating. Shortly after, she received a call from a friend recruiting for a facial recognition company and was immediately intrigued. At the time, in 1999, the idea of facial recognition and biometrics was virtually unheard of. She jumped in with the hunch that this would become something big.

Zelazny loved it. The environment was intellectually stimulating, populated by brilliant individuals, many of whom held PhDs. Weekly seminars and constant knowledge sharing were the norm, given the academic backgrounds of most employees. "What struck me most was the significant policy work surrounding facial recognition, particularly concerning privacy considerations," she said. "Immediately, I recognized the immense potential of this technology, not only from an inclusive standpoint but also in terms of its capacity to change the way we bank, travel, interact at work, the possibilities were endless." Despite its novelty, its promise was palpable, and she knew she was part of something groundbreaking. "Joining as the 18th employee at this start-up, I felt privileged to be at the forefront of such innovation," she said. "Little did I know, this experience would not only shape my career but also alter the course of my personal life – I met my husband there."

Over the next 13 years, Zelazny worked for Visionics and then L-1 Identity Solutions, a company deeply entrenched in biometrics and identity solutions. "Our portfolio included producing US driver's licenses, passports, and visas and facilitating voter registration programs globally," she said. "From India's Aadhaar to a wide array of biometric and identity-related projects, we left no stone unturned."

She was working in marketing, but in a start-up environment, working in marketing meant product marketing, policy advocacy, lobbying, investor, and media relations – essentially wearing multiple hats. Her proudest accomplishment was striking a deal with the World Bank, becoming a leading authority on leveraging biometrics and identity for inclusive development. The significance of such initiatives cannot be overstated. Many individuals worldwide lack basic documentation like birth certificates, perpetuating a cycle of exclusion. Addressing this issue can unlock access to essential services like land titles, education, and healthcare, catalyzing financial and societal progress. Yet, amidst these noble endeavors, privacy remained paramount. Refugees, the disenfranchised, and vulnerable populations faced heightened risks in an era of data management and security concerns. From her experience, Zelazny understood the delicate balance between leveraging biometric data for societal good while safeguarding individual privacy rights. The company was eventually sold in 2011.

Upon leaving the company post-acquisition, Zelazny ventured into consulting, specializing in assisting Israeli start-ups in their US market launches. One of her notable clients was a mobile payments company, pioneering features like bill splitting and payments via smartphone – an innovation ahead of its time. "However, that excitement turned to dismay as we discovered rampant fraud perpetrated through the app, particularly by users associated with a major US restaurant chain," she said. "The revelation was jarring, especially from my background in biometrics, where security and fraud prevention were paramount." Witnessing how fraudsters exploited the app to launder credit cards and make illicit purchases was deeply troubling, and the experience propelled her into the world of fintech.

But she wasn't quite ready to jump into entrepreneurship, so she took up one more job, this time at BioCatch, an Israeli start-up focusing on biometrics and fraud prevention in banking. "They had recently closed their Series A funding round and needed a chief marketing officer," she said. So, she stepped in.

Working at BioCatch would round out her expertise as a bridge between biometrics, identity protection, fraud prevention, and financial services. Given her leadership role, Zelazny delved into the intricacies of fraud prevention in the banking sector, gaining valuable insights into the tactics employed by fraudsters. "Yet, amidst tackling these challenges, I found myself continually questioning the underlying issue: Why were we constantly chasing fraudsters instead of addressing the root cause?"

It became evident that the prevailing methods of authentication, relying on stolen personal data available on the dark web, were fundamentally flawed. Traditional authentication methods like usernames, passwords, and security codes were easily compromised, perpetuating a cycle of breaches and fraud. "This realization fueled my determination to seek a better solution," she said. In 2020, she was ready to build her own start-up – leading to the inception of Anonybit.

To explain the fundamental concept of Anonybit to me, Zelazny provided me with a scenario. "Imagine this," she said. "A breach like the recent AT&T incident, where 73 million consumers' data was compromised. It's a wake-up call. This data, once on the dark web, becomes a playground for fraudsters. They impersonate customers, exploiting personal information to gain access to accounts. Take 'Nicole Casperson' as an example. A hacker armed with her stolen data calls AT&T, posing as her, easily convincing them to transfer the phone number. Then, armed with the number and basic personal info, they target her bank, exploiting weak authentication systems. It's not about flaws in individual companies; it's systemic. The ecosystem lacks security, leaving everyone vulnerable."

The scenario is common, and when we think about it, every new breach triggers a surge in fraud. The T-Mobile breach caused chaos for months. Banks and businesses scramble to contain the fallout. But we can't keep playing catch-up. We need a paradigm shift. That's where Anonybit comes in. "Fraud thrives because personal data sits in vulnerable central-ized databases," she said. "Siloed processes compound the problem. We enable a new approach. By securely storing biometrics, we eliminate the risk of data breaches. It's a game-changer. We're not just selling a product; we're offering peace of mind."

Zelazny's ambition to solve the root cause of problems is a trait typi-cally found in female leaders. Research shows women have been associated with more proactive cognitive processing, and women with proactive personality traits are more likely to develop stronger entrepreneurial intentions.[8] The idea for Anonybit, Zelazny told me, stems from where the heart of fraud lies – in the storage of personal data within vulnerable databases, creating enticing targets for cybercriminals. "Paradoxically, while we seek to combat fraud, we rely on this compromised data for authentication across various sectors – enterprises, fintechs, banks, healthcare, telcos, and beyond," she said. "However, the fear of becoming the next victim of a data breach has hindered the adoption of biometrics, when it's actually the most potent tool for fraud prevention."

So Zelazny designed Anonybit to confront this challenge head-on, enabling a way for biometric data to be fundamentally protected so more institutions can use it. The platform actually breaks down employee biometric data into anonymized bits (hence the company name) and distributes them via a multi-cloud environment. This method aims to thwart hackers from pilfering employee credentials and biometrics from centralized repositories, commonly referred to as "honeypots." By preventing cybercriminals from impersonating legitimate employees and gaining unauthorized access to company systems and data, Anonybit's approach adds a new layer of protection to digital assets. "By doing so, we not only mitigate the risk of data breaches but also eradicate fraud," she said. "This breakthrough gets to the root of the problem, a proactive approach instead of reactive." By overcoming the hesitancy surrounding biometric data management, Zelazny found, we can revolutionize fraud prevention and usher in a new era of cybersecurity and efficiency.

It's a technological advancement that is critical to the future of financial inclusion. On 10 December 2020, International Monetary Fund Managing Director Kristalina Georgieva delivered a speech during a virtual conference stating that efforts to expand financial inclusion and strengthen cybersecurity must go hand in hand.[9] While policymakers continue to make progress by turning to fintech to close wealth gaps and bring finance to the most vulnerable, the reliance on digital financial services also means cyberattacks are growing. In fact, attacks have tripled over the last decade, and financial institutions continue to be the most targeted. For example, what if a cyberattack takes a bank down and a remittance doesn't go through? What if a mobile money app is hacked, and a family cannot get a cash transfer and must pay for food? These cyber-threats can have a grave impact on financial stability, and by threatening financial stability, cyberattacks can also deny people the benefits of financial inclusion.

In 2022, Anonybit, Zelazny's New York and Tel-Aviv-based start-up, officially burst onto the scene from stealth mode, with a $3.5 million funding round. The platform isn't a conventional fintech venture, considering it actually provides services to fintech companies and other financial institutions – her way of playing an impactful role in ensuring inclusive innovation among financial services. Fast forward to May 2024, and Anonybit has raised $8 million in capital and is continuing the journey of replacing Band-Aids on problems by redefining what innovation looks like.[10]

Zelazny's journey from her childhood steeped in diverse narratives and dual identities to her pivotal role in revolutionizing biometric security with Anonybit is a testament to the power of addressing the root causes of complex issues. As the specter of data breaches loomed larger in the digital age, Zelazny's experiences underscored the critical importance of safeguarding identities and combating fraud from its core.

Her career trajectory, from her formative years at the United Nations to her tenure at L-1 Identity Solutions, laid the foundation for her deep understanding of the intersection between identity management and technological innovation. This knowledge crystallized into action when she spearheaded the creation of Anonybit, a disruptive force in biometric security.

Anonybit's mission is not just about building trust or delivering services; it's about fundamentally reshaping the cybersecurity and financial services landscape. By daring to confront the prevailing norms and championing a proactive approach to fraud prevention, Zelazny and her team are leading the charge toward a more secure and resilient digital future.

The lessons from Zelazny's journey are clear: By challenging assumptions, embracing innovation, and tackling problems at their roots, we can effect meaningful change in even the most daunting arenas.

ACCESS TO DATA TO DRIVE INNOVATION DIFFERENTLY

As our world becomes more interconnected, data emerges as the backbone of innovation. The insights provided by data are invaluable in understanding societal shifts, market trends, and environmental dynamics. Access to reliable and high-quality data is crucial for fintech businesses to develop a range of financial products, including personal finance apps, trading platforms, AI models, credit tools, and other products that fundamentally shape society. However, obtaining such datasets can be quite costly, and it can cost up to $200 000 for new entrepreneurs to test their products and business models.[11] This high cost and limited accessibility of quality data pose a significant challenge for early-stage start-ups. Without democratizing access to data, we risk narrowing the possibilities for women and diverse entrepreneurs to enter the fintech space and contribute to its growth and development.

Ten years ago, Sarah Biller, a woman with a talent for innovation and the ability to link seemingly unrelated information, decided to take on a challenge that had stalled her and other fintech entrepreneurs building the next generation of products and services for a rapidly digitizing financial services sector. Biller, who grew up in the Appalachian area of West Virginia, had experienced firsthand how isolation and a lack of access to essential resources could hinder creativity and progress. Still, she considers this upbringing in Appalachia as a wellspring of resilience that has helped her overcome the obstacles of entrepreneurship.

Before entering the fintech industry, Biller acquired years of professional experience in various sectors, from corporate treasurers to venture capitalists and telecommunications. She had even worked in the life sciences field. However, it wasn't until 2006, when she began in the global asset management industry, that she gained a comprehensive understanding of the financial system and witnessed the 2008 economic crisis firsthand. During her tenure at one of the world's largest financial institutions, where she oversaw efforts supporting a multi-billion-dollar mutual fund contract renewal analytic process, she realized that conventional portfolio optimization techniques and modern portfolio theory typically using a core set of factors had limitations. "It became apparent to me that there was an incomplete view of the markets when relying solely on these conventional methods," she said. Consequently, she sought to leverage data analytics, natural language processing, statistical models, and early applications of artificial intelligence for predictive modeling to enhance risk assessment. "It was during this time that I developed a deep passion for the intersection of data analysis and what we commonly refer to as scoring – essentially, how to leverage quantitative techniques like Bayesian methods to interpret transient factors in financial services," she said.

Combining these statistical techniques with unstructured data gleaned from analyst reports enabled Biller's team to also measure sentiment. This work underpins today's quantification of bias in institutional as well as individual credit models that incorporate AI, which can unfairly penalize individuals, for example, with traditionally feminine names like Nicole or Sarah. "To address the pitfalls of generative AI," she emphasized, "we must confront inherent biases." To ensure that financial services are accessible to everyone, addressing data biases within AI systems is essential. One way to do this is by using a diverse range of data points from different financial domains to ensure that the data is representative of the global population. Despite the technological advancements in finance, it is essential to remember that the industry is still fundamentally human and, therefore, must take steps to address biases and foster equitable financial systems that reflect the diversity of humanity.

This would lead her down her path to fintech, obsessing over data access as a force for innovation and a source for good.

In 2009, she co-founded Capital Market Exchange to set out on her mission. She developed the company to use advanced technologies like predictive analytics, big data, machine learning, text analysis, and visualization to convert bond investor sentiment into trading strategies. In the aftermath of the credit crisis, they generated ideas, provided transparency on emerging factors from professional investors' opinions, and predicted their impact on near-term corporate bond/credit default swap spread changes. "Our goal was to begin to aggregate those non-financial factors by using crude natural language processing models and machine learning, as well as more systematically aggregating and quantifying what the investment community collectively viewed as important, or what else they thought was going to drive credit risk," she said.

Few forces rival the potency and influence of the capital markets on our society. The key lies in harnessing this power for positive change. "For me, directing capital, often through a credit model, toward addressing pressing issues has been particularly impactful," Biller said. "Women, I believe, possess a unique empathy that enables us to excel in this realm. This empathy catalyzes change, irrespective of one's career or life trajectory."

As a financial services professional and a breast cancer survivor, Biller saw similarities between the appearance of a tumor on an MRI and the concept of risk in credit markets. "Just as a tumor starts in one area and spreads out," she said, "so does risk, forming concentric rings of contagion." Data proliferates and intertwines with financial services, enriching our understanding of risk. For instance, we can examine various indicators of climate change, a topic of particular interest to Biller. Moreover, she is deeply intrigued by the significance of individual movements in shaping urban landscapes. "Observing someone navigating through Hell's Kitchen might foreshadow developments like Hudson Yards," she explained. "By analyzing such movements, we can anticipate opportunities for financial services and better support small businesses, which are vital drivers of our economy." Biller, early on, saw value in historical data and metrics of private company financial health as they offer insights into market trends at a micro level, which ultimately contribute to the broader economic landscape.

Biller's experiences and discoveries led her to commit considerable resources and time building technology and data access to predict the next credit crisis. She envisioned a platform that could represent risk in a novel way, taking inspiration from the progression of cancer in the body. Drawing from her expertise in life sciences, she proposed a new approach to credit scoring that would identify risk factors in a manner more akin to how cancer cells spread and metastasize throughout the body. This innovative approach could offer a fresh perspective on managing risk in the credit industry, potentially leading to more effective and proactive strategies for mitigating financial risk.

While unconventional, integrating social science insights into financial services, Biller fundamentally believes in connecting the dots from other industries to improve financial services. "Innovation often springs from the fusion of disparate knowledge," she said.

Biller secured a small round of venture funding for Capital Market Exchange to build out this brilliant idea, but she found gaining access to the necessary data difficult. Initially, financial data providers only offered limited data options when she needed much more. They seemed unwilling to put in the effort required to help her succeed since selling data to massive corporations was more lucrative. Frustrated by this experience, Biller joined forces with entrepreneurs and fintech investors to create a solution to this problem.

So, she co-founded Fintech Sandbox, a platform to provide fintech start-ups access to the different data they need to succeed. In parallel with the development of Fintech Sandbox, Biller was also working on Capital Markets Exchange. Juggling both start-ups, she eventually joined State Street Bank, where she assumed the Chief Operating Officer for Innovation and Head of Innovation Ventures roles. It was an exciting position, with Silicon Valley's reputation for innovation meeting the traditional finance sector. Leveraging these capabilities, she developed novel applications to identify new quantitative trading signals and address identity-related issues, which she remains deeply invested in today.

One area of focus was applying technology to Anti-Money Laundering (AML) and Know Your Customer (KYC) procedures. However, what truly ignites Biller's passion is the ongoing need for innovation in the infrastructure and frameworks that underpin our financial services. "If we fail to address fundamental issues like identity verification and the digitization of processes, especially in community banking, we'll continue to rely on outdated methods that hinder progress," she said. This backward approach doesn't just impact efficiency; it also hampers our ability to serve diverse communities, including women, effectively. This realization is what motivates her to drive change in the financial industry.

With Fintech Sandbox, Biller opened the door for entrepreneurs to solve for these pressing issues in our financial infrastructure. Launched in 2014 in Boston, Fintech Sandbox was established as a nonprofit organization to provide early-stage start-ups worldwide access to critical datasets and infrastructure through its Data Access Residency program. By collaborating with leading data providers, Fintech Sandbox offers start-ups free access to a diverse range of financial and non-financial datasets. This enables entrepreneurs to develop and test their applications more efficiently and to a higher standard, paving the way for groundbreaking innovations in fintech.

Currently, Fintech Sandbox has 41 dedicated data partners that provide their premium datasets for free to start-ups participating in the Data Access Residency program. These data partners include MT Newswires, Polygon, Benzinga, Dow Jones, FactSet, Moody's, Nasdaq Data Link, and Plaid, who are making additional datasets available to fintech start-ups.

In 2023 alone, the organization welcomed 51 new start-ups from across four continents, facilitated more than 145 connections between its start-ups and data partners, and expanded its reach to three new countries: Albania, Ghana, and Kuwait. Fintech Sandbox continues to build a global community of entrepreneurs, industry executives, and investors dedicated to innovating within the fintech industry.

Data quality is paramount in a landscape increasingly dominated by AI and automated decision-making. With the rise in generative AI use, Fintech Sandbox today is hyper focused on ensuring start-ups can access the high-quality, representative, and unbiased data necessary to train their models effectively and drive meaningful change in the financial industry.

"By breaking down barriers to data access and fostering collaboration, we empower entrepreneurs to harness the power of data for good and drive innovation forward," Biller said.

Thanks to her relentless pursuit to ensure access to data could redefine innovation, Biller's contributions to the fintech space have created a surge of opportunity for other start-up founders facing the same roadblocks as she once did as a founder. Today, Biller is a versatile professional who adeptly juggles several responsibilities. Her recent role as the Executive Director of Vantage Ventures stands out, as she leads a team that actively supports and invests in visionary founders who are building cutting-edge and impactful tech start-ups in the Appalachian region.

It's a full circle moment as Biller gives back to her community, creating an innovation cycle in diverse areas, like where she grew up. "It's not fatal where you're born or where you came from," she said. "As an Appalachian, what matters is what you do with it – there's been no greater honor for me." Her passion and ability to foster a thriving start-up ecosystem make her an invaluable asset to the fintech industry.

TACKLING STUDENT DEBT – AND ITS RIPPLE EFFECTS

For those of us who see education as our pathway to a better future, it's crucial to recognize student debt's role in our economic well-being, both for ourselves and our families. Education is critical to financial freedom, yet for 70% of students with a bachelor's degree, financing education means taking on debt with a payback period spanning 17 to 20 years.[12] This reality has important implications for savings and retirement planning. It creates a cycle that traps most Americans in endless debt, making it difficult to have a comfortable retirement or achieve financial prosperity. They are forced to pay for higher education, placing them in debt to qualify for a high-paying job, which forces them to work continuously while struggling to catch up with their expenses. *Ironic.*

Given these implications to Americans and the ripple effect on our economy, student debt relief has dominated discussions for years, thanks to some significant policy shifts. In summer 2022, the Biden administration unveiled a plan to cancel up to $20 000 in federal student loans.[13] Then, in December 2022, Congress signed the SECURE 2.0 Act into law, introducing provisions for employers to match student loan payments while bolstering retirement accounts.[14] February 2023 saw the Supreme Court deliberating on a lawsuit challenging President Biden's debt relief initiative.[15]

The ongoing pause on federal student loan payments, spanning three years due to the global pandemic and its end in June 2023, has intensified concerns.[16] Another problem with student debt, typically the first debt that a young person takes on, is the intense focus it puts on the borrower to relieve themselves from debt at the expense of building wealth. Compounded by the revelation that most Americans lack $500 for emergency expenses, there's a clear opening for fintech companies to innovate solutions, addressing student debt as a societal and economic priority.[17]

Fintech entrepreneur Laurel Taylor experienced the weight of student debt firsthand, coming from a household where college and the inherent student debt that comes with it were expected. "What I didn't anticipate was the opportunity cost – missing out on two decades of compound interest on wealth while repaying loans," she said. "Reflecting on this, I've come to realize the profound impact of forgoing those crucial years of investment growth."

This problem demands attention, and it's alarming to see the statistics. With 47 million Americans currently burdened by student debt, totaling nearly $1.8 trillion, it's the second-largest liability in our country, growing by approximately $100 billion annually.[18] Student debt has become the norm, particularly in the workplace. As our workforce increasingly skews toward millennials, with projections of 75% or more by 2025, addressing student debt becomes even more urgent. However, even Taylor hesitates to use the term "student debt" alone – it's more than that. "It's mom's debt, dad's debt, spouse's debt, grandparent's debt – it's everyone's debt," she said. Recognizing this broader impact is essential to uncovering solutions that can alleviate the burden and pave the way for a brighter financial future for all.

Taylor was working in a leadership role at Google when she felt a calling to tackle student debt. She refers to this moment as the realization that her "purpose was solving for financial freedom," she said. Taylor always wanted to build something bigger than what her then role at Google could provide. Due to her personal experience struggling with student debt and her technology background, she was ultimately surprised by the lack of progress in addressing this pressing issue. So, she stepped into fintech entrepreneurship to tackle it while proving that profitability and purpose go hand in hand.

In 2016, she founded the fintech platform Candidly, an AI-driven student debt and savings optimization platform that enables employers to help employees manage student loans through self-serve tools and sponsored benefits, like employer contributions to student debt. Her mission is clear: to obliterate student debt and empower hardworking Americans to transcend financial stress and achieve true prosperity. "This isn't just a catchy tagline; it's our core purpose," she said. "We recognize that the student debt and savings crises are deeply intertwined."

Instead of following a traditional sales approach or targeting individual consumers, Taylor's go-to-market strategy for Candidly was a B2B2C approach. This involved embedding Candidly's artificial intelligence-driven student debt and savings optimization products into the infrastructure of its partners, such as employers, financial institutions, retirement, and wealth management firms. By doing so, Candidly was able to integrate its products into employee benefit engines for the benefit of their customers. "There's so much market demand for our offering because of major policy changes that it's a challenge to keep up with," Taylor told me in an interview. "We're not just another AI-driven platform; we're the market's sole solution dedicated to optimizing student debt and savings," she said.

Taylor built Candidly based on the observation that students with debt often navigate their financial goals linearly, which isn't practical for economic freedom. First and foremost, they prioritize paying down their student debt. A study conducted by MIT's AgeLab in collaboration with TIAA revealed a stark reality: regardless of the remaining debt amount, a staggering 84% of those burdened by student debt delay saving for retirement or other financial goals until their debt is fully cleared.[19] This sequential approach to economic management can be financially crippling, as it delays the opportunity to harness the power of compound interest for wealth-building early in one's career trajectory. Indeed, data underscores the consequences of carrying student debt. Individuals with student debt at the age of 30 typically possess only half the retirement savings of their debt-free counterparts[20] – a situation Taylor personally experienced.

"Driven by my struggles and the stigma surrounding student debt, I felt compelled to take action," she said. "Despite graduating from institutions like Texas State and MIT, student debt remained taboo among my peers." There was a pervasive sense of shame and envy surrounding the issue. So, she set out to change that narrative, to normalize and destigmatize student debt, and to leverage technology to provide a modern solution. "Anticipating regulatory shifts and policy changes incentivizing employers to address student debt," she said, "I recognized the potential for widespread adoption." After all, the Treasury had a vested interest in recouping student debt owed to the government.

Today Candidly partners with industry giants such as Empower, Guild, Lincoln Financial Group, PNC, UBS, Vanguard, and more. The platform has even attracted partners outside of the typical financial services realm.

In February 2023, American Eagle Outfitters leveraged Candidly to assist employees in paying more than $100 000 in student loan debt.[21] "We've achieved this goal, and have now delivered over $1.4 billion in impact to the users we serve," Taylor said.

During our interview, I asked Taylor how investors initially responded to the idea of Candidly. Taylor admitted to experiencing a swell of emotions in response to the question; it wasn't just one reaction but rather a multitude. The impact of Candidly's solution seems like a no-brainer for any investor.

Still, Taylor could barely believe the underlying sense of snobbery from some investors around the Candidly product and mission. "I vividly recall one instance during a pitch where someone suggested that offering student debt benefits would attract subpar employees, a notion that struck me deeply on a personal level," she said.

The reality is that two-thirds of student debt is held by women – close to $929 billion.[22] On top of that, women are not paid as much as men, even when working full-time and year-round. On average, women are paid 83.7% of what men are paid.[23] This inequity is even greater for Black and Hispanic women. Making such dismissive comments is offensive and indicative of broader systemic issues. It was a moment that left Taylor reeling, but unfortunately, it wasn't the only one. "There were other instances where my vision for a new category in the market was met with condescension," she recalled. "As if addressing student debt in the workplace was naive or philanthropic."

Let's be clear: while Taylor's start-up is mission-driven and aims to make a positive impact, Candidly is unequivocally for-profit. "We've seen employers offering Candidly to their employees reduce turnover between 33% and 76%, depending upon the program design," she said, "while delivering tangible returns on investment." Despite the dismissals and doubts, Taylor's unwavering commitment to her company's vision and conviction that this problem was worth solving carried her through. "That conviction drives me forward each day," she said.

Taylor's bet on herself, and the problem she is solving, paid off. In March 2023, Candidly announced $20.5 million in Series B funding; following a year of record growth, the company saw 10x revenue growth, Taylor said.[24] With this runway, the company is developing tools that allow employers to match employees' student loan payments, contribute to emergency savings, and provide tax-advantaged retirement contributions. "I'm going to write a thank you letter to the people who doubted the idea when we ultimately exit," Taylor said.

Taylor mentioned that operating in a dynamic market has been quite a journey, especially when it comes to navigating the challenges that COVID-19 has brought about. Building in such an environment has been a significant part of the platform's story, as it serves as an opportunity to gather data and innovate to make Candidly an ideal solution to resolve the most pressing issues related to the student debt crisis.

For instance, the three-year moratorium on student loan payments added another layer of complexity. However, it's important to clarify that it wasn't a continuous three-year break; instead, it consisted of eight instances of 90-day delays. This constant uncertainty created a unique set of circumstances for the 47 million Americans grappling with student debt, 43 million of whom hold federal student loans. "Imagine the rollercoaster of emotions as borrowers were repeatedly told that payments would resume in 90 days, only to have that deadline pushed back again and again – eight times in total," Taylor said.

In such a climate of confusion, Taylor decided to collect insights to uncover how this back-and-forth impacted borrowers. "We recently reviewed 500 hours of coaching calls, providing invaluable support and human touch alongside our high-tech digital solutions," she said. "Before the announcement of the moratorium's end, our data revealed a mix of dread, fear, confusion, and frustration among borrowers who had been bracing themselves for its continuation."

Taylor initially observed a positive trend in the aggregated user data when the moratorium on student loan payments was first implemented.

There was a notable increase in savings and a decrease in revolving consumer debt. Borrowers used this opportunity to build up their savings and tackle existing debt. "However, we've since witnessed a significant shift," she said. "Now, there's been a decline in savings and a substantial rise in consumer debt, accompanied by a notable increase in rent, attributed to the ongoing inflationary period." Having access to this comprehensive data allows Taylor to build Candidly to offer personalized guidance and assistance, easing the anxiety and uncertainty experienced by many.

From employers' perspective, the Consolidated Appropriations Act of 2021 marked a pivotal moment. "This legislation empowered employers to leverage their tuition assistance or reimbursement budgets, which typically go largely unused – up to 95% annually, in fact," Taylor said. "Despite 71% of employers offering tuition reimbursement, most of these funds remained untapped." The Consolidated Appropriations Act changed the game by allowing employers to redirect these funds toward alleviating their employees' student debt burden.

By tapping into the budget previously allocated for tuition assistance, employers could now provide tax-free aid of up to $5250 to help employees pay down their student debt.[25] This innovative policy shift unlocked a powerful tool for employers to support their workforce's financial well-being. "As a result, we witnessed a remarkable surge in employer contributions flowing through our platform – increasing by an astounding 3600% in 2022 alone," she said. This demonstrates the profound impact that policy initiatives can have in addressing the student debt crisis and empowering borrowers and employers.

Going into more detail, the SECURE 2.0 Act made an impact when enacted on 29 December 2022. It introduced a groundbreaking provision similar to the 401(k) introduction, which enables employers to offer retirement savings contributions in combination with student loan payments. Taylor has a vivid memory of the happiness that the passing of this act brought her and how it cemented Candidly's position in the economic ecosystem.

"Consider an individual spending half of the 20-year paydown period – let's say 10 years – receiving a matching contribution for each student loan payment made during this time," she said. "Without making any additional contributions to retirement savings, this individual could amass a staggering $450 000 in retirement savings by the time they retire." That's four times the retirement savings amassed by many boomers today.

"The thought of my mom having an extra $450 000 at retirement, along with 47 million other Americans, is truly transformative," Taylor said. "For many households, it can mean the difference between financial uncertainty and security." The beauty of it all is that it just makes sense. It's a win-win scenario for individuals, employers, and the financial industry. What's even more exciting is the broader societal impact. This provision addresses the needs of low- and middle-income earners, women, people of color, and even high earners who are stretched thin by college expenses. For the industry, it represents growth and a new net revenue stream. It's a moment where everyone comes out ahead.

As a founder tackling one of the most significant economic issues our society faces today, Taylor has three key elements that keep her going as an entrepreneur: stamina, surrounding herself with amazing people, and good old-fashioned discipline.

Firstly, maintaining stamina and spirit is essential. It's about deeply connecting to the why – the mission of the organization. "For instance, reaching the milestone of generating a billion dollars of projected student debt impact for our users is incredibly fulfilling," she said. "But what's even more exciting is envisioning where we'll be next year and the impact we'll continue to make."

Secondly, surrounding yourself with amazing people is paramount. "In the early stages, especially when you're pursuing something perceived as radical, finding the right people can be challenging," she said. "But it's crucial to be deliberate about the company you keep."

Lastly, discipline is critical. "This encompasses a range of practices, from consistent daily habits to maintaining physical and mental health," she said. "Being a founder is like running a marathon with intervals – it's about understanding what works for you and sticking to it, even when balance seems elusive."

Finally, stand firm in your belief that purpose and profit are not opposing forces; they are aligned. "This is what enlightened capitalism looks like to me – recognizing that our mission drives our profitability," she said. "Every day, I consciously devote myself to this belief."

DEFEATING INEQUITY WITH DATA

Danielle Sesko's journey into the world of fintech was unexpected. She started her career in financial services at a financial consulting firm during one of the most tumultuous periods in recent economic history: the 2008 financial crisis. At the time, Sesko was tasked with navigating the complexities of mergers and acquisitions (M&A) for failed banks. This was no easy feat, as the housing market's historic collapse triggered an unprecedented surge in bank failures. Between 2008 and 2010, approximately 322 banks failed, according to data from the Federal Deposit Insurance Corporation (FDIC). This surge in bank failures, far exceeding the average of about three per year, highlighted the severity of the crisis. By comparison, in 2023, there were only five bank failures compared to 157 in 2010.[26]

During an interview, Sesko shared with me valuable insights regarding bank closures. She explained that such closures usually occurred on Fridays and her work would start the following week. The primary focus during that time was to ensure that depositors had access to their funds throughout the turmoil. Sesko played a critical role in managing the instability caused by the crisis by facilitating FDIC-assisted transactions. "Initially, I perceived our purpose as safeguarding the communities affected by these transitions, ensuring that people could access their funds," she said. However, what stood out the most to her was the realization that most people do not understand the impact of poor decisions made by leaders. She recalled that post-mortem analyses conducted 15 years later revealed a sobering reality: the communities where banks failed had suffered adverse effects, including higher unemployment and increased poverty rates. Marginalized and underserved communities still experience these effects to this day.

As Sesko looks back on her past experiences, she realizes how significantly they have influenced her perception of the financial services industry. Back then, "fintech" was not yet a part of everyday language, and technology was not a common topic in banking discussions. In 2008, banks focused mainly on physical infrastructure, believing that grand buildings would provide reassurance of financial stability. However, Sesko discovered that beneath this facade lay a need for financial robustness within these institutions. "It became evident to me that appearances can be deceiving, and the emergence of fintech represented a missing piece of the puzzle," she shared. "Had these banks invested in technology and modernized their infrastructure, they could have expanded access to credit, offered more competitive rates, and provided better deposit services."

That's when the lightbulb clicked. Sesko's experience in bank M&A early in her career made her gravitate toward innovating one of the oldest products of the financial services industry: insurance. While insurance as a product doesn't prevent risks from occurring, it serves as a financial safety net in the event of a catastrophe. "Insurance is not just a product of protection but a product that enables rational risk-taking and allows people to make choices," Sesko said. "It enables people and empowers them to live their best lives – it's fundamental to the fabric of our society." For most of us, the total loss from a house fire would be financially devastating, and businesses would struggle to recover from a crisis without insurance coverage. While we can't eliminate the occurrence of unfortunate events, we can mitigate their impact by providing support for individuals and businesses to recover. Insurance is about managing and navigating risks, allowing society to progress despite setbacks.

After the financial crisis, Sesko pivoted her career from M&A and shifted her focus to identifying gaps within the insurance industry. She discovered the sector needed more efficiency in distributing its products, particularly in reaching broader consumer segments. This is especially true for life insurance, which "peaked in market penetration in the 1970s at 85.4%," according to Sesko. Fast forward 40 years, and only 52% of consumers reported having life insurance.[27] This disparity is because insurance companies have historically targeted wealthier segments, neglecting middle-market consumers. This oversight has resulted in a staggering $25 trillion mortality gap in the US, exacerbating the wealth divide across generations.[28]

Motivated to address this issue, Sesko embarked on a mission to redefine insurance accessibility and affordability. One of her first ventures, SafetyNet Insurance, aimed to offer cash flow protection products to enhance the financial well-being of millions of consumers. "One phrase resonated deeply throughout my interactions with consumers: "Insurance is for the rich. I can't access it," she recalled. This sentiment fueled Sesko's determination to challenge the status quo even more. "I've dedicated considerable time to engaging with consumers, listening to their pain points, and understanding precisely how insurance offerings serve as lifelines during critical moments," she shared. "Whether it's covering unexpected car repair costs, providing support during job loss, aiding individuals facing disabilities, or even in cases where pet owners lack the means to care for their beloved companions, leading to difficult decisions like euthanasia. It was a profound realization that insurance is pivotal in enabling individuals to navigate life's uncertainties."

This insight ultimately propelled Sesko to become the Director of Product Management and Innovation at TruStage in January 2023. A venerable company with a century-long legacy, deeply committed to serving middle-market America, TruStage is a financially strong insurance, investment, and technology provider. The company has prioritized inclusivity in every aspect of its operations, from its hiring practices to its choice of vendors, all geared toward ensuring that insurance becomes accessible to traditionally overlooked consumers. With more than 4200 employees, Sesko's leadership role has a heavy hand in developing the Madison, Wisconsin–based company's Digital Lending Insurance (DLI) initiative, reimagining insurance, which has remained essentially unchanged since the mid-twentieth century.

Sesko explains TruStage's mission with the new category of products is to spread risk across large populations, allowing banks and lenders to make capital more accessible to a broader range of people. "My vision was to modernize insurance by integrating it into the lending process," she said. "By embedding insurance as a component of the loan itself, we become the financial safety net for the lending institution." That way, in the unfortunate event of a borrower experienced hardship, the goal of the products is to help provide the cash flow, facilitating rehabilitation of the loan and safeguarding consumers' credit scores. Through this proactive approach, TruStage mitigates the impact of defaults and makes credit more accessible to a broader demographic. By mitigating the effects of common causes of defaults, such as job loss and disability, the new category of products is designed to reduce default rates by at least 20%, providing lenders greater capital flexibility and the potential to expand their underwriting aperture. "Where a lender may have previously said no to someone deemed high credit risk," Sesko said, "they can now say yes and help that person access cash." Plus, the products are designed to help lenders improve conversion rates and reduce client acquisition costs.

Research shows that female leadership and a commitment to inclusive innovation have a positive impact on a company's product performance. Additionally, businesses that embrace gender diversity, especially at the senior and management level, tend to perform better, as highlighted in a 2019 report from the Bureau for Employers' Activities of the International Labour Organization.[29] The report, titled "Women in Business and Management: The Business Case for Change," surveyed nearly 13 000 enterprises across 70 countries. More than 57% of respondents acknowledged that gender diversity initiatives positively impacted business outcomes. Furthermore, almost three-quarters of companies that monitored gender diversity in their management reported profit increases ranging from 5 to 20%, with the majority experiencing gains between 10 and 15%.

In an industry where legacy institutions often prioritize maintaining the status quo instead of empowering more people economically, products like the ones created from the DLI initiative, led by innovators like Sesko, are essential. The benefits extend beyond lenders, too, Sesko emphasized. Unlike traditional deferment programs, these products offer consumers a lifeline by helping to make their loan payments in the case of unexpected losses of income, sparing individuals from the crippling consequences of default.

During our interview, Sesko reflected on her encounters with individuals struggling to access credit due to traditional underwriting constraints. "I spoke to people over my career who just needed a small dollar loan to pay for their kid's school pictures, and they couldn't get that," she shared. "Or they wanted to get a house that they could afford and had a $100 000 down payment on the home but couldn't get a mortgage because they were new to the country and had a thin credit file."

These interactions also make Sesko well aware of the challenges of democratizing access to financial services through insurance products. Only one in five people trust their insurance company, reflecting a pervasive skepticism within the industry. This mistrust in traditional lending insurance results from systemic issues within the industry. Many financial institutions, hungry for non-interest income, have grown reliant on the commission revenue generated from selling insurance, thus becoming dependent on its margins. This fuels the complexity of insurance contracts, further exacerbating the issue. Legal jargon and convoluted benefit structures make it difficult for consumers to understand what they're purchasing. Often, agents are incentivized to push these overly complicated products, leading to cost-prohibitive and untrustworthy offerings. The friction they introduce into the credit process is substantial, leading modern consumers – who value their autonomy – to dismiss such offerings outright due to their inconvenience and lack of transparency. Sesko's passion for insurance stems from her deep-seated belief in its power to address these societal challenges. "One approach is to integrate insurance products with non-insurance brands that consumers already trust," Sesko said. "By partnering with well-known companies, we can personalize insurance offerings and enhance the overall customer experience."

Leaders like Sesko at legacy institutions like TruStage show us how technology redefines traditional financial services products as an inclusion catalyst, especially when partnering with fintech companies. But, historically, that has not been the case. Traditional insurance models have frequently drawn criticism for their complexity, high costs, and barriers to entry. Income inequality worsens insurance coverage accessibility. This is particularly evident in advanced economies, where inequality has only increased over the years, leading to a stall in expanding insurance coverage. Research has shown that if income distribution reflected 1990s levels, households would have an additional $252 billion in insurance coverage, as the Swiss Re Institute reported.[30] However, due to the widening income inequality from 1990–2019, the gap in natural catastrophe protection has also widened by 2.5%. This suggests that an additional $1.7 trillion worth of assets could have been protected against natural disasters if income inequality had not increased. There's a silver lining. Affordable insurance can stimulate economic activity by aiding individuals in managing risks and navigating challenging circumstances.

Lending and insurance are evolving together. However, legacy lending insurance is not designed to transition to the digital world. Most insurance plans were cooked up in a time when face-to-face interactions were the norm; back during the days when loan officers and financial advisors would try to upsell you on extra coverage, often making the whole process slow, confusing, and frustrating. And let's be honest, that's just not cutting it anymore. Modern digital consumers are burned out from the misaligned incentives of some insurance providers, who are more concerned with their profits than consumers' financial well-being. It's a harsh reality for many consumers of digital financial services. Insurance was initially designed to make our lives easier, but now it often seems like just another way for financial service providers to boost their bottom line.

Leveraging rising trends, digital lending-focused companies can build products that offer higher returns on investment and faster profitability while advancing economic equity.

These trends include:

1. **The Rise of E-commerce:** More transactions are happening online, and this trend became even more pronounced during the pandemic. Global e-commerce sales are expected to total $6.3 trillion in 2024. Even in asset-heavy purchases such as vehicles, furniture, and electronics – traditionally segments driven by physical retail – consumers are leaping to complete their purchases online.

2. **Componentization of the Digital Banking Stack:** With technological advancements, digital banking products are now easier to launch. The banking-as-a-service (BaaS) model has enabled companies to assemble their banking systems using pre-built software components, reducing development time and costs without the need to integrate with a bank's core legacy systems. Now, a trend

has emerged in which the various components of digital lending, such as origination and servicing, are readily available to product teams. This has significantly reduced time to market for lenders, neobanks, and widespread consumer platforms like Apple Pay Now to provide credit to their users.

3. **Embedded Lending:** Embedded lending means integrating loans directly into other services or products. You could be offered a loan right when you purchase or sign up for a service online.

Lending is an ideal product category for embedded finance, given how widely software connects various B2C and B2B interactions. Integrating financial services into software systems is easy, creating many new opportunities for B2C and B2B loan products. Plus, lending-as-a-service (LaaS) platforms are becoming more popular as an alternative to the discrete software components of lending, which require orchestration and integration.

LaaS offerings abstract the complexity of the lending value chain, making it easier for digital consumer platforms to expand their product footprint by embedding loans powered by these full-service add-ons. Although LaaS platforms reduce implementation time and make it easier to bring lending products to market, product teams will have to give up some flexibility and control over the user experience. However, the benefits of increased stickiness and revenues associated with lending can outweigh this.

Access to previously unavailable data has brought fresh insights into underwriting practices. Innovations like account aggregation have empowered a new breed of digital lenders – such as cash advance fintechs and Buy Now, Pay Later (BNPL) platforms – to emerge. These lenders leverage alternative data, such as cash flows in and out of checking accounts, to gauge an individual's borrowing capacity. This breakthrough has paved the way for digitally extending credit to a broader spectrum of borrowers, a feat unimaginable offline. DLI is, ultimately, vital to this contemporary tech landscape. The advancements in digital lending owe much to integrating API-delivered components developed by tech leaders like Stripe, Plaid, Twilio, and Okta. These components are becoming a standard for delivering new financial products and services. Few newcomers to digital banking or lending are developing their technology; instead, they opt for a range of packaged components that accelerate time-to-market, reduce development costs, delegate maintenance, and – with the support of sponsor entities – navigate the complexities of compliance.

Insurance innovation has always been challenging, with limited product innovation observed in the industry. However, with a seasoned history building digital insurance products, Sesko is up for the challenge. "Understanding the problem you're solving and connecting with the consumers or business entities affected by those problems fosters empathy throughout the innovation process, building resilience and perseverance," she said. As insurance innovation trends in fintech, the key to remaining relevant in today's market is ultimately leveraging empathy to enhance user experience. We need the right technology and motivated leaders to get us there.

FROM THE MILITARY TO FINTECH

In 2018, Nasdaq announced they relocated their corporate headquarters from downtown Manhattan to the heart of Times Square, where, via the Nasdaq MarketSite, they had already been broadcasting the market opening and closing bell ceremonies since the year 2000.[31] Nasdaq, established in 1971, is a global electronic marketplace for buying and selling securities via a computerized, speedy, and transparent system – symbolizing innovation in traditional financial services. As the world's first electronic stock market, Nasdaq carefully reimagined its headquarters to serve as a global experience hub to welcome and nurture the next generation of innovative companies to launch their initial public offering (IPO). Nasdaq's relocation bridged the storied legacy of finance with the bold promises of modern technology. The emblem of this transition? None other than the 48-story skyscraper, featuring an iconic 7-story Nasdaq tower, casting its luminous gaze of Nasdaq clients over the bustling streets of New York City below.

As I made my way to the Nasdaq MarketSite for the first time in late May 2022, the hustle of a morning commute to Times Square felt calm compared to the excitement of stepping onto the Nasdaq floor for the first time. The resilient spirit of entrepreneurship, historical transactions, and epoch-making events charged the floor's atmosphere like a corporate sanctuary where vital decisions were made and shaped the course of history. I was invited to the Nasdaq MarketSite to interview Brandis DeSimone, a Nasdaq executive celebrating more than 10 years of calling the exchange her work home. As I settled into the embrace of the glass-enclosed broadcast studio overlooking a busy Times Square, it quickly became evident that DeSimone and I shared a joint reflection as we got mic'd up for our interview. Much like mine, her thoughts wandered through the corridors of Nasdaq's history, pausing to pay homage to the trailblazing women who had graced its stage. The prior year, 2021, had borne witness to a procession of female leaders guiding their companies into the public arena.

In 2021, Nasdaq hosted 52 IPOs with female CEOs, more than any other US exchange. Among these IPOs were Bumble, which had the second-largest tech IPO by proceeds raised; Olaplex, the third-largest consumer IPO; and Lyle Healthcare, one of the largest healthcare IPOs. Additionally, 15% of the female CEOs were under 40.[32]

Anne Wojcicki, with the DNA-testing company 23 and Me, had charted a course for IPO in Nasdaq's virtual halls in June 2021.[33] In February of that same year, Whitney Wolfe Herd, donning a radiant yellow power suit and her son on her hip, had heralded the IPO of her dating app, Bumble, etching her name into the annals of history as the youngest woman to steer a company public at 31.[34] Jennifer Hyman, co-founder and CEO of Rent the Runway, added her chapter to this narrative in October 2021.[35] Their ascension to the IPO stage was significant against a backdrop of sobering statistics that remind us that female founders and CEOs had shepherded a mere fraction of IPOs. More than 2000 companies went public in the US between 2013 and 2020. But only 18 of them were led by a female founder and CEO.[36] The numbers spoke volumes, painting a stark picture of the systemic barriers that had long hindered women's access to the IPO market.

As DeSimone and I explored the complex relationship between finance and femininity, it became evident that Nasdaq's halls were not only a testament to the accomplishments of the past but also a harbinger of a more equitable future. The potential for transformation lies in the intersection of tradition and innovation. Amidst the grand tapestry of history, I felt a sense of quiet optimism as I saw the way female leadership from DeSimone and Nasdaq's Chair and Chief Executive Officer, Adena Friedman guide us toward a future where diversity, equity, and inclusion advance companies toward a pathway of profitable and sustainable growth.

DeSimone's journey to leadership at Nasdaq can be traced back to her education at the US Naval Academy in Annapolis, Maryland, and her service in the US Navy. She joined the Navy before the 11 September attacks and continued to serve until 2008. Looking back on her experience, she said, "During my tenure [in the military], we were in a state of war. The military and armed forces underwent a significant transformation."

DeSimone views the US Naval Academy as a center for developing leadership abilities, where disciplined followership is prioritized to cultivate leadership skills in students throughout their academic journeys. Despite its mostly male composition, she acknowledged the Academy's ongoing efforts to address gender imbalances, which are similar to initiatives in the financial services industry. A 2023 press release from Commander, Naval Information Forces revealed that more than 20% of the Navy's active force comprises women, with 22 female admirals and 1580 female master chiefs and senior chief petty officers leading from the front.[37] In contrast, although women constitute more than half of the entry-level finance workforce in the United States, only about 6% hold senior positions in top public financial institutions.[38]

Attending the Naval Academy guaranteed DeSimone a comprehensive education in technology. She described it as an engineering-focused institution, conferring a Bachelor of Science degree to all students regardless of their majors. This emphasis stems from the belief that every leader must grasp the technology they oversee. Whether troubleshooting ship engines or addressing missile malfunctions, understanding technological fundamentals is imperative for effective leadership.

"Understanding the fundamentals of technology has carried me through my career because that's really how finance is," she said. "It's all about grasping the backbone of market structure and technology." Proficiency in navigating these domains is synonymous with genuine understanding.

Today, as the Head of Data Sales for the Americas at Nasdaq, DeSimone leads sales in the Americas for the exchange's data business, providing fintech companies with essential content data to integrate into their applications and technology during development. Imagine a scenario where a founder, perhaps a technologist with an engineering background, approaches Nasdaq with a brilliant idea but needs insight into market structure, particularly within the retail brokerage domain. Nasdaq helps bridge the gap between creativity and realization by equipping founders with the necessary tools and knowledge. "We're not just building one fintech," DeSimone emphasizes. "We're fostering a flywheel effect." From pre-seed rounds to Series A and B investments and ultimately going public on Nasdaq, the company supplies fintech startups with the data they need to challenge the status quo. After all, 92% of job growth occurs after a company goes public.

Ultimately, Nasdaq seeks what most fintech start-ups crave: partnership. DeSimone's role revolves around nurturing enduring partnerships with start-ups. In an era dominated by automated transactions, DeSimone's "let's build a relationship" ethos underscores the profound understanding that genuine human connection is the ultimate sales catalyst. Like any successful partnership, values and connections take precedence.

DeSimone learned this lesson well before joining the upper echelons of corporate America. Before venturing into finance, she served aboard a Navy Destroyer, contributing to Operation Iraqi Freedom and the Global War on Terror. "We were conducting anti-piracy operations off the Horn of Africa," she recalled. "I led a sizable team as an officer in the Navy." Following this experience, she harbored a singular career aspiration: Wall Street.

In 2008, she relocated to New York but quickly realized that her military background didn't make her a prime candidate on Wall Street. "No one would take a chance on me because I lacked a finance background," she said. The finance industry appeared as an impenetrable fortress, leaving her feeling isolated – a solitary "female island" rather than an attractive prospect. DeSimone shed light on the hurdles veterans encounter during their transition to civilian employment, particularly in finance and technology. Military training emphasizes self-sufficiency and task completion without seeking assistance, traits that, while beneficial for military roles, can hinder networking skills essential for civilian employment.

Lacking networking know-how, she resorted to sending hundreds of online resumes daily. Then, one night, while watching television, she stumbled upon an interview with Janet Hanson. Hanson's story as the first woman to attain the position of managing director on the sales and trading floor at Goldman Sachs in 1986, resonated deeply with DeSimone's struggles. "I felt a connection watching her interview," she recalled. "Here I was, having served my country, yet feeling overlooked on Wall Street."

Researching Hanson's background led DeSimone to discover 85 Broads, initially established as a women's network of professionals working at Goldman Sachs' former headquarters on 85 Broad Street.

"I reached out to 85 Broads' customer service in the middle of the night," she recounted. In her email, she introduced herself as a military veteran seeking a career in finance. In a stroke of luck, she received a response from Hanson herself, offering assistance with a condition: she needed to refine her networking skills.

Hanson subsequently connected DeSimone with three influential women and encouraged her to meet them personally. Following these encounters, Hanson imparted a networking strategy to reshape DeSimone's trajectory. "She advised me to ask each woman I met for three additional connections," DeSimone explained. This approach exponentially expanded her network, catalyzing her eventual success. These women became her mentors, guiding her toward her inaugural finance role on the trading floor of Merrill Lynch in 2008.

By 2013, more than 30000 pioneering women from various career paths had joined the 85 Broads network. Sallie Krawcheck, a former Wall Street executive turned fintech entrepreneur, acquired 85 Broads in 2013 and rebranded it as Ellevate in 2014, focusing on women empowering women.[39]

After more than a decade at Nasdaq, DeSimone has carried forward the same ethos of female support, enriching her community. She attributes her successes to the women who extended a helping hand when she needed it most. She recognized the power of networking and human interaction and established Nasdaq's inaugural women's network group upon joining the organization. This initiative reflects her commitment to paying forward the support she received, fostering an environment where women uplift and empower one another. Additionally, she led the establishment of Nasdaq's veterans' program, acknowledging veterans' unique challenges when transitioning to civilian life. DeSimone is also leveraging her role at

Nasdaq to ensure that more fintech start-ups rise and continue to open access to financial tools to more people.

As we emerged from the shadow of COVID-19, a surge in market interest became apparent. Individual stock trading transformed with the advent of user-friendly platforms and real-time information. During Covid, approximately 30 million brokerage accounts were opened in the US between 2020 and 2022 due to advancements in new technologies.[40] With sports suspended and businesses shuttered, the markets became a primary avenue for engagement. While tragic, this unforeseen consequence of the pandemic showed us a silver lining – a newfound enthusiasm for market participation.

In DeSimone's view, Nasdaq operates within a business-to-business (B2B) and a business-to-consumer (B2C) framework, with the former often intertwined with the latter being crucial. "We rely on fintech applications to continue delivering value to their customers, thereby sustaining retail interest and broadening market access," she said. This democratization of finance is pivotal. It's not confined to a particular demographic; anyone with a smartphone and a savings account can now partake in market activities, potentially paving the way for generational wealth.

In light of this, it's mutually beneficial for Nasdaq to leverage data to support fintech companies focused on reshaping the finance narrative, empowering them to grow and potentially become the next IPO company. To ensure the viability of these fintech platforms, Nasdaq must prioritize low barriers to entry and cost-effectiveness. This entails facilitating easy access through APIs and offering data at reasonable rates. Moreover, Nasdaq must cater to retail investors who, despite their involvement, remain cautious amidst market volatility. The key lies in empowering them with knowledge and tools for prudent investing. "So how do we keep them interested? By saying, "Let's teach you how to be smarter investors. Let's give you the tools to stay in the markets but maybe diversify your portfolio in a way you hadn't been doing in 2021," she said.

Beyond mere investment in stocks, Nasdaq is now focused on facilitating more innovative investment strategies for individuals, prioritizing protection while maintaining market participation. This shift involves exploring diverse datasets to achieve this goal.

While individual stocks held allure in 2021, today's market environment necessitates a more balanced approach. Encouraging allocation toward ETFs and index-linked products, renowned for their stability, can help mitigate risk. For instance, the Nasdaq 100® has consistently outperformed broader markets over the past decade. Furthermore, Nasdaq's focus extends beyond traditional stock data. It explores datasets to aid investors in portfolio analysis, encompassing thematic evaluation, risk assessment, and environmental, social, and governance considerations. By comprehensively scrutinizing portfolios, Nasdaq can offer tailored insights to enhance clients' resilience.

Advancing the economy through technology is a vital mission for Nasdaq and leaders like DeSimone who understand that innovative fintech ideas from entrepreneurs, coupled with the rise of women supporting women, are essential for the ecosystem's cohesive success. Together we've created the Nasdaq Fintech Trailblazer contest as an effort, every year, to combine our resources to discover the next fintech company that will fundamentally rewrite tomorrow.

There are a few key learning lessons for women in fintech to take away from DeSimone's story. The importance of seeking inspiration, being unafraid to ask for assistance, and using the power of our networks. DeSimone recognized a unique opportunity and pursued it with tenacity while seeking support and guidance from those around her. This approach resulted in a positive snowball effect, ultimately allowing her to secure her dream job. In addition to her personal success, she is deeply committed to empowering others and supporting more women to attain leadership roles in the traditional financial sector and as start-up founders. Through her work and advocacy, she hopes to influence and transform the business practices of these institutions and start-ups, paving the way for greater diversity and inclusivity in the field. And as a reminder, just like Hanson believed in her, it only takes one person believing in you to become a leader. Turns out, reaching out for help is not a flaw, but a superpower of a great leader.

NOTES

1. Federal Trade Commission. "Equifax Data Breach Settlement." Accessed May 20, 2024. https://www.ftc.gov/enforcement/refunds/equifax-data-breach-settlement.
2. T-Mobile. "T-Mobile Data Breach in 2023." Accessed May 20, 2024. https://www.t-mobile.com/news/business/customer-information.
3. Dropbox. "A Recent Security Incident Involving Dropbox Sign." May 1, 2024. Accessed May 20, 2024. https://sign.dropbox.com/it-IT/blog/a-recent-security-incident-involving-dropbox-sign.
4. Evolved. "Cybersecurity Incident." Accessed May 20, 2024. https://www.getevolved.com/about/news/cybersecurity-incident/.
5. Franceschi-Bicchierai, Lorenzo. "Yieldstreet Says Some of Its Customers Were Affected by the Evolve Bank Data Breach." TechCrunch, July 2, 2024. Accessed May 20, 2024. https://techcrunch.com/2024/07/02/yieldstreet-says-some-of-its-customers-were-affected-by-the-evolve-bank-data-breach/.
6. PYMNTS Intelligence. "PYMNTS FinTech Tracker July 2023." Accessed May 20, 2024. https://www.pymnts.com/wp-content/uploads/2023/07/PYMNTS-FinTech-Tracker-July-2023.pdf.
7. PYMNTS. "Smaller Fintech Issuers Lose Nearly 60 Percent More Revenue to Fraud Than Larger Ones." Accessed May 20, 2024. https://www.pymnts.com/fraud-prevention/2023/smaller-fintech-issuers-lose-nearly-60-percent-more-revenue-to-fraud-than-larger-ones/.
8. Karali, Nansy, Christos Livas, and Faidon Theofanidis. "Technological Innovation, Entrepreneurial Proactiveness and Performance: The Perspective of Female Executives." 2024. Proceedings 3. 10.3390/proceedings2024101003.
9. International Monetary Fund. "Financial Inclusion and Cybersecurity in the Digital Age." December 10, 2020. Accessed May 20, 2024. https://www.imf.org/en/News/Articles/2020/12/10/sp121020-financial-inclusion-and-cybersecurity-in-the-digital-age.

10. Anonybit. "Anonybit Has Raised $8 Million in Capital." Accessed May 20, 2024. https://www.anonybit.io/press-releases/3m_seed_extension.
11. FinTech Sandbox. "Why Is Data So Important?" Accessed May 20, 2024. https://www.fintechsandbox.org/why-is-data-so-important.
12. Urban Institute. "Many Students Borrow to Fund Their Education." Accessed May 20, 2024. https://collegeaffordability.urban.org/covering-expenses/borrowing
13. Federal Student Aid. "Debt Relief Announcement." Accessed May 20, 2024. https://studentaid.gov/debt-relief-announcement.
14. U.S. Department of the Treasury. "Secure Act 2.0 Report to Congress." Accessed May 20, 2024. https://www.treasurydirect.gov/files/savings-bonds/secure-2.0-act-2023-report-to-congress.pdf.
15. NPR. "Student Loan Forgiveness Supreme Court." February 28, 2023. Accessed May 20, 2024. https://www.npr.org/2023/02/28/1159606491/student-loan-forgiveness-supreme-court.
16. U.S. Department of Education. "A First Look at Student Loan Repayment After the Payment Pause." December 2023. Accessed May 20, 2024. https://blog.ed.gov/2023/12/a-first-look-at-student-loan-repayment-after-the-payment-pause.
17. Yahoo Finance. "Nearly Half of Americans Have Less Than $500 for Emergency Expenses." Accessed May 20, 2024. https://finance.yahoo.com/news/nearly-half-americans-less-500-120012475.html.
18. Candidly. "FutureFuel.io Acquires College Finance Company to Expand Beyond Student Debt, Rebrands to Candidly." Accessed May 20, 2024. https://getcandidly.com/futurefuel-io-acquires-college-finance-company-to-expand-beyond-student-debt-rebrands-to-candidly.
19. Business Wire. "TIAA MIT AgeLab Study Finds Student Loan Debt Significantly Impacts Retirement Savings, Longevity Planning, and Family Relationships." July 30, 2019. Accessed May 20, 2024. https://www.businesswire.com/news/home/20190730005618/en/TIAA-MIT-AgeLab-Study-Finds-Student-Loan-Debt-Significantly-Impacts-Retirement-Savings-Longevity-Planning-and-Family-Relationships.
20. Federal Reserve. "The Effect of Student Loan Debt on Retirement Savings." Accessed May 20, 2024. https://www.federalreserve.gov/econres/feds/files/2022019pap.pdf.
21. Candidly. "Candidly's Partnership with American Eagle Outfitters Helps Pay Down More Than $100,000 of Student Debt for Associates." Accessed May 20, 2024. https://getcandidly.com/candidlys-partnership-with-american-eagle-outfitters-helps-pay-down-more-than-100000-of-student-debt-for-associates.

22. American Association of University Women. "Fast Facts: Student Debt." Accessed May 20, 2024. https://www.aauw.org/resources/article/fast-facts-student-debt.

23. U.S. Department of Labor. "5 Fast Facts: The Gender Wage Gap." March 14, 2023. Accessed May 20, 2024. https://blog.dol.gov/2023/03/14/5-fast-facts-the-gender-wage-gap.

24. Business Wire. "Candidly Raises $20.5 Million to Help Millions of Americans Repay Student Debt and Build Savings." March 7, 2023. Accessed May 20, 2024. https://www.businesswire.com/news/home/20230307005464/en/Candidly-Raises-20.5-Million-to-Help-Millions-of-Americans-Repay-Student-Debt-and-Build-Savings.

25. Internal Revenue Service. "Reminder: Educational Assistance Programs Can Help Pay Workers' Student Loans." Accessed May 20, 2024. https://www.irs.gov/newsroom/reminder-educational-assistance-programs-can-help-pay-workers-student-loans.

26. Federal Deposit Insurance Corporation. "Bank Failures in Brief." Accessed May 20, 2024. https://www.fdic.gov/resources/resolutions/bank-failures/in-brief/index.html.

27. LIMRA. "2023 LIMRA Life Insurance Awareness Month Fact Sheet." Accessed May 20, 2024. https://www.limra.com/siteassets/newsroom/liam/2023/0859-2023-liam-fact-sheet-2023_final.pdf.

28. Swiss Re. "Mortality Protection Gap: $25 Trillion in the U.S." Accessed May 20, 2024. https://www.swissre.com/reinsurance/life-and-health/reinsurance/america-lh.html.

29. International Labour Organization. "Women in Leadership Bring Better Business Performance." Accessed May 20, 2024. https://www.ilo.org/resource/news/women-leadership-bring-better-business-performance.

30. Swiss Re. "The Role of Insurance in Reducing Income Inequality." May 11, 2022. Accessed May 20, 2024. https://www.swissre.com/dam/jcr:978cea72-60d6-410b-acf0-071a3393d69c/2022-05-11-sigma03-role-of-insurance-in-reducing-income-inequality-en.pdf.

31. Nasdaq. "Nasdaq to Move Global Headquarters to 4 Times Square." Accessed May 20, 2024. https://www.nasdaq.com/about/press-center/nasdaq-move-global-headquarters-4-times-square.

32. Nasdaq. "Nasdaq Welcomed 743 IPOs and 35 Exchange Transfers in 2021." Accessed May 20, 2024. https://ir.nasdaq.com/news-releases/news-release-details/nasdaq-welcomed-743-ipos-and-35-exchange-transfers-2021.

33. 23andMe. "News: 23andMe on Nasdaq." Accessed May 20, 2024. https://blog.23andme.com/articles/news-23andme-on-nasdaq.

34. Bumble. "Bumble IPO: Whitney Wolfe Herd Speech." Accessed May 20, 2024. https://bumble.com/en-us/the-buzz/bumble-ipo-whitney-wolfe-herd-speech.

35. Reuters. "Fashion Firm Rent the Runway Struts into Wall St. with $1.7 Billion Valuation." October 27, 2021. Accessed May 20, 2024. https://www.reuters.com/business/retail-consumer/fashion-firm-rent-runway-struts-into-wall-st-with-17-billion-valuation-2021-10-27.

36. Visual Capitalist. "Female Founders in U.S. IPOs." Access ed. May 20, 2024. https://www.visualcapitalist.com/female-founders-in-us-ipos.

37. U.S. Navy Information Warfare Forces. "NAVIFOR Celebrates Women's History Month 2023." Accessed May 20, 2024. https://www.navifor.usff.navy.mil/Press-Room/Press-Releases/Article/3342594/navifor-celebrates-womens-history-month-2023.

38. Deloitte. "Diversity and Inclusion in Financial Services Leadership." Accessed May 20, 2024. https://www2.deloitte.com/us/en/insights/industry/financial-services/diversity-and-inclusion-in-financial-services-leadership.html.

39. Ellevate Network. "Krawcheck to Acquire 85 Broads from Former Ex-Goldman Executive." Accessed May 20, 2024. https://www.ellevatenetwork.com/press/21-krawcheck-to-acquire-85-broads-from-former-ex-goldman-executive.

40. Sweaterventures. "The Rise of Retail Investors in Alternative Investments: A Decade-Long Trend." Accessed May 20, 2024. https://www.sweaterventures.com/insights/the-rise-of-retail-investors-in-alternative-investments-a-decade-long-trend.

CHAPTER EIGHT

THE ROOM
WHERE IT
HAPPENS

B orn in Ethiopia, Lule Demmissie traveled and lived in numerous countries before finding her anchor in the United States at 16. Her sharp intelligence and drive led her to Smith College, where she graduated with a degree in economics in 1996. By the early 2000s, she was in Columbia Business School when the tech-heavy Nasdaq-100 dropped by 80% due to the boom and subsequent bust of new-age start-ups.[1] The US economy, also reeling from the fallout of the 11 September attacks, plunged into an eight-month recession. She eventually graduated in 2001 and soon after began her career on Wall Street, working in equity research, saddled with student loan debt and supported by a work visa. She was an analyst and financial consultant at JP Morgan and Merrill Lynch, prior to business school. After her MBA from Columbia, she took up executive director roles at Morgan Stanley and TD Ameritrade and eventually climbed the ranks to become the President of Ally Invest in 2019. During those two decades, she absorbed the lessons of Wall Street like a sponge, realizing that behind the scenes, money, economics, and capital markets lie a source of individual empowerment, particularly for those unrepresented communities overlooked. She survived the last three market meltdowns – the dot-com bubble, the Global Financial Crisis, and the COVID-19 pandemic – as a person, an investor, and an industry leader. Her mental framework of "this too shall pass" enabled her to work through these challenging economic times in our history because she could lean on her understanding of investing and finance, as it provides a lens to decipher the enigmatic "matrix" of our ever-shifting world, she shared.

In 2021, Demmissie advanced further in her career and assumed the role of CEO and Board Member of eToro US, one of the largest global fintech platforms for retail investors with millions of users across the globe. For Demmissie, joining a fintech company as CEO stemmed from her belief that wealth creation is a right and is power. Through her representation, she aims to provide easy access to capital markets and digital assets, enabling wealth creation and broadening capital formation and inclusion to a broader group beyond the typical ultra-wealthy individuals with access to and understanding of such resources. Her determination has made working in financial services more than just a source of income; it has become a calling, a higher purpose.

NOT THROWING AWAY OUR SHOT

Few CEOs stand as uniquely equipped to tackle the pressing issue of inadequate representation in financial institutions than Demmissie. With a distinguished career spanning both Wall Street and fintech start-ups, she deftly leverages her potent blend of finance expertise, emotional intelligence, and diverse identity facets – as a Black woman, immigrant, and member of the LGBTQ+ community – to propel her career to unparalleled heights. Her roadmap as a trailblazer is grounded in how she strategically navigates obstacles, shattering barriers and reshaping the future of fintech. The best part about her is that she's always ready and willing to teach others how to masterfully circumvent obstacles when climbing the upper echelons of corporate America. I am lucky to call her a friend and mentor over the years. Her inspiring teachings have influenced what I built as founder and CEO of my media company, Fintech Is Femme, and how I continue to lead with curiosity as a journalist. In this section, I'm breaking down the key lessons I've learned from Demmissie so you can leverage them, too – including her tactical strategies for successfully navigating corporate environments by building supportive networks and advocating for diversity.

Before diving into her insights, let's take a moment to recognize just how impressive and vital her leadership is. With experiences in high-profile leadership roles across banks, brokerages, and fintech companies, she has created a historical mark for women in the industry, especially considering women hold less than 10% of leadership positions as founders and members of executive boards of fintech firms, and only 5.6% of CEOs in fintech are women, according to research from the International Monetary Fund.[2] While there is limited data on the demographic breakdown of fintech CEOs, Black women in America face a significant disparity in leadership roles across business sectors. Only four Black women have ever been CEOs in a Fortune 500 company. Ursula Burns served as CEO of Xerox Co. from 2010 to 2016, and Mary Winston was the interim CEO at Bed Bath & Beyond in 2019. In March 2021, Rosalind Brewer became the third Black female CEO when she assumed the role of CEO of Walgreens Boots Alliance. In May 2021, Thasunda Brown Duckett was appointed as the fourth Black woman to join the ranks of CEOs as she became the President & CEO of TIAA.

"I don't want to be a unicorn; I want to be a farm horse," Demmissie shared, her voice carrying its usual blend of determination and warmth. As a journalist, my encounters with Demmissie have been as varied as they've been enriching. It's not surprising, considering she has sat in the decision-making room of institutions that wield significant influence over our societal fabric and economic landscape. Yet she continuously brings forth a perspective dedicated to propelling positive change within the financial sector – evident in every exchange we've shared. Over the years, I've learned that Demmissie's multicultural upbringing is the foundation for her ability to relate to diverse individuals and maintain an aspirational mindset. "What's helped me is expanding my closest network to include people from dozens of countries," Demmissie shared. "The more diverse my connections, the more I realize bridges and tunnels exist for all cultures."

Research shows leaders with a global mindset do more than uphold equity and inclusion – they fundamentally understand how cultural identity influences the communication styles, values, and needs of communities worldwide. Embracing her intersectionality, Demmissie refers to her heightened emotional intelligence as her "third eye," a tool she strategically wields to connect with people from all walks of life. It's a strategy she credits with propelling her up corporate leadership ranks to build diverse teams. "People are willing to connect and be open when they feel seen," she said. "They're motivated by it."

As the fintech industry grapples with many challenges, ranging from banking sector instability to high-profile crypto trials, Demmissie relies on her innate ability to empathize, communicate effectively, and see multiple diverse perspectives. She recognizes that these qualities are crucial in navigating the complex landscape of the financial world. Despite the obstacles, Demmissie remains resolute in her conviction that, amidst the chaos, there lies an opportunity to transform financial outcomes and promote inclusivity on a global scale. She understands courage is born from facing our fears head-on and is determined to leverage her expertise to create a more equitable and prosperous future for all.

As she likes to say, "I wore my Hamilton scarf because I'm not going to waste my shot."

She certainly has put in the work. As a Black woman in finance, Demmissie acknowledges that she has encountered her fair share of obstacles and failures throughout her career. She directly experiences and recognizes the systemic barriers that Black women face in corporate America, enabling her to navigate them – and teach others – becoming an even more innovative and trailblazing CEO. Unfortunately, Black women in the workforce are subjected to a specific set of systemic discrimination that results from the intersection of sexism and racism, which limits leadership opportunities due to a lack of representation. Even as entrepreneurs, Black female founders earned just 0.34% of venture capital funding in 2021, according to Crunchbase data.[3] That shows how few influential and impactful products and companies are being built to serve Black women. Despite having the highest labor force participation when compared to other women, Black women are paid only 67 cents for every dollar paid to white men.[4] With the ongoing attacks on diversity, equity, and inclusion initiatives, particularly in the aftermath of the rollback of affirmative action in higher education and the ripple effect that has had on corporate America's DEI programs, the environment for Black women looking to advance in their careers has become even more hostile. As a result, the representation of Black female senior leadership remains disproportionately low. Therefore, it is crucial to stop expecting Black women to fix themselves and instead tell companies to treat them fairly.

These realities are complex, no doubt; however, as Demmissie has always said, "As the saying goes, you don't eat an elephant all at once; you take one bite at a time." She speaks from personal experiences, and while her knowledge of the system doesn't immunize her from its impact, it did help her manage her response to it. "I'd describe my approach as deliberate and incremental yet impatient," she said.

Demmissie means we shouldn't be patient for change but must strategically plan incrementally to effect it. Eating the elephant one bite at a time illustrates this philosophy. Sometimes, the desire for immediate change without a structured plan can lead to disappointment and disillusionment. Several factors contribute to meaningful change. Diversity in decision-making is paramount. CEOs must actively pursue it.

Furthermore, diversity is essential because homogeneous teams often share the same blind spots and assumptions, which can stifle innovation. Embracing diversity mitigates blind spots, enriching products and decision-making processes – a necessity in an industry like fintech designed for innovation. In terms of diversity, inclusion, and equity, intentional cultural design and courage are required from all involved. "It's a combination of cultural intentionality and programmatic design," Demmissie shared.

A part of that design means when Demmissie hires diverse teams, she insists on seeing a wide swath of talent. As CEO of eToro US Demmissie loves serving future generations in finance because millennials, and younger generations, are the first minority-majority demographic. So ultimately, it makes moral and business sense to ensure that her employee base is diverse. Demmissie believes that diversity and merit are not in conflict. She believes only the lazy mind would see them in conflict. Yes, it takes intention but in the long run, it is well worth the effort. Throughout her career, she has ensured the interviewing circle is also diverse. As a pro tip, Demmissie always discusses why being inclusive is essential. It's not necessarily the conversation piece for innovation we hear from all CEOs. Many studies have shown that organizations benefit from diverse thinking, staff heterogeneity, and inclusiveness when formulating and executing new ideas. For instance, in 2018, Boston Consulting Group conducted a research study analyzing 1700 entities worldwide. The study found that companies with more diverse leadership teams generated higher innovation-related revenues. BCG considered various factors such as diversity in gender, ethnicity, professional background, age, and sexual orientation. The study discovered that companies with below-average diversity at the leadership level generated, on average, about 26% of their revenues from innovation and change (i.e. new products, services, and features launched in the past three years). On the other hand, companies with above-average diversity at the leadership level derived almost half (45%) of their revenue from innovation.[5] To ensure that your company benefits from diversity, it all starts with the routines established by the founder and CEO.

"Tone at the top is necessary to establish those routines," she said. "But you also need to have the sticky glue of a cohesive culture – because routines are useless without it." As a leader, how do you ensure that you have that culture? Look for people who will be an extension of cultural transformations. When I asked her about overcoming biases in talent evaluation, Demmissie emphasized the importance of cultural malleability. The more types of people one knows, the less likely bias is to creep into decision-making processes. Creating a company culture that resembles a tossed salad, where people mix and get to know each other's stories, can mitigate biases when promotions and opportunities arise.

"So, I don't have to go around saying I need to do this," Demmissie said. "I just empower people who have that kind of vision." Then, you can rely on those cultural champions within the company to start incubating a petri dish of ideas. One of Demmissie's routines throughout her career when an employee joins a company she has led is an onboarding process that ensures they've met all the leaders they'll be working with in an informal setting.

"For a lot of people who have that sense of 'otherness,' that 'imposter' feeling, they don't necessarily reach out as much, right?" she said. "Because they feel like, 'Okay, I don't have the right, you know, it's not the right group. It's not my crew.'" To combat these feelings, Demmissie meets every new person who comes in through a Zoom call or an in-person meeting. "From the very start, we instill the idea that people matter," she said. From the beginning, Demmissie signals to employees that "your story matters."

Every Friday, during stand-up meetings, Demmissie champions models that encourage people to share about themselves. Because at the end of the day, regardless of our ethnic or gender identity, the core human desire is to be seen. Demmissie's success results from her endeavor to engineer programs, cultural elements, and actual policies that nurture what needs to be seen. Once somebody feels seen, they'll go to the moon for you and their teammates. "Money is one component, for sure, but when people feel seen and helped to improve their skills, it's this intangible thing that makes them want to break through walls for you and their team," she said.

However, putting routines in place takes practice – like any new opportunity. It takes a few reps to get it right. "If your company hires from diverse ethnic groups, but they all segregate during mealtimes or social events, you haven't truly achieved diversity and inclusion," Demmissie said. "You may have the numbers, but the goal remains unmet. And if you fail to achieve genuine inclusivity, it inevitably fosters the rise of other forms of discrimination due to the inability to integrate. Resentment of one group over another may end up rising." Ultimately, there is success on the other side of intentionality in designing routines and cultural practices that foster that connective glue between people.

It is essential to build diverse teams and advocate for diversity without considering it a zero-sum game where one person's inclusion means another's exclusion. To promote diversity, CEOs and leaders can take note of Demmissie's suggestions:

1. Encourage employees to share their stories in open forums.
2. Invite emerging talent to present at management meetings.
3. Organize roundtable discussions where different teams can ask questions and share perspectives.

4. Ensure leaders are accessible to employees, as it helps them feel valued and seen.

5. Provide employees with rotational role, or project, opportunities to diversify their knowledge and skills.

As we see incremental steps toward progress, Demmissie urges that ultimately, as individuals, playing it safe doesn't encourage personal or professional growth. Women like Demmissie believe in bold actions as they believe fortune favors the brave. As she said, it's all about rethinking how you perceive risk. "Are you ready to embrace disruption and shape a more exciting and equitable world," she said, "or will you resist it?" Her advice for leaders is to build the infrastructure that supports it instead of resisting change. It's what drew Demmissie to join fintech in the first place. "One reason I value this disruptor fintech platform is because I've always approached investing with an 'and' mindset rather than an 'or,'" she recalled. "I find it intriguing when people frame progress in binary terms, such as declaring social investing bad because traditional investing is good. Both approaches have merits and drawbacks, and we should evaluate both their good and their potential moral hazards as discerning consumers. The individual investor is not a child that needs parenting. Such thinking only leads to less innovations that can expand their access."

As Demmissie explains, we live in an era of "and," where an inclusive mindset allows us to extract value from disruptions. Conversely, resisting change and thinking in terms of "but" risks falling behind or losing out entirely as change inevitably prevails. The question is: Are you adaptable enough to harness change for personal transformation, or will it sweep you away? Fintech, like many other disruptive industries, stands at this critical juncture.

Demmissie's perspective and strategies around leadership have a unique lens; she seemingly – and seamlessly – combines purpose-driven and a "happy warrior" orientation to execution. Purpose-driven leadership is about helping employees find meaning in their work and creating a committed workforce that shares common objectives that are anchored in value-based decisioning. Happy warrior leaders find a "yes" and "can" in their ability to make decisions and execute. Both leadership styles overlap and take intentional effort to succeed. The hardest part? Both approaches value humility, a lack of ego, and a belief that joy can be at the center of excellent execution and a pursuit of high performance in business.

One of the central pillars in Demmissie's leadership philosophy revolves around instilling inclusivity and excellent execution as a core value within a fintech company. She knows this is easier said than done. "It's a very complex challenge our society has and will take repeat practice to address," she said. "Ultimately, where I find my center of gravity and being able to change things is showing instead of telling, which means that representation matters – not just speaking about our desire for diversity." Per Demmissie's blueprint, this means making sure that representation is incorporated into:

1. Your friendship circles
2. Your network
3. Your hiring practices

If you need a diverse friendship circle, go to meetups, do other things, and open your world. "When the center of your friendship circle diversifies, your work network changes and you become a recruiter," she shared. "You become a valuable recruiter when opportunities come about." So, step one: Make sure your nest egg of network and friendship is intentionally diverse.

The other thing that helps is that your life will be more enjoyable. "Because, as I always say, you're not eating rice pudding daily, right?" Demmissie told me. "I guarantee you your life is more enriched by having different people in your life." The other part is figuring out how to be in a diverse ecosystem business; it takes work. "If you're not practicing it in your personal and network circles, how are you supposed to be good at it in your work circles?"

A mountain of research shows that professional networks lead to more job and business opportunities, broader and deeper knowledge, improved innovation capacity, and faster advancement. Over the years, we've learned that leaders who create the space for actual vulnerability build psychologically safe work environments where people feel welcome to be themselves.[6] We've learned that when people are willing to be authentic at work, they're also more willing to take creative risks, share their perspectives without fear of a consequence, and make valuable contributions that can only be expressed within a culture that values trust and inclusion.

However, Demmissie urges us to be careful with our desire to seek "safe spaces" because courage is essential for growth. Building resilience is crucial to engage in diverse conversations without constantly flinching. "Safety alone isn't sufficient," she shared. "It can lead to a reliance on others to do the work. It's a two-way street; we must also put in the effort ourselves and risk engaging even if we falter."

People often seek Demmissie's career advice, even if they no longer work for her. As you can tell, she provides tough love, emphasizing the importance of building oneself up, taking risks, and not outsourcing risk-taking. One commonality in human behavior she has observed leading teams of thousands of employees is that we often create stories in our heads to avoid admitting our mistakes or weaknesses. This tendency can be a hindrance. It's okay to indulge in this self-pitying narrative momentarily, but it becomes problematic if it becomes habitual and obstructs your progress. She does not mean we should not be kind to ourselves. She merely stresses that it's crucial to objectively analyze the situation and the story you're telling yourself as you diagnose the take-aways. "Sometimes, you may realize you don't fit into that narrative," she said. "In such cases, you have two options: change your environment or develop the resilience and networking skills needed to secure your place." Everyone faces moments where they must make a choice. The critical mental framework to remember is: "Am I constructing a self-serving story rooted in some denial, or am I observing the facts?"

Work is a significant part of our lives; if it's unhealthy, it can impact our overall well-being. Before leaving a toxic workplace, address the narratives you've told yourself. Sometimes, it's not just the place; it's the stories you've internalized. In terms of tough love, Demmissie has "learned to trust advice from those who've faced failures, as I have," she said. "The courage to fail out loud gives you credibility to advise others."

However, when mentoring, she first assesses a mentee's readiness. Not everyone is prepared for tough love; some may have unresolved issues. So, it's essential to gauge their readiness. Don't come in with a heavy dose of tough love for someone struggling – calibration is critical. The second step is to ask mentees questions to understand their troubles. "People will listen to advice if they feel cared for," she said. "I build them up by leading with questions and listening. Even though I enjoy talking!" Next, Demmissie repeats what they've said to ensure she understands correctly. "Retelling their grievance helps them self-correct their version of the truth. It is a natural antidote that encourages self-reflection and mental breakthroughs for people," she shared. Finally, Demmissie asks permission to provide tough love, emphasizing that she has their best interests at heart. This step only happens if the person is ready for it, as it can be overwhelming for others without the proper preparation.

TONE AT THE TOP

Unfortunately, we're all likely to experience a toxic work culture at some point in our careers, which often begins at the top. If leadership fails to set an aspirational value-based tone, it's tough to effect change. "So, imagine you've worked in such an environment where the leader was closed off, didn't listen, and didn't make themselves vulnerable," Demmissie said. "If you carry that baggage to a new company, it's like bringing cynicism and resentment in your suitcase."

When transitioning to a new environment with slightly better leadership, it's essential to recognize that taking small risks can be beneficial. Rather than jumping in headfirst, taking calculated risks in small bites can be a valuable tactic. "Engaging in small risk-taking teaches me to ensure that the light we often shine on feelings of inadequacy or job insecurity gets redirected towards our power center," Demmissie said. "Your power center isn't about going to an employer and complaining about how the company sucks. It's about mastering the art of communication and self-awareness." Demmissie told me it's about understanding different cultures, leading with vulnerability, and courage to address issues. "I'm not referring to black and white HR themes; I'm talking about the more nuanced aspects of company culture," she said. If we all approached situations generously, giving each other the benefit of the doubt, it would facilitate discussions within our community. When nobody extends this courtesy, tensions rise. So, the key is to communicate your concerns with the mindset of assuming the best intentions and avoiding the trap of self-storytelling. We all have a finite amount of energy, and it's essential to redirect it from dwelling on negativity toward self-care and personal growth. Plus, by taking calculated risks frequently, you learn to recover quickly from any setbacks that may occur. This rapid recovery is crucial to prevent the baggage of a previous toxic environment from affecting your new one. As Demmissie said, "Faster and frequent recovery ability is the key to ensuring that whatever bad environment you're in doesn't come with you in a suitcase to the next environment." So, take those small risks, focus on your strengths, and progress toward personal growth and success. "No matter my situation, I'm a Black woman in finance. Hello, you know what I mean? I've had some pretty tough rides," she told me. "But as I've grown wiser and older, the favor I want to do for myself is not to let those experiences define me entirely or bring me down."

This is why Demmissie emphasizes the power of not telling ourselves false stories simply to feel good. "Because if we either need to blame some-one or dwelling on those negative narratives it dims our light. What we focus on is what our life outlook is made up of. We have a choice to protect our light," she said. "I can channel that light into toxic thoughts or focus it on things that make me stronger, brighter, and more resolute."

When I asked her about some of the best partners she's ever worked with and their characteristics, she admitted that as an experienced CEO, she's intensely drawn to pragmatic optimists who see the glass as half full. "That's something they all have in common," she recalled. "They're the ones who don't squander their opportunities." Also, success often comes hand in hand with those who understand the art of reciprocity. There's nothing inherently wrong with taking, but one must also grasp the importance of giving. Sometimes, in business, leaders who have yet to be vetted for simply being excellent human beings are prematurely elevated to high places.

"In my experience, successful partnerships are built on two pillars," Demmissie said. "Firstly, there must be a sound business logic, and I can't delude myself on a business model that is broken, or non-viable. This does not mean we are not aspirational on new ideas, but we need to be grounded. Secondly, there's the quality of being open-minded, giving as much as one takes, and embodying a generous, servant-leader mentality." That's been a consistent theme, although she acknowledges it's also her bias. "We must be cautious not to elevate our ideals of what constitutes an excellent human being to the point of bias," she said.

Demmissie has experienced successful partnerships with individuals who were the opposite of what she just described, but they are rare because they require substantial effort to make work. Nevertheless, she always sees the learning lessons from those difficult relationships because they offer a different perspective. "Therefore, I seek out experiences that challenge my thinking and bring new insights, including emotional intelligence, into every business endeavor I undertake," she admits.

Why? Because change always wins. So, are you adaptive and able to take that change and use it as diesel for your transformation? Or are you going to be a victim of it?

PLAYING THE CARDS WE'RE DEALT

Jenny Just has a track record of shattering barriers in finance. When asked about her journey, she openly acknowledges her initial lack of expertise in the industry. "I'd say I was pretty average with money," she told me. "I didn't connect to why having a deeper understanding of money was so important. While money isn't everything, everything is money."

Hearing her share this admission can feel striking, considering she's now a billionaire who has played a pivotal role in the success of fintech giants like SoFi, eToro, Betterment, and Webull. What ties these companies together is their reliance on Apex Fintech Solutions for back-end trading services, a platform owned by Just and her husband, Matt Hulsizer, through their Chicago-based investment firm, PEAK6. Since acquiring Apex in 2012, Just has transformed it into a "fintech for fintechs," providing trading and technology solutions for more than 200 clients – think most investment platforms. But you haven't heard her name before despite her heavy hand impacting a large swath of the fintech ecosystem. That's intentional. She has been quietly building her empire in fintech, and only in recent years has she come out of the shadows to show there are opportunities for women to succeed in fintech.

Starting as one of the few women to trade on the floor of the Chicago Options Exchange, she's crossed the ranks of Wall Street in the upper echelons of corporate America. Growing up in Wisconsin with the ambition to work in Chicago, Just interviewed with three firms – a bank, an advertising agency, and a company called O'Connor and Associates – after graduating from the University of Michigan. She took a job with O'Connor and Associates, where she eventually went to work on the trading floor. According to Just, it's like what you've seen in movies – a huge room with tons of men trying to scream over each other. She worked her way through the company, trading in different aspects, and when Swiss Bank came in to do a joint venture, she moved into something called over-the-counter equity derivatives, a non-exchange traded product. Just's experience building that business helped her prepare for her entrepreneurial journey after she left the firm and built PEAK6 under the fundamental belief that the technology side of fintech is the driving force to make any traditional or outdated system work better for everyone.

When I interviewed Just for an episode of my podcast in the summer of 2023, we immediately dove into her belief that anyone can work in finance, tech, or fintech. "The smartest person isn't necessarily the best fit for a lot of what we do at our business today," she said. "They have to be intelligent, of course, but curiosity and hard work far outweigh raw intellect." The notion that you can only excel if you possess a certain IQ level isn't accurate. Just understands that diversity in perspectives – and strong EQ – enriches her company's approach to market dynamics, which evolve constantly. Different viewpoints are invaluable in navigating this ever-changing landscape. "Bringing in someone who offers a fresh perspective has been key to the longevity of our business," Just said.

She loves building her company but has never been one to seek the spotlight despite being one of the most formidable figures in fintech. "Perhaps that's been my greatest risk," she shared. "Despite being approached for years to take on public appearances, my answer was always a firm 'no.'" Recently, she realized that if she didn't step up, who would become a role model for women in finance, technology, and fintech? Sure, the numbers slowly improved over her 25-year career, but setbacks like COVID-19 posed new challenges. Someone needed to step up, and Just felt compelled to fill that void. Another crucial aspect for her was ensuring that her presence would tangibly benefit women, offering insights that could inspire change in their professional lives.

Just recalls that she was only 29 when she leaped, starting PEAK6 without a clear roadmap. Back then, there wasn't the same level of scrutiny or social media saturation. "No one told me I couldn't do it, and I wasn't surrounded by start-up culture," she shared. The decision to venture into entrepreneurship stemmed partly from practical reasons – she didn't want to relocate when her firm was acquired. So, she simply replicated what they were doing but with a technological edge, which turned out to be fortuitous. Her learning lesson from that move: Entrepreneurship isn't reserved for a select few; anyone with determination can embark on this journey.

At PEAK6, Just ensures the employee experience is transformative. She wants women, especially young women, to understand the massive impact of working in fintech. "You're at the heart of the economy, influencing and being influenced by every development," she said. "Every corporate story directly ties into your work, making you an integral part of the cultural zeitgeist."

She's right. The pace of this industry is exhilarating, with ample opportunities for financial growth. "I find it gratifying to empower young women who, like me, didn't come from a finance background," she shared. "The field is wide open, waiting for those willing to leap."

She takes pride in having created something unique to ensure a positive impact on women of all generations – and it isn't just how she runs her business with an open mind or her decision to step into the spotlight after several decades. Her biggest passion and secret to success? Poker.

AIN'T NO HOLD 'EM

She has gleaned a few observations from her time building in fintech and as a mother to a daughter. Women tend to wait till we're comfortable and we have enough information. Men tend to run in quickly and take risks early without full knowledge. As women, we'll do our homework, which takes a little longer. That's why Just is also committed to empowering women, mainly through her company, Poker Power, which in 2020 she created to train one million girls and women in Texas Hold 'em.

"I've been surrounded by poker players my whole career," she said. "And I always thought it was just another guy thing wasting time. And as it turns out, it wasn't. And we are teaching women every single day."

Learning poker can help women better understand strategy, risk, and capital allocation. "The most important thing about it is that you're practicing making decisions," she said. Those decisions allow you to build confidence and have a tangible way to help you in your everyday work.

As women, we need to embrace the concept of risk-taking and grasp and internalize what it feels like because that's entrepreneurship. And what better way to do that than with a game many of us know and love – or at least have heard of in some capacity, from seeing it in movies?

Poker Power is a passion project close to Just's heart. "We have a small operational team dedicated to it, but a large group of teachers who work tirelessly every day to educate more people about this game," she said. "It's fascinating because poker has been hiding in plain sight for so long. Despite its negative stereotypes, it's a game of skill, and the skills it teaches apply professionally and in everyday life."

Men have been leveraging these skills for years, with more than 100 million poker players worldwide. However, less than 7% of them are women. Boys learn strategy, risk-taking, and capital allocation through poker from a young age. These are essential skills for success in various fields, especially finance and technology.

Just's journey with poker began only four years ago, purely by chance. Her youngest daughter, a talented athlete, was struggling in a tennis match. "My husband suggested she learn poker to understand strategy and decision-making," she recalled. Initially skeptical, Just eventually embraced the idea and hired a local high school teacher who plays poker to teach her daughter and her friends. The transformation she witnessed was astounding. From shy whispers to confident players, it was clear that poker was more than just a game – it was a tool for empowerment.

What started as a local initiative spans more than 40 countries and includes partnerships with major corporations and organizations. Poker Power has become a vehicle for women to develop confidence, strategy, and resilience. It's not just about the cards; it's about understanding your opponent and making calculated decisions – skills crucial in both professional and personal settings.

Like any skill, the key to mastering poker is practice. Men often have more opportunities to play and hone their skills, giving them a competitive edge. But Poker Power aims to level the playing field, providing women with the tools and confidence to thrive. The principles of poker are at play in classrooms, negotiation rooms, and boardrooms. By empowering women to take risks and trust their instincts, Just's initiative reshapes the narrative and breaks down gender barriers.

So, the next time you're faced with a challenging decision, remember: it's not about the cards you're dealt; it's how you play your hand. And with women in fintech like Just and her company Poker Power, women everywhere are learning to play – and win – the game of life.

With this mindset, Just said she believes there's a tremendous opportunity to address the gender gap in leadership, which is particularly impactful considering that nearly half of the workforce in finance comprises women. However, when it comes to leadership roles, that percentage drops significantly, hovering around 10% or even lower. So, what's causing this disparity? It's a complex interplay of various factors we've already gone over, but at the root of the problem is a system that needs to be fixed – not women.

In December 2023, Tori Dunlap, founder and CEO of herfirst100k, invited me to learn and play at a Poker Power event in New York City. The game is remarkable in many ways; it's edgy, different, and incredibly eye-opening. However, it can also be tricky for some to understand why teaching poker is valuable. I've noticed a recent trend where there's been discussion about the importance of teaching women golf, even suggesting that companies should sponsor their employees to learn. While I appreciate the sentiment, I find poker a much more accessible and enjoyable skill. After one night of playing, I realized I had been playing poker my entire life – I just didn't know it. The skills I learned from playing poker helped me learn to take calculated risks. Here are some key lessons I learned from playing poker:

1. **Play to Win** – Bet big and use your knowledge from observing others to your advantage.
2. **Take Risk** – In life, you don't always get dealt the best cards. Get comfortable with being uncomfortable. Take calculated risks with imperfect information. You have to have an opinion, and you have to act on it. Make a judgment call and bet on it.
3. **Be Confident** – Bluffing is just acting confidently in a negotiation to increase your chances of winning. Act with confidence even when you don't have a winning hand. Trust yourself. You're doing the right thing.

As women, we're often told to play small, but in poker, it pays off to play big. Women must practice setting the price and taking control of the power dynamic in any given situation. During one night, I learned that poker is an excellent way to do that. Imagine how different our world would be if millions of women learned those lessons earlier.

"At PEAK6, we make it a point to offer poker lessons to all employees, regardless of gender," Just shared. While it's true that some may already know how to play, it's not a gender-specific skill. CEOs and leaders are responsible for fostering diversity within their workforce, including providing opportunities for skill development beyond traditional avenues.

"We've conducted numerous tests, including having senior teams play poker together, and the results have been enlightening," Just said. "Playing poker breaks down barriers and allows individuals to see each other in a different light." It's a game that requires strategic thinking, adaptability, and a keen understanding of human behavior – invaluable skills in any setting.

One of the most intriguing aspects of poker is how it mirrors real-life scenarios. Take this story, for example:

One day, Just got off a call from one of the CEOs of one of PEAK6's businesses looking for advice. It's a big deal that they are negotiating. She notes that everyone knows they have more to give but asks the CEO what cards they think the other company has. "I think they're bluffing, and we should call," they said. Every hand is different, just like every business negotiation or project collaboration. By playing poker, individuals develop a common language and framework for discussing strategy and decision-making. So, what happened when Just and her team decided to call their opponent? Well, they were right. It turns out the company on the other side of the table was bluffing, and ultimately, PEAK6 got the deal it wanted.

Every hand is different, just like every business negotiation or project collaboration. By playing poker, individuals develop a common language and framework for discussing strategy and decision-making.

Poker also provides a unique opportunity to teach women to play to win, which isn't always emphasized in our upbringing. "Our goal isn't just to teach a million women to play poker; it's to achieve gender parity in the world," Just said. That's why she developed the Poker Power Play app – what Just considers to be the first gender-neutral platform where anyone can learn and practice poker. Whether you are a beginner or an experienced player, the app provides the tools and resources you need to know.

Just shows us that poker isn't just a game – it's a vehicle for change. It's about leveling the playing field, breaking gender barriers, and empowering women to thrive in any competitive arena.

With the app ready to go, Just's next task was the challenge of mass distribution. "How do we make poker more accessible and appealing? How do we position it as something different, something more engaging? Getting the engine up and running was just the first step," Just recalled. "Now, we're focusing on enhancing the user experience. We want to create a soft landing for users, a place where they can continuously improve their skills – a sort of 'Peloton of poker' concept."

Just wants users to track their progress, like monitoring steps on a fitness app. How many hands are they playing? How many are they folding? Users can gain insights into their style and strategy by analyzing their gameplay patterns. This, in turn, can help them in real-world scenarios like negotiations or decision-making.

The app offers daily community games, providing players with a fun and supportive environment. "It's fascinating to observe how people play and learn from each other's strategies," she said. "While nothing can replace the joy of in-person events, the app offers a convenient way to connect and enjoy the game."

Just says they're also planning various events like poker brunches and lunches to foster community engagement further. "Poker isn't just a late-night activity; we host games throughout the day at PEAK6, bringing our team together for shared experiences," she said. "As we move into phase two, we focus on expanding the app's reach. While the technology is ready, we must ensure it reaches as many people as possible." That's Just's next big step in making poker more accessible and inclusive for everyone.

Community is truly the heart of this app. I'm thrilled by the idea of integrating it into existing female-led communities like Fintech Is Femme. Imagine hosting a virtual poker party where members from different locations can join online to play and connect. It adds a tangible, engaging element to community-building beyond traditional cocktail parties. While in-person events are fantastic, having an online version allows for broader participation and accessibility, too.

For women in fintech, this app offers more than just community – it encompasses decision-making, strategic thinking, risk assessment, and even money mindsets. These skills are particularly crucial in the fintech space, where innovation and leadership are driving forces for positive change. I'm excited to see how this ecosystem evolves and empowers women in fintech to become even stronger leaders and innovators.

One key takeaway to share is the importance of embracing a growth mindset as fintech leaders. Learning poker and honing these skills isn't just about the game – it's about cultivating a mindset that embraces challenges, learns from setbacks, and continuously seeks improvement. It's about proactively shaping your success and driving positive change in your industry. So, to all the women in fintech reading this, embrace the opportunity to learn and grow with poker – it's more than just a game. It's a pathway to empowerment and success.

Just has put a lot of effort into increasing female representation in her trading business, especially since trading is the backbone of the company's operations, fueling everything it's achieved over the years. The challenge was getting more women to make money decisions, essentially becoming capital allocators. It wasn't an easy journey. "We faced setbacks, but eventually, after multiple attempts, we launched programs like the Women's Trading Experience and the Women's Technology Experience, running for eight to ten weeks during the summer," she said. "I've realized through this process that it's not just about being around money; it's about being part of the conversations about money, no matter your role."

Whether you're in product development, engineering, finance, or operations, understanding how your work impacts the financial aspects of the business is crucial. Even in a non-profit organization, finances matter because, without financial sustainability, the mission can't thrive. For example, if you're an engineer, consider how your innovations can save or generate money for the company. Consider how your decisions contribute to the bottom line if you're in finance. Even if you're not directly involved in financial tasks, understanding the financial implications of your work can lead to better decision-making and, ultimately, a more significant impact on the organization's success. So few people are at the table regarding financial discussions because they're not naturally inclined to think about money in their day-to-day tasks. But by consciously connecting your work to financial outcomes, you train your brain to think differently and more strategically. This mindset shift doesn't just benefit you professionally; it also translates into better financial decision-making in your personal life.

Whether you're making decisions about your morning coffee or managing your household budget, staying connected to the financial aspect of your life empowers you to make informed choices. So, regardless of your gender or role, being financially savvy and understanding the impact of your decisions on the bottom line is essential for maximizing your impact in the workplace and beyond.

"Interestingly, I've had conversations with numerous senior women in the finance and fintech sectors, and an overwhelming majority, around 65 to 70%, revealed that they grew up playing poker," Just said. "It's remarkable, isn't it? These women, including those managing trillions in assets, all attribute poker to shaping their perspective on money, even though it's not commonly associated with women." Imagine the impact it could have if more research were conducted on this topic.

Just has taken that step – initiating research collaborations with institutions like Harvard and USC, exploring the link between poker and financial mindset, she shared. Poker Power has even partnered with a group in East Kenya that focuses on empowering marginalized girls through the Global Give Back Circle. "They've integrated our poker curriculum into their leadership program, and the results are astounding," she said. "These girls are learning valuable negotiation skills through poker." They've even built their poker tables, and Poker Power conducts lessons over Zoom. Now, they're elevating this initiative by training local teachers in Kenya to become certified poker instructors. "It's incredible to witness how poker enables these young women to negotiate for opportunities beyond their current circumstances," Just said. Each layer of research and every success story adds to the foundation of evidence supporting the positive impact of poker.

As more individuals like you – the reader – embrace poker and share your experiences, coupled with ongoing research efforts, we'll continue dismantling negative perceptions and highlighting the game's transformative power. It's a journey of personal discovery and collective advocacy; we're making strides toward change together.

AN UNCONVENTIONAL FINTECH CEO

Sarah Kirshbaum Levy grew up in New York City, surrounded by parents who aligned their passions with their career choices. Her father, a book publisher, would spend his weekends engrossed in books or browsing bookstores, while her mother, an antiques dealer, frequented fairs. It was a privilege Levy is hyper aware of because her parents' dedication to their interests shaped her understanding of how crucial it is to find a career that ignites passion. So, naturally, she began her career journey in media, a field she felt drawn to as a lover of movies and television. Levy has carved a path for herself in business sectors she's passionate about, thinking more about what she wants her life to look like holistically rather than focusing on a specific job. It's a recipe for success that has served her well.

In December 2020, Levy was appointed as the CEO of Betterment, the largest independent digital investment adviser that as of March 2024 served more than 850 000 customers and managed assets exceeding $45 billion. Her appointment took place during a transformative period in financial services, marked by pandemic-induced lockdowns and societal shifts that placed investing platforms at the forefront of the cultural zeitgeist. Although her background as a media executive might seem unconventional, Levy's leadership is critical to a new era that is fundamentally reshaping the cultural landscape of wealth management-focused fintech start-ups.

Betterment founder Jon Stein's decision to bring in an external CEO with a fresh perspective and a proven track record in launching and nurturing new brands was a strategic move. It reflected the evolving nature of fintech, which was undergoing its own rebrand as an industry in response to changing societal needs and behaviors around money and technology. In today's landscape, where social and environmental issues are at the forefront, investors are increasingly leveraging their wealth to advocate for change. Levy's experience as a media operator, aligning brands with the audience's values, makes her a perfect fit as a fintech CEO. Her strategic approach to business, focusing on brands that inspire her and businesses with significant growth potential, resonates with the evolving needs of the fintech industry.

"As I reflect on my journey and what ignites my passion, it boils down to two key elements," she told me in an interview on my podcast in December 2021, just one year after landing the CEO role. "Firstly, it's about aligning with a brand that truly inspires me. Secondly, it's about identifying a business with significant growth potential." Early in Levy's career, she learned that one of the pathways to success is diving into an industry and a company that's on the upswing, riding the wave of growth. Fresh out of college she joined Disney, a powerhouse brand experiencing a resurgence in animation with hits like *The Little Mermaid*, *Aladdin*, and *The Lion King*. Her tenure at Disney not only taught the importance of loving what you do but also instilled in her a thirst for knowledge and curiosity. After Disney, Levy spent 18 years at Nickelodeon, 11 as Chief Operating Officer, and 3 years in the same role at Viacom Media Networks. With a media background, Levy can place a lens on financial services most fintech executives that come from traditional finance or tech backgrounds struggle to hone,

one that understands that when it comes to branding, it's about more than just logos and slogans. Great brands have meaning; they inspire employees and customers, evoke positive emotions, and foster strong connections with their audience. One of the first initiatives Levy encountered was the launch of Betterment's socially responsible investing portfolios, which "felt like a pivotal moment for our brand," Levy recalled. "These portfolios became our fastest-growing ones ever, attracting over a billion dollars in less than five months."

Individual investor interest in sustainability is on the rise, according to a 2024 report by the Morgan Stanley Institute for Sustainable Investing.[7] More than three-quarters (77%) of global individual investors say they are interested in investing in companies or funds that aim to achieve market-rate financial returns while considering positive social and environmental impact. In addition, more than half (57%) say their interest has increased in the last two years, while 54% say they anticipate boosting allocations to sustainable investments in 2025.

Today's workforce and consumers desire to engage and use their investment dollars to support businesses they believe in – aligning with their values. Socially responsible investing taps into this sentiment perfectly. Betterment's climate, social justice, and broad impact portfolios reflect the movements of our time that resonate deeply with today's generation of investors. The new portfolios represented a shift toward personalization and choice, concepts not traditionally associated with Betterment at the time. "It hinted at future opportunities for our business," Levy said. "For me, it was more than just a successful launch – it sparked ideas for our next growth phase." So, she began exploring how Betterment can apply this personalized approach more broadly.

At its core, initiatives like this are about crafting a brand with a resonant mission and values that shape internal culture and ignite consumer passion. "The very essence of the word 'Betterment' embodies constant improvement," Levy said, "which sets a high standard for us to raise the bar continuously."

The crucial part is effectively reaching this digitally savvy, values-driven investor audience. This is where fintech companies like Betterment outpace traditional competitors. Levy told me all about how the fintech company had been honing its presence on social media, developing a distinct voice, and building a dedicated team to engage with its audience. They ventured into podcasting, connected TV, and formed partnerships with unexpected content platforms. This multi-faceted approach drew from Levy's background in the media business – breaking free from the traditional confines of brand communication, reaching new audiences, and igniting fresh conversations, setting Betterment on a path to connect with even more potential customers.

Transitioning to a new CEO amid the challenges of COVID-19, especially one the team had never met in person, was an unusual scenario. However, Levy says the company's culture served as the glue that held everyone together during this period of uncertainty. "If you're a true believer in what we're striving to achieve, it becomes easier to navigate through the storms of change," she shared.

When Levy joined Betterment, its investing platform was primarily focused on selling to retail consumers. However, Betterment had also realized there were diverse paths to reaching these retail consumers, each with unique preferences. Some investors prefer a digital solution, while others prefer initiating their investing journey through their employer's 401(k) plan. And then, a third group seeks personalized guidance from human advisors. Knowing these trends, Betterment had nascent products for all three pathways.

As Levy and I talked about financial wellness and the "great resignation" trend, a significant wave during the pandemic, she saw the massive opportunity gap for employers to differentiate themselves in the benefits space. It all starts with a 401(k) plan, but Levy envisioned an expansion into broader financial wellness initiatives. She and the team saw an opportune moment in the market due to regulatory changes as well. While large enterprises have traditionally offered comprehensive benefits packages, smaller companies have yet to catch up. Addressing employees' long-term financial independence becomes paramount as we contemplate the fragile state of Social Security for the next generation. Levy is particularly thrilled about the opportunity to reshape the landscape in this area.

While the government imposes limits on 401(k) contributions each year, additional savings often exist. Betterment is increasingly assisting employees in exploring options such as opening an IRA or building up an emergency savings fund. Betterment aims to offer individuals peace of mind by addressing these aspects comprehensively. "The connection between our holistic financial services on the retail side and the offerings we provide to employers creates a truly impactful experience for the end user," she said. "It's an innovative approach that hasn't been seen before."

To further lock in Betterment's diverse offerings, the fintech company even provides a modern custodian for financial advisors, which includes technology to simplify their back-office support and practice management needs. The all-in-one solution brings retirement and wealth together and frees advisors to focus on expanding their client base while the fintech handles the administrative tasks. Initially, Betterment primarily served start-up registered advisors. However, the platform started hearing from medium-sized registered investment advisory firms seeking advanced technology and the ability to customize portfolios for their clients.

So, in Levy's fashion to listen to audiences, Betterment responded by launching new tools exclusively for advisors, empowering them to create tailored portfolios for their entire practice or individual clients. Providing advisors and end-users with easy-to-use applications, particularly on mobile devices, has proven to be a potent combination. This expansion into the advisor space represents an exciting growth area for Betterment as Levy sets up the company with a multipronged distribution model that gives the company a competitive advantage.

By catering to diverse consumer pathways – through employers, direct-to-consumer channels, or partnerships with advisors – Levy is leading Betterment to bolster its position as a fintech powerhouse.

This level of innovation stems from Levy's intentional focus on diversity and inclusion both externally and internally. "When I reflect on this, I tend to emphasize the internal aspect more," she said. "Upon joining Betterment, I found diversity a fundamental pillar and cultural priority, supported by a robust process to foster inclusion and belonging." However, despite these commendable efforts, the representation metrics didn't align with the company's core beliefs. This misalignment presented an opportunity for improvement that Levy eagerly seized upon.

Why is building a diverse team imperative? Simply put, it's beneficial for business and product development. Embracing different perspectives, whether regarding gender, ethnicity, or other dimensions of diversity, enriches the decision-making process and enhances a company's ability to create a personalized product that resonates with a diverse user base. "After all, we're catering to a generation with varied needs and backgrounds, and meeting them where they are is essential," she said.

But how do you move from a grand theory of inclusivity to excellent execution? "I was told many years ago, back in my media days, that what gets measured gets done," Levy said. "It's a pretty simple idea. But putting explicit measurements in place is one of the keys to ensuring this doesn't fall to the bottom of the list. So, for the first time, Levy included diversity and inclusion goals in company bonuses. That's important because, as fintech leaders, we need to cultivate an inclusive dialogue, and we're going to do that by getting people engaged in the conversation. So that's how Levy thinks about it internally. "Externally, we talked about the fact that I was kind of an unconventional choice for this job," she said. "The fact of my appointment can begin to impact [the external environment]."

In other words, Levy is determined to show the industry that anyone from any background can step into a high-profile role as a fintech leader.

"If you have a curious mind and a humility about what you don't know, because certainly there's a lot I don't know, I think you can have a real impact," she said.

By reading Levy's story, and all the women you've met in this book, I hope more female leaders will follow and not be afraid to jump into fintech as a worthwhile avenue to find passion and fulfillment in your career.

NOTES

1. eToro. "The Bear Necessities with Lule Demmissie, eToro's US CEO." Accessed May 20, 2024. https://www.etoro.com/en-us/news-and-analysis/market-insights/the-bear-necessities-with-lule-demmissie-etoros-us-ceo.
2. Khera, Purva, Sumiko Ogawa, Ratna Sahay, and Mahima Vasishth. "Women in Fintech: As Leaders and Users." IMF Working Papers. Accessed May 20, 2024. https://www.imf.org/en/Publications/WP/Issues/2021/12/17/Women-in-Fintech-As-Leaders-and-Users-511783.
3. Crunchbase News. "Something Ventured: Black Women Founders." Accessed May 20, 2024. https://news.crunchbase.com/diversity/something-ventured-black-women-founders.
4. American Progress. "Women of Color and the Wage Gap." Accessed May 20, 2024. https://www.americanprogress.org/article/women-of-color-and-the-wage-gap.
5. Boston Consulting Group. "How Diverse Leadership Teams Boost Innovation." 2018. Accessed May 20, 2024. https://www.bcg.com/publications/2018/how-diverse-leadership-teams-boost-innovation.
6. Harvard Business Review. "The Best Leaders Aren't Afraid of Being Vulnerable." July 2022. Accessed May 20, 2024. https://hbr.org/2022/07/the-best-leaders-arent-afraid-of-being-vulnerable.
7. Morgan Stanley. "Sustainable Signals: Individual Investor Interest in Sustainability Is on the Rise." Accessed May 20, 2024. https://www.morganstanley.com/content/dam/msdotcom/en/assets/pdfs/MSInstituteforSustainableInvesting-SustainableSignals-Individuals-2024.pdf.

CHAPTER NINE

PROGRESS IS POSSIBLE

As I approached the completion of writing this book, I was packing my bags to head to Amsterdam to moderate a panel discussion on success metrics for founders outside of profits. The room was filled with entrepreneurs, investors, and executives eager to network and gain new insights. As the discussion began with simple introductions, one of my panelists – a founder of a female-run VC firm – shared her belief that women have a confidence problem and need to adjust to the system, not the other way around. She claimed that discrimination is unintentional (tell that to the 2% of female founders who receive funding despite showcasing greater ROI). Honestly, it left me shocked on stage. I rebutted, sharing that from my experience and countless others I've interviewed, it's not women who have an issue but the structure that has an issue. A structure that chooses, time and time again – from funding, wealth, and pay gaps to the investing gap – to discriminate against women. This moment reminds me how easy it is to enter a cynical mindset. With female VCs like that, what hope is there? But, as Shaina Taub writes in her Tony-winning Broadway musical, *Suffs*, "progress is possible, not guaranteed." How do we know progress is possible? By looking to the trailblazing women who came before us and successfully pushed for systemic change. You just met more than 30 of them in this book.

THE NEXT ERA

Encounters like what I experienced on stage are a stark reminder that change happens with each and every one of us. There will always be distractions – people, companies, lawsuits – that will attempt to slow progress. The narrative that women have a confidence issue is one of the noisiest distractions – a false narrative that wastes our time, energy, and money when we should be placing all our efforts into combating the system, not changing women.

So, what can we do at both an individual and systemic level to improve the representation of women in fintech? Here are some actionable steps:

1. **Mandatory Disclosure of Investment Data:** There's currently no official data on how venture capital firms invest their money, which funds the backbone of our innovation economy. California's new bill requiring demographic data disclosure of venture capital investments to the Civil Rights Department is a start. Let's expand this policy nationwide to ensure transparency and accountability in funding decisions.
2. **Pressure for Diversity:** Limited partners should demand that venture capital firms hire more women partners and present clear diversity plans. Both male and female investors need to prioritize funding women and diverse founders.

3. **Equal Pay for Equal Work:** CEOs and board members must commit to paying women at the same rate as men. This is straightforward – just do it. Companies should regularly audit their pay practices to ensure equity and transparency.

4. **Reduce Isolation:** Minimize instances where there is only one woman in the room. This can be achieved by hiring more women and promoting them to leadership positions, thereby creating a more inclusive and supportive work environment. Hiring a diverse workforce at the early stages of your start-up is crucial, as it sets the trajectory for the rest of your company's lifetime and can significantly impact its success.

5. **Mentorship and Sponsorship Programs:** Establish programs that provide women with mentors and sponsors who can advocate for their advancement within the organization.

6. **Network Is Your Net Worth:** Create and support networks and organizations that focus on women in fintech. These networks can provide resources, opportunities for collaboration, and platforms to share experiences and strategies for overcoming challenges.

7. **Highlight Success Stories:** Celebrate and promote the achievements of women in fintech to inspire and motivate others. Media and industry events should feature more stories of female leaders and innovators. At Fintech Is Femme, we prioritize this regularly. Our industry events attract 300 attendees and feature all-female panels of industry experts. My newsletter, Fintech Is Femme, profiles *badass* women in fintech weekly.

8. **Advocate for Policies Supporting Work-Life Balance:** Push for policies that support parental leave, flexible working arrangements, and affordable childcare. These policies can help women, who represent the majority of caregivers, balance their careers and personal lives more effectively.

9. **Regular Assessments:** Conduct regular assessments of diversity and inclusion efforts within companies and across the industry. Use the findings to make informed decisions and improvements.

10. **Collaborate Across the Industry:** Companies, investors, and industry groups should work together to share best practices, develop standards, and create a unified approach to increasing female representation in fintech.

By implementing these systemic solutions, we can create a more equitable and inclusive fintech industry. Change starts with each of us, and together, we can build a future where women are fully represented and valued in fintech. Let's shift the narrative and focus on transforming the system by listening to the women who navigate it.

CAUSE I SLAY

In Japan, there's a traditional repair method called kintsugi. When pottery breaks, it is repaired using Japanese lacquer and dusted with gold or silver powder, making the pottery not only usable again but also more beautiful by highlighting its cracks.

Iyandra Smith Bryan's career embodies this philosophy. She's embraced all the cracks and challenges, turning them into something unique and beautiful. Born in Nassau, The Bahamas, Smith Bryan is a trailblazer and advocate for women in finance. With more than 14 years in financial services, she's now the Chief Operating Officer at Quantfury, a global fintech brokerage, where she champions transparency in trading and governance.[1]

Smith Bryan's journey started as an attorney working with commercial organizations. She quickly realized she wanted to contribute more than legal opinions; she wanted to shape business strategy. She found her perfect blend when she entered the fintech industry. At Quantfury, the dynamic environment and flat hierarchy where everyone collaborates to improve the product is exactly what she needed.

Demanding systemic change while also undergoing introspection and embracing your personal cracks and imperfections is a profound way to step into your power as a woman in fintech. As I've learned from trailblazing women like Smith Bryan, this dual approach acknowledges the external barriers that exist while also celebrating the unique strengths and vulnerabilities that shape our individual journeys.

Understanding that perfection is a myth and that our flaws are part of what makes us resilient and innovative is key. In fintech, an industry driven by innovation and constant evolution, acknowledging our imperfections can be a powerful tool. It allows us to approach problems with a fresh perspective, fostering creativity and resilience. By embracing our imperfections, we can turn perceived weaknesses into strengths, using them to fuel our drive and determination.

Retrospection is another critical element in this process as it leads into our metamorphosis, Smith Bryan told me. Regularly reflecting on our experiences, both successes and failures, provides valuable insights and learning opportunities. This self-awareness helps us understand our motivations, recognize our achievements, and identify areas for growth. It's through this reflective practice that we can continuously improve and adapt, staying ahead in the fast-paced fintech landscape.

Simultaneously, working toward systemic change is essential. The fintech industry, like many others, has biases and barriers that need to be addressed to create a more inclusive environment. Advocating for transparency in funding, equal pay, and diverse leadership are not just necessary steps for equality but also strategic moves for the betterment of the industry. Diverse perspectives lead to better decision-making and more innovative solutions. *Period.*

Combining these approaches – personal growth through retrospection and the embrace of imperfections, along with the advocacy for systemic change – is a holistic strategy that pushes us to shape the industry not just for ourselves but for the women who will follow in our footsteps. It's about building a legacy of resilience, innovation, and inclusivity.

By taking action, we create a ripple effect. Our actions inspire others, breaking down barriers and opening doors. We become role models, showing that strength comes from authenticity and that real change is possible when we work collectively.

In essence, stepping into your power as a woman in fintech means recognizing and celebrating your whole self, advocating for systemic change, and continuously striving for personal and professional growth. It's a journey that not only transforms your own path but also paves the way for future generations of women in fintech.

Reflecting on her journey, Smith Bryan told me she is grateful for her diverse career path – from attorney to bank CEO and now to fintech. Each step has been valuable. All of her learnings can be distilled into her formula for success as a woman in fintech, which she calls her S.L.A.Y. method:

S – Social Networks: "Your social circle significantly influences where you are and where you end up," she said. Building a network, especially within a community of women excelling in the industry, is crucial for thriving in a male-dominated field like fintech.

L – Living Fearlessly: "Successful people jump in with fear right behind them," Smith Bryan says. Embrace the steep learning curve and keep moving forward despite the fear.

A – Authenticity: "Be yourself – the best version of yourself that you know how to be," she advises. Know your values and what you're willing to negotiate before entering any environment. Find an environment where you can truly be yourself, flourish, and succeed. Authenticity helps you find the right cultural fit in organizations and the right investors when you're building a start-up and ensures long-term success and fulfillment.

Y - Understanding Your Why: "Discover your passion and take action," she said. Reflect on what you love to do and what you're great at. Find where your passions and skills intersect and pursue opportunities in those areas.

Smith Bryan is determined to show that fintech is for everyone, not just white males or tech guys. It's an opportunity for women and people of color to work, own, and generate substantial wealth. Inclusivity in fintech means there's room for everyone, whether you're technical or not. By embodying openness and encouraging more women to join, she aims to make fintech more inclusive and ensure its growth and success.

THE FINTECH FUTURE IS FEMALE

Many fintech companies are struggling with unsustainable spending, overhiring, and poor management, leading to many start-ups facing the possibility of shutting down within the following year. Despite these challenges, we can work toward increasing recognition of female co-founders and leaders' and their crucial role in driving better decision-making, product insights, sales strategies, and overall growth in the industry.

Female leadership is critical to the lasting success of fintech companies. Throughout this book you've discovered how research shows that organizations with more women in executive positions tend to outperform their peers. Decades of studies consistently highlight that women leaders boost productivity, enhance collaboration, foster organizational commitment, and increase profitability. Women represent less than 10% of leadership – both as founders and as members of executive boards of fintech firms.

Still, female leaders in the fintech industry are pivotal in developing, marketing, and supplying financial products that better suit women's needs – which will further help in bridging the gender gap in digital financial inclusion.

In October 2023, I recorded a live podcast at Money20/20 to discuss the future of women in fintech with Kathryn Petralia, founder of Kabbage and Keep Financial, and Sasha Pilch, a former principal at FinCapital and co-founder at GTM Guild.[2]

Petralia is a fintech trailblazer who co-founded Kabbage in 2009. The company focuses on providing cash flow management and credit lines for small businesses. It raised $250 million from Softbank, achieving "unicorn" status with a valuation of more than $1 billion, and was eventually acquired by American Express in 2020. Petralia and her co-founder, Rob Frohwein, are working on Keep Financial, which ties employee compensation to retention and performance.

"Fintech has this amazing power to democratize access to all kinds of things," Petralia said. "Not just basic financial services, but growth, personal growth, and education. Fintech is unique in that way."

Pilch, who also founded NYC FinTech Women, believes more female investors will get more female founders funding, creating a positive cycle of representation and success. Our podcast discussed the importance of networking and community in fintech. Joining networks can connect founders, operators, and investors with the necessary resources to succeed. It's one of the most effective growth strategies.

Here are the essential action items for women in fintech to take from our conversation:

1. **Embrace Leadership Roles:** Female leadership enhances productivity, collaboration, organizational commitment, and profitability. Women should seek and embrace leadership roles to drive better decision-making and innovation within the industry.
2. **Build and Leverage Networks:** Join communities like Fintech Is Femme or NYC FinTech Women to connect with founders, opera-

tors, and investors. Building a solid network provides resources, support, and opportunities for career advancement.

3. **Promote Female Representation:** Advocate for increased female representation in investment roles. More female investors can lead to more female founders receiving funding. As Asya Bradley said in Chapter 3, "If I find myself in a position where I am the only woman in a room, I make it a priority to change it."

4. **Become Industry Experts:** Master your field. Continuous learning and staying updated on industry trends and data make your contributions undeniable. Read fintech news daily and stay up to speed on what's happening in the ecosystem – you can do so through some of your favorite fintech influencers' newsletters.

5. **Support Each Other:** Foster a supportive environment among women in fintech. Share experiences, offer mentorship, fund each other's companies, and collaborate to navigate challenges. Give freely, give often.

6. **Adopt a Growth Mindset:** Embrace challenges as opportunities for learning and development. Shift from a scarcity mindset to a growth mindset. Outsource anything you aren't great at – the best leaders know how to hire great talent.

7. **Focus on B2B & Consumer Fintech:** Consider making small pivots to your business model to fall under B2B fintech (embedded finance, payments, employee benefits), or even have a B2B2C approach, which tends to attract higher valuations and funding. This strategic focus can enhance business growth and success for female founders.

8. **Drive Inclusion and Diversity:** Advocate for inclusivity in fintech. Highlight the importance of diverse perspectives in driving innovation and better customer experiences. Arm yourself with the data in this book to push diversity and innovation forward. Don't get distracted by the *BS*.

9. **Capitalize on Fintech's Democratizing Power:** Leverage fintech's potential to democratize access to financial services, personal growth, and education. Develop solutions catering to your community's specific needs and underserved populations.

10. **Learn from Success Stories:** Study successful women in fintech to understand their journeys, challenges, and strategies. Use these insights to inform your own career path.

BUILD AS FINTECH FEMINISTS

We're at a critical moment in our world, where political, economic, and cultural tensions are palpable. However, we must not lose sight of what this book provides. The stories and blueprints laid out in this book have the potential to reach thousands of people, inspire more women to build in fintech, and perpetuate a cycle of feminist perspectives that could truly transform our economy.

I wrote this book because I believe women are the key to unlocking a better financial future for the world. My goal for this book is to provide you with these women's knowledge, data, and real-life stories so that you can also advocate for yourself, whether that's your next project pitch, funding round, or job interview. By understanding how and why women play an integral role in the future of our global economic system, female innovators in fintech can reshape finance, redefine success, and transform the digital revolution into a goldmine for entrepreneurial success. The results are increased global GDP, more profitable businesses, and a society that everyone would benefit from.

As we conclude this journey, I urge you to take this book's inspiration, strategies, and insights and apply them to your path. The stories of the women highlighted here aren't just inspiring. They demonstrate a blueprint – or roadmap – for how to achieve success in this industry while continuing to transform it into a realm where diverse perspectives can drive transformative change. Whether you are a fintech professional, an aspiring entrepreneur, or an investor, your contributions can help create a more inclusive and innovative economic landscape.

The world of fintech needs more women leaders – innovators who can tackle the industry's challenges, harness opportunities, and contribute to the ongoing transformation of the digital era. Your unique perspective and skills are invaluable in this journey. So, go forth and build. I can't wait to see what innovative solutions you come up with. While you do, remember that the future of fintech is female, and our economic prosperity will thrive in the hands of your feminist values.

Thank you for joining me on this journey. Let's continue championing the cause, supporting one another, and shaping a future where fintech and its ripple effects are more inclusive and impactful for all.

NOTES

1. Humans of Fintech. "Episode: Building Inclusive Fintech Solutions." Accessed May 20, 2024. https://open.spotify.com/episode/03TI3pULd0ZBS2hgH4Wahe?si=cKT9iVQ5SXad5wp3Oq0_Hg.
2. Humans of Fintech. "Episode: Empowering Women in Fintech." Accessed May 20, 2024. https://open.spotify.com/episode/5cRbKRFqGQwVjYs45Lcep6?si=lA4wlBT6R22uoDAxu10ZZQ.

ABOUT
THE AUTHOR

Nicole Casperson is an award-winning journalist, content director, podcast host, global speaker, and community builder. As a leading figure in the fintech sector, she is known for her dedication to covering the industry's impact on the global economy with a focus on inclusivity and innovation. As the founder and CEO of Fintech Is Femme Media, she offers authoritative insights into the convergence of gender equity, finance, and technology through her industry-leading newsletter, podcast, and event series. In less than a year, Nicole transformed her twice-weekly newsletter into a thriving media brand, attracting more than 50 000 subscribers in the fintech industry and securing partnerships with some of the world's largest financial institutions.

Nicole's journey, shaped by her Filipina American heritage, fuels her mission to amplify the voices of dynamic women entrepreneurs and leaders in fintech. As a news editor and reporter, she witnessed the stark underrepresentation of diverse female voices in media and financial services and its profound impact on society. This realization inspired her to establish Fintech Is Femme.

In addition to her role as a founder, Nicole imparts her expertise as a professor of Financial Management at the Parsons School of Design and is a regular contributor to *Forbes*. Her achievements have earned her the accolade of Top Inspiring Female in Fintech in 2022 by NYC Fintech Women, recognition as a Top Influencer in Financial Twitter by ETFtrends .com, and finalist status in the Fintech Nexus DEI Trailblazer Awards.

Nicole's work extends to uniting female fintech leaders through engaging, sold-out events, largely hosted in New York City. Her profound insights have graced the pages of publications such as the *LA Times*, *Forbes*, and *Nasdaq Trade Talks*, firmly establishing her as a respected authority within the industry. She is a highly sought-after speaker at major industry events, from the Women's World Banking Summit in Mumbai to Money20/20 in Amsterdam and Las Vegas.

Nicole calls Brooklyn, New York, her home, where she collaborates with her partner to champion greater equality and diversity within the financial world.

INDEX